# NO NONSENSE
# MINISTRY

# NO NONSENSE MINISTRY

*By*
*John H. Muller*

**Companion Press**
**P.O. Box 310**
**Shippensburg, PA 17257-0310**

"Good Stewards of the
Manifold Grace of God"

ISBN 1-56043-508-9

For Worldwide Distribution
Printed in the U.S.A.

# Contents

# Foreword

Referring to the high-priesthood in Israel, the writer to the Hebrews says, "No one takes this honour upon himself; he must be called by God." If that was true of the Jewish high priest, it is no less true of the Christian preacher and pastor. The demands made by this way of life are so far-reaching that no one who gives any thought to it could contemplate embarking on it without the assurance of being called by God and empowered by God for this exacting ministry.

This is not the way of life to which I myself have been called; mine is much less demanding. But I have over the years been closely associated with many who have been divinely called to the preaching and pastoral ministry, and who have obeyed that call. I have the utmost admiration for them. Robertson Nicoll tells somewhere how he attended the funeral service of a Baptist pastor who had served the same church for sixty years. The service was conducted by another pastor of comparable age, and he preached from the text, "His hands were steady until the going down of the sun." It was Moses' hands, uplifted in prayer for his people, that were steady until victory was won, and they were steadied by another power than his own. Such upholding power is indispensable for anyone entrusted with the cure of souls, whether in one congregation or in several.

These are the remarks of an observer, but they are intended to introduce the wise words of one who has had long experience of the pastoral ministry in various parts of the United States and more recently in Australia—not to speak of a spell as chaplain in Korea, of which he has given an account in one of his earlier books: *Wearing the Cross in Korea.* I have known Dr. Muller for many years, and have been impressed from our first meeting by his single-hearted devotion to the ministry. Over and above his wide-ranging experience as a preacher and pastor, he has read widely in the field of pastoral theology and has made the fruit of his experience and study available to others by lecture-courses delivered to ordinands. What he has given to them he now gives in these pages to a larger public. I cannot think of any aspect of the ministerial calling, public or private, on which he does not touch. I found the book so interesting I couldn't lay it down. What he has written is bound to be enriching and helpful to many others, who are anxious to know how their own ministry in turn can be made more effective.

F. F. Bruce
Emeritus Professor
University of Manchester, England
(Dr. Bruce went to be with the
Lord in September 1990)

# Preface

Of the making of books on preaching there seems to be no end. However, to find one that covers both aspects of the ministry, preaching and pastoring, is not easy. They really should be tied together.

While serving in Australia for six and one-half years I found little that was written from an Aussie point of view.

Hence we have sought to combine the many aspects of the ministry into one book, and also add an Aussie flavor to it. Behind it is forty-seven years of full-time ministry in varied situations in the United States, Korea and Australia. Much of this material has been presented to the students of the Presbyterian Theological College in Melbourne, Victoria, Australia.

We are indebted to Dr. Fred F. Bruce, Dr. Allan Harman, and Rev. Peter Hastie, who have read the manuscript and made helpful suggestions. Special thanks is due to my faithful wife of 48 years, Sunny, who has typed all of my books and theses through the years, and has done so again with this book.

We send it forth with the hope and prayer that it will benefit those who go out to serve our Lord, and encourage and help many who are already in His work.

John H. Muller

# Part 1

# PREACHING

1

# Chapter 1

# The Importance
# of Personal Commitment

We cannot start talking about preaching or its importance without establishing a base from which we take off. It is too easy to take this for granted. Nearly every book on preaching does. The base is the matter of personal commitment.

Every preacher and pastor needs to have a personal experience of salvation through Jesus Christ. Too many times this has not been the case. Witness the famous instance of Thomas Chalmers preaching in Scotland for seven years before he was converted. This is a well-known example, but, unfortunately, it could be multiplied many times.

There is nothing that can replace a full and complete personal commitment to Jesus Christ. We first recognize our sin and unworthiness, and then turn to Christ for forgiveness of sin. We follow Paul's advice that he gave to the Philippian jailor when he requested what he should do to be saved. (Acts 16:31 NIV)—"Believe in the Lord Jesus, and you will be saved." Romans 10:9 NIV, also lays it out clearly: "If you confess with your mouth, Jesus is Lord, and believe in your heart that God raised Him from the dead, you will be saved." The core of the Gospel is given to us in the famous John 3:16 verse: "For God so loved the world that He gave His only begotten Son, that whosoever believes on Him may not perish but have everlasting life." You can also personalize the familiar 23rd Psalm by emphasizing that "the Lord is *my* shepherd." When you can wholeheartedly say that Christ is your own personal Saviour, you then have made the commitment that is a requisite for every preacher and pastor, no matter where or how you may serve.

If you plan to preach in Presbyterian or Reformed churches, you must also commit yourself to the Reformed faith. You accept the Sovereignty of God as the pivot around which you build your faith. You take the five points of Calvinism as a base for your understanding of the Scriptures—Total depravity, unconditional election, limited atonement, irresistible grace, and the perseverance of the saints (eternal security). You accept the Bible unconditionally as God's holy and inspired Word.

You also are committed to this type of worship, which is always reverent and deep with meaning. You shun the back-slapping, knee-jerking, sentimental and highly emotional forms of worship for dignified, reverent, yet happy approaches to God.

Now you have a reason to preach and teach the Gospel.

# Chapter 2

# The Call to the Ministry

Second only to the matter of a personal commitment to the Lord is the issue of a call to the ministry. How a person enters the ministry is of tremendous importance. There is a "door" into this sheepfold, and there is "some other way."

There are many influences that can play a part in one's desire to enter the ministry. It is indeed one of the professions. It is one way to earn a living, although seldom a lucrative one. It is a way of exercising leadership, and becoming a respected person in the community. It has its own aura of social distinction. None of these reasons are above the horizontal level. We need the vertical vision.

The way J. H. Jowett put it is excellent: "I hold with profound conviction that before a man selects the Christian ministry as his vocation he must have the assurance that the selection has been imperatively constrained by the Eternal God."[1] Paul put it this way: "For though I preach the Gospel I have nothing to boast of, for necessity is laid upon me, yea, woe is unto me if I preach not the Gospel."[2]

It is not possible to describe for you the way in which you are called. Each man's circumstances differ. Our own call may be unique. We need not always expect a bolt of lightning from heaven such as Martin Luther experienced. The call may come by way of the "still small voice." The variety of ways in which God calls is typified by the biblical calls to Amos, Isaiah and Jeremiah.

Amos was a shepherd out in the pastures of Tekoa. He had heard of problems developing in the high places of Israel. Wealth and luxury were breeding grounds for injustice and "truth is fallen in the streets." As the shepherd mused, the fires began to burn within. He heard a mysterious call and saw a beckoning hand. He had no alternative. "The Lord took me as I followed the flock, and said, Go, prophesy."[3]

The setting for Isaiah's call is quite different. He was a friend of kings who felt at home in courtly circles. Isaiah had pinned his hopes on long-time king, Uzziah. But now Uzziah was gone. On that empty throne Isaiah discovered the very presence of God. "In the year that king Uzziah died, I saw the Lord."[4] The human pillar had crumbled, but the Pillar of the whole world remained stable and firm. Isaiah mourned the fall of a king and heard the call from above. The call to service came: "Whom shall I send and who will go for me?"[5] Isaiah's heart was smitten, he heard the call, and answered "Here am I, send me."[6]

The circumstances surrounding Jeremiah's call are different again. The meditative type, a shift of circumstances changed his

---

1.  J. H. Jowett: *The Preacher: His Life and Work*, p. 12.
2.  I Corinthians 9:16
3.  Amos 7:15
4.  Isaiah 6:1
5.  Isaiah 6:8a
6.  Isaiah 6:8b

4

meditations into conviction, and he heard the voice of the Lord God saying unto him, "Before you came forth out of the womb I sanctified you, and I ordained you a prophet unto the nations."[1] This was a clear call to Jeremiah. With some reluctance, he accepted it.

For more detailed discussions of the call one can turn to Edmund P. Clowney's booklet, *"Called to the Ministry."* He analyzes the call to service in chapter two, and then deals in detail with "What is God's Calling to the Ministry" in the last two chapters. In Al N. Martin's booklet, *"Prepared to Preach,"* his third chapter is called "The Call and Commission of the Preacher." He discusses II Timothy 2, Romans 12, James 3:1, and I Timothy 3:1. Then he contrasts Spurgeon and Dabney, as representing extreme right and left in their views of the call. He himself speaks of three indispensable elements to the call 1) A desire to serve born out of right motives, 2) A genuine, balanced, and matured Christian experience, and 3) An evidence of gifts necessary for the edification of the people of God. There is also a chapter by Joel Nederhoed on "The Minister's Call" in the anthology on *"Preaching,"* edited by Samuel T. Logan, Jr. He even deals with false forms of the call. He lists four attitudes flowing from a sense of obedience to Christ that must be present in anyone called to the ministry: 1) Self-discipline, 2) Self-sacrifice, 3) Self-giving, and 4) Self-control.

---

1.    Jeremiah 1:5

# Chapter 3

# Maintaining the Devotional Life

An essential part of the preacher's life is the maintaining of a close walk with God, commonly known as the devotional life. The minister is great only when he is God-possessed. When Moses came down from Mt. Sinai, we read in Exodus 34:29 that he was not aware that his face was radiant after he had spoken with the Lord. The preacher will reflect his devotional life in his conduct as well as in his preaching.

Andrew Bonar vowed "not to speak to men until I have spoken to God, not to do anything with my hand until I have been on my knees, not to read other books until I have read the Holy Scriptures."

McCheyne wrote to a missionary: "In great measure, according to the purity and perfections of the instrument, will be the success. It is not great talents which God blesses so much as great likeness to Jesus. A holy minister is an awful weapon in the hand of God."

It is said of Martin Luther that he gave three hours of each day to prayer. Ofttimes he prayed aloud with compelling earnestness and deep reverence. This is nothing short of amazing when you consider his voluminous writings, his frequent preaching, his administration, his extensive correspondence, and his family life. John Calvin bore up under tremendous work pressures only because of his deep devotional life.

The greatest example set before us of a life lived in closeness to the heavenly Father is that of our Lord Himself. The Gospels record much of His prayer life. In fact, a study of the prayer life of Jesus is well worth your time.

The Christian minister must live in "heavenly places with Christ,"[1] and must learn to pray without ceasing, or pray continually,

---

1.    Ephesians 1:3

as the NIV puts it.[1] Our habits must be kept under control. Total abstinence from smoking and the use of alcoholic beverages is best for the Christian minister. The example principle of I Corinthians 8 is the final answer to those who would argue for moderation rather than abstinence.

By all means the Christian minister must learn to keep sex under control. Paul uses the figure of boxing in I Corinthians 9:27 and refers to keeping his own body under control so that he himself "will not be disqualified for the prize." The tragedy wrought by sexual aberrations of men of the cloth is beyond telling.

Ralph Turnbull wrote a whole book on the perils that a minister faces in his work.[2] J. H. Jowett[3] has a chapter on "The Perils of the Preacher." His perils as listed are: 1) The danger of men who are busy among holy things becoming profane. We may lead others into the heavenly way and we may lose the road ourselves, 2) Deadening familiarity with the sublime. We may become mere guideposts when we were intended to be guides. We may indicate the way and yet not be found in it. We may live in mountain country, and lose all sense of the heights, 3) Deadening familiarity with commonplace. The pathetic may cease to melt us and the tragic may cease to shock us. We may become "past feeling," or lose all our sensitivity,[4] 4) The possible perversion of our emotional life. The emotions can become unhealthily intense and inflammatory. They may become defiled, and even neurotic. Moral defences can be imperilled. Exaggerated emotion can flood us. This is in evidence when leaders of the heavily emotional church groups are so frequently drawn into immoral situations, 5) The perilous gravitation of the world. The spirit of compromise means sacrificing moral ideals of popular standards and subjecting personal conviction to current opinion. We may

---

1.    I Thessalonians 5:17
2.    Ralph G. Turnbull, *A Minister's Obstacles*
3.    Jowett, op. cit., p. 41ff
4.    Ephesians 4:19 KJV and NIV

often-times find ourselves in a gray area, but the Scripture counsels us to keep our garments white.[1] The tempter worked on Jesus with this compromising approach, and he has not ceased to work on His ministers ever since. We can seek to be showy, rather than Spirit-filled. We can become more intent on full pews than on redeemed souls, to add large numbers to our membership rolls rather than seeking to have our people included in the Lamb's book of life. Worldliness seeks more for the praises of men than for the praises of God.

These and other perils can best be overcome by a healthy devotional life. What can easily defeat us can thus be turned into life's true victory.

# Chapter 4

# The Object and Purpose of Preaching

Why preach? What is the ultimate purpose of preaching? The traditional answers to these questions have usually been twofold, referring to the saved and the unsaved, or the believer and the unbeliever. Simply stated—to save sinners, and to edify and sanctify the saints—or—to make bad people good, and to make good people better.

D. J. Burrell puts it this way: "Preaching is persuasion towards God. The business of the preacher is to counsel, to convince, and to convert; i.e., to bring men into immediate vital touch with God."[2] Jay

---

1. Revelation 3:4-5
2. David James Burrell: The Sermon, Its Construction and Delivery, p. 295

Adams[1] discusses purpose from the viewpoint of three Greek words used in the New Testament. *Kerusso* and *euangelizo* describe heralding and announcing the Gospel, while *didasko* has to do with the proclamation of truth among those who already believe the Gospel. He concludes that there are two kinds of preaching; evangelistic preaching and pastoral preaching. J. I. Packer states that "the purpose of preaching is to inform, persuade, and call forth an appropriate response to the God whose message and instruction are being delivered."[2] From R. L. Dabney [3] we choose three statements: "The preacher is a herald; his work is heralding the King's message," "The preacher's task may be correctly explained as that of instrumentally forming the image of Christ upon the souls of men," and "The preacher's business is to take what is given him in the Scriptures, as it is given to him, and to endeavor to imprint it on the souls of men." Writing some 160 years ago Charles Bridges said: "For the instruction of all sorts of men unto eternal life it is necessary that the sacred and saving truth of God be openly published unto them. Which open publication of heavenly mysteries is termed preaching."[4]

Jesus turned to Isaiah 61 when He described His ministry. He entered the synagogue in Nazareth, opened the Scriptures, and read from Isaiah. Then He applied the passage as referring to His ministry. Look at it: "The Spirit of the Sovereign Lord is on Me, because the Lord has anointed Me to preach good news to the poor. He has sent Me to bind up the broken-hearted, to proclaim freedom for the captives and release from darkness for the prisoners, to proclaim the year of the Lord's favor and the day of vengeance of our God, to comfort all who mourn and provide for those who grieve in Zion—

1. Jay Adams: *Preaching With Purpose*, pp. 5-6
2. J. I. Packer: "Why Preach?" In *Preaching*, ed. by S. D. Logan, Jr., p.9
3. R. L. Dabney *On Preaching*, pp. 36-37
4. Charles Bridges: *The Christian Ministry*, p. 188

to bestow on them a crown of beauty instead of ashes, the oil of gladness instead of mourning, and a garment of praise instead of a spirit of despair."[1] Note the headings:

> "Preach good news."
> "Bind up the broken-hearted."
> "Freedom for captives and prisoners."
>
> Proclaim 1. The Lord's favor,
>       2. Vengeance of God.
> "Comfort mourners."

As these were characteristic of our Lord's ministry, so they should be of ours. Jowett summarized that "in all these words there appears to be this general sense of emergence and release. There is an opening of mind, an opening of heart, an opening of eyes, and opening of doors. In every word the iron gate swings back and there is the sound of the song of freedom."[2]

Jesus said:"As the Father has sent Me, I am sending you."[3] We have good news to tell—about God, our heavenly Father—about Jesus Christ, God's Son—about the wonder of God's grace in the forgiveness of sins—about how broken and shattered lives can be mended and rebuilt—about how we can overcome worry and care, sorrow, death, and the grave. These truths we not only need to teach and proclaim, but we also need to incarnate them—live them—before our fellow men.

Jesus also laid out our task to the Apostle Paul when He commissioned him to go to his people and the Gentiles: "I am sending you to them to open their eyes and turn them from darkness to light, and from the power of satan to God, so that they may receive forgiveness of sins and a place among those who are sanctified by faith in me."[4]

---

1.     Isaiah 61:1-3 NIV
2.     J. H. Jowett, op. cit., p. 32
3.     John 20:21 NIV
4.     Acts 26:17-18 NIV

This commission to Paul clearly lays out priorities for us. We are to open men's eyes, bring them into the light of the Gospel, deliver them from the power of the evil one. We are to so proclaim God's truth that they will experience the forgiveness of sins and become a part of the family of God.

We must preach about the great themes of the faith. We cannot drop the big themes and expect to create great saints. We need to preach on the great biblical texts, the fat texts. We must grapple with big truths—truths that are deep and abiding, and that permanently matter. We are not in business just to give good advice, we are to proclaim Good News—about the love of God, the grace of Christ, the power of the Holy Spirit, the wonders of the cross, and the home our Father has prepared.

Men who speak from years of experience give varied counsels as to what to emphasize. Parker said: "Preach to broken hearts." Ian Maclaren said: "The chief end of preaching is comfort." Dale said: "People want to be comforted. They need consolation." Macartney said to present the cardinal doctrines and truth of the Christian faith—concerning the soul, sin, the person of Christ, the atonement, regeneration and salvation. There can be no true Gospel preaching without them.[1] F. B. Meyer begins his book with: "The one supreme object of the Christian ministry is to preach Christ, and Him crucified. All sermons must culminate and find their loftiest purpose in the Divine Redeemer."[2] D. M. Lloyd-Jones concludes "that the primary task of the Church and of the Christian minister is the preaching of the Word of God."[3]

We are placed in the position of the prophets of old who spoke for God. We must call men and women to hear the Word of the Lord.

Our God is bountiful and has given us abundant resources. We have as our allies the Triune God, the grace of our Lord, the love of

---

1. Clarence Macartney: *Preaching Without Notes*, p. 19
2. F. B. Meyer: *Expository Preaching*, p. 11
3. D. M. Lloyd-Jones: *Preaching and Preachers*, p. 19

the Father, and the communion of the Holy Spirit. With such helpers and with such a message, we cannot fail to bless.

# Chapter 5
# Study Methods and Reading Habits

"Preaching that costs nothing accomplishes nothing. If the study is a lounge the pulpit will be an impertinence. It is, therefore, imperative that the preacher go into his study to do hard work—There is no man so speedily discovered as an idle minister, and there is no man who is visited by swifter contempt."[1]

Be systematic about your study habits. Enter your study at an appointed hour. Let the hour be as early as those of the farmers and businessmen in your church. They work for their daily bread. Shall their minister be behind them in his search for the Bread of Life? Put first things first. You will win the respect of your people when they see that you mean business.

Claim your morning hours for study. The creative faculty is often strong at night, but our minds are fresh and clear in the morning.

You don't cease to be a student when you leave the Theological College (Seminary). Preachers must remain students all of their lives. Calvin said: "No one will ever be a good minister of the Word of God unless he is first of all a scholar." Spurgeon said: "He who has ceased to learn has ceased to teach. He who no longer sows in the study will no more reap in the pulpit." Phillips Brooks said: "The preacher's life must be a life of large accumulation." Billy Graham

1.    J. H. Jowett, op. cit., p. 114

said: "If I were to start my ministry all over again, I would study three times as much as I have done."

James Montgomery Boice outlines some guidelines: 1) Get all the formal training you can get. Work toward an advanced degree if possible. 2) Never stop learning. The ministry should be self-educating. 3) Set aside specific times for study. 4) Tackle some big problems. It will broaden your knowledge.[1]

In a life lived for God's service there must be control of time. We must discipline the hours, and bend them to God's purpose. Self discipline is of tremendous importance in the ministry. To a large degree you are your own boss. Set your mind to diligence and faithfulness. Remain a student to the end. A preacher with a mind closed down is a tragic figure.

The Scriptures give us some good advice along this line. "Give attendance to reading."[2] "Search the Scriptures."[3] "Study to show thyself approved unto God."[4]

"The craftsmanship of preaching is not to be belittled or despised—Because the message entrusted to us is of such paramount importance—we should labour at it night and day, sparing no pains to become skilled in our craft and to make the earthen vessel as worthy as we can of the treasure it contains—Slovenly work, careless technique, faulty construction and inarticulate delivery have had their day: they will pass muster no longer. Surely the preacher's task, undertaken at God's command for Christ's dear sake, demands the very best that unremitting toil and care and disciplined technical training can bring to it."[5]

While students for the ministry we are wise if we determine at the outset to know our Bibles. First hand knowledge of the Bible is

1. James M. Boice, "The Preacher and Scholarship" in "*Preaching,*" S. T. Logan, ed., pp. 94-99
2. I Timothy 4:13
3. John 5:39
4. II Timothy 2:15
5. James S. Stewart, *Heralds of God,* p. 103

the firm foundation on which a preacher can erect a temple of truth which will draw humanity to its holy light. Stott suggests soaking our minds in the Scriptures. Lloyd-Jones recommends that all preachers read through the entire Bible at least once each year!

We should read our Bibles "slowly but persistently. Take time to do it prayerfully. Read it chapter by chapter and book by book. Then study books on the Book that summarize its contents like G. Campbell Morgan's "*Living Messages*" or his "*Analyzed Bible*." The most solemn obligation rests on all preachers to master the Bible, and to be mastered by it."[1]

"Spurgeon said, 'I do not know how my soul would have been kept alive if it had not been for the searching of Scripture which preaching has involved.'—The very nature of our calling compels us to live daily in the pages of the Bible.—Let us give ourselves day by day to prayerful and meditative study of the Word, listening to hear what the Lord will speak: lest when we seek to interpret the Scriptures to others, it should have to be said of us, in the words of the Samaritan woman 'Thou hast nothing to draw with, and the well is deep' " (John 4:11)[2].

Memorize the Scriptures. Hide the Word in your heart. Set your mind to learning three verses each day, and in a year you will have a storehouse of Scriptural truth that will stick with you throughout your life. It will prove invaluable to you. Please set a goal to memorize Scripture verses and passages.

Then use good Bible commentaries. Read a commentary on a specific book of the Bible. Also consult Bible dictionaries, standard works on Systematic and Biblical Theology, and special books on Christian doctrine.

Every person who answers God's call to preach must become an inveterate reader of the Bible, of literature about the Bible, and of all books that promote the Gospel and the building of the Church. Read as if your life depended on it.

---

1.   Simon Blocker, *The Secret of Pulpit Power*, pp. 24-25
2.   James S. Stewart, op. cit., pp. 108-109

Refresh your soul with great spiritual classics like Augustine's *Confessions*, Baxter's *Reformed Pastor*, Wesley's *Journal*, David Brainerd's *Diary*, Bunyan's *Pilgrim's Progress* and *Imitation of Christ*, by Thomas á Kempis.

Even include some enemies of the faith in your reading. The damaging arguments of the skeptics can be turned to the greater glory of Christ.

Read, too, in history and biography, literature, fiction, and poetry. To have companied with Shakespeare, Tolstoy, Charles Dickens, Sir Walter Scott, and T. S. Eliot is to find your horizons stretched and widened.

Give attendance to reading. Set a goal of reading at least 25 books a year. Keep adding choice books to your library. Start with standard works and commentaries, and build from there. No one is expected to read everything in their library. What is important is to know what you have available, and where to find it when you need it. To that end, skim all your books to discover what they are about. Then you know where to go when a need arises.

No matter how often one has preached and taught, we still have much to learn. With good study methods and reading habits you will always be adding to your knowledge and understanding.

# Chapter 6

# Organization of the Sermon and the Theme

The sermon has been called a thrust—a thrust with the sword of the Spirit, which is the Word of God. Therefore, it takes our very best effort to properly prepare it.

Stott[1] tells of an Anglican clergyman who was lazy. He couldn't be bothered to prepare his sermons. He had considerable native intelligence and fluency of speech, and his congregation were simple people, so he got by fairly well with his unprepared sermons. Yet, in order to live with his conscience, he took a vow that he would always preach extempore, and put his trust in the Holy Spirit. Then one day, a few minutes before the morning worship began, who should walk into the church and find a place in one of the pews but the bishop, who was enjoying a Sunday off. The clergyman was embarrassed. It was one thing to bluff his uneducated congregation, but it was another thing to hoodwink his bishop. He went over to welcome his unexpected visitor and, in an endeavor to forestall his criticism, told him of the solemn vow he had taken always to preach extemporaneous sermons. The bishop seemed to understand, and the service began. Halfway through the sermon, however, to the great consternation of the preacher, the bishop got up and walked out. After the service he found a scribbled note on the vestry table which the bishop left. It read: "absolve you now from your vow."

"There was a young American Presbyterian minister, whose besetting sin was not laziness, but conceit. He frequently boasted in public that all the time he needed to prepare his Sunday sermon was the few minutes that it took him to walk to the church from his manse next door. Perhaps you can guess what his Session did—they bought him a new manse five miles away!"[2]

We can agree with Spurgeon that "habitually to come into the pulpit unprepared is unpardonable presumption."[3] What would we think of a lawyer who enters court to defend his client without having prepared his case? After the death of Dr. Leslie Weatherhead of London in 1976 a personal appreciation was written which said: "What was the secret of his extraordinary influence with people?

1. John R. Stott, *Between Two Worlds*, p. 211
2. Ibid.
3. Charles H. Spurgeon, *Lectures*, p. 4

Poor and rich, powerful and dispossessed, known and unknown, all came and all received his undivided attention. And what was the secret of the spell he could cast over a huge congregation who had withdrawal symptoms when he finished preaching? I must have asked him this twenty times, and always he replied, '*Preparation.*'"[1]

How, then shall we prepare? It is a subjective matter. There is no one way to prepare sermons. But there are some good guidelines to follow.

*First*, choose a subject, or a passage of Scripture, or both. There are several factors which can influence our choice. The liturgical year should be considered. Advent and Christmas, Lent and Easter, Ascension and Pentecost are illustrations of important seasons which must be taken into account. External events can play a part in your selection. A national experience, an issue of public debate, a disaster, or a catastrophe can call for sermonic treatment. Pastoral experiences will lead us to subjects which are geared to our people's need in their spiritual pilgrimage. Series of sermons on the Apostles' Creed, the Ten Commandments, various books of the Bible, on the Parables of Jesus, and on Bible characters all give us much direction in choosing sermonic material.

Once you have found your text or your Scripture passage, then meditate on it. Incubate it. Read it, reread it, and read it again. Turn it over in your mind. Probe at it, like a physician who is operating. Suck on it, like you would a piece of candy (lolly). Chew on it, like a cow chews its cud. Ask —What does it mean? What does it say? What is the context about? What can it say to our day?

Then we have to pray over it. R. W. Dale said: "Work without prayer is atheism, and prayer without work is presumption."

"Work as if it all depends on you and pray as if it all depends on God."

Now it is time to develop your theme. The theme seeks to express the essential spiritual message of the sermon in a single sentence. It is the sermon boiled down to its essential meaning. "The theme is the sermon condensed, the sermon is the theme expanded."

---

1.    *Church of England Newspaper,* 9 January 1977

"The theme states a proposition, enshrines a truth, conveys a meaning. It is drawn from the Bible verse or passage. It expresses its abiding, universal, contemporary and redemptive significance. It should be comprehensive enough to suggest directly or by implication the development of the theme in the body of the sermon."[1]

The theme should be timeless. Bible characters and Bible events are not put in the theme. For example—You would not say, Daniel and his friends stood up for God regardless of the cost, but, young men today must stand up for God regardless of the cost. Give Christ the preeminence in your theme. State the theme after the introduction, before the body of the sermon. Repeat it at intervals to keep the melody of the message in tune to the proper key. Then state it at the conclusion, or just before it.

Now work up an outline, and then begin to develop the body of the sermon. Let it fall into divisions or points. Three seems to be the sacred division, but two or four is also permissible. Be cautious about using too many points. Don't force the points, let them come naturally. It's nice to use alliteration, but don't press that too far.

Progress in your sermon. Stick to your subject. Don't ramble. You won't, if you stay by your theme, and progress within the organization you've set up. Vary your methods and style, so that your people don't always know what to expect. Beecher once said: "When you have finished your sermon, not a man of your congregation should be unable to tell you, distinctly, what you have done: but when you begin your sermon, no man in the congregation ought to be able to tell you what you are going to do."[2]

Let the divisions be clearly stated. Man must have a skeleton if he is to function. So must the sermon. But don't make too much issue of the skeleton. We must put flesh on it, so that the bones don't stick out. The hearers must be able to get hold of our scheme and follow us intelligently.

1.    Simon Blocker, *The Secret of Pulpit Power*, p. 18
2.    From James Black, *The Mystery of Preaching*, p. 99

Morgan[1] gives us an example of how not to do it. The text is John 4:24, a great text. A certain preacher started with this scheme of divisions. First, the transcendental properties of the Divine nature. Second, we have the anthropomorphic relations under which those transcendental properties of the Divine nature stand revealed and become apprehensible. Third, we have the Scripture symbolism by which these relations and mysteries of the transcendental properties of the Divine nature are apprehended, which constitutes worship.

The divisions are excellent. He had the right ideas. But to put his ideas before the congregation in such language was fruitless. Scarcely one in a hundred would grasp his point.

Now if the body of the sermon is nearly complete, you are ready to work on the introduction and the conclusion. Black says that you are to set your goal first.[2] That is okay, but the actual conclusion can come later.

An introduction is essential, and should be neither too long nor too short. Its purpose is to catch attention, and then you move on into your subject. Houses usually have a porch and books have a preface. The introduction arouses interest, stimulates curiosity, and whets the appetite for more. It introduces the subject by leading the hearers into it. It should be characterized by simplicity, pertinence to the subject, and courtesy. Paul's experience in Athens is very much to the point. "Men of Athens, I see that in every way you are very religious."[3] He began where they were. He knew their faults, but he was courteous.

Now to move on to the conclusion. Don't be slow in coming to it. Don't forget to conclude when the sermon should be ending. Don't conclude two or three times. For goodness' sake, don't say— to be continued next week. That is unforgivable!

"Everything in the sermon is a means to an end, and it is the end that counts."[4]

---

1.    G. Campbell Morgan, *Preaching*, p. 78
2.    James Black, op. cit, p. 90
3.    Acts 17:22, NIV
4.    James Black, op. cit., p. 105

The conclusion is the application. You have given them a message—now—so what? What are they to do about it? What difference should it make to them? The appeal to the will is the final thing. A discourse which makes no spiritual or moral appeal or demand is not a sermon. Truth is something which must be obeyed. Preach for a verdict. The last sixty seconds are the dynamic moments in preaching. Make the most of them!

How can we master all these details? It comes naturally in its own time, if we work at it and ask God for His help. It's like a child trying to walk. Failures—and then success.

"There is only one excuse and justification for all this talk about the art and craft of preaching—A LOVE FOR GOD and a passion for the souls of men, so that we are willing to submit ourselves and our gifts for the invasion of the Holy Spirit. Without the grace of God and a passion for others, the most finished discourse is a tinkling cymbal!"[1]

# Chapter 7

# **Illustrations**

The word illustration suggests a figure of light, whether through a window by day, or by electricity at night. It makes an obscure matter clear. Illustrations help to see and understand the truth being proclaimed.

Various writers give different ratings to illustrations in respect to sermons. First, we note some who rate them highly.

Arthur W. Hewitt, writing especially to rural preachers, says: "Probably the greatest function of the preacher's imagination is in

---

1.   Ibid., p. 106

sermon illustration. And this is a matter of supreme importance to the rural preacher. Thought must have definite incarnation for country people who live out-of-door, active lives, and think plainly and usually in practical terms. Illustrative preaching is gripping, convincing, and memorable."[1]

Faris D. Whitesell puts the issue strongly: "A sermon is virtually worthless without good illustrations. We live in a visual-minded generation. Magazines and newspapers use photographs or drawings to accompany good articles. This carries over into preaching…Since we learn 85 percent by sight, sermonic material must be made vivid and picturesque."[2]

James D. Robertson emphasizes the pictorial aspect of illustrations. "Abstractness is a great curse. God reaches men not through abstractions but through persons and through concrete situations of day-to-day personal life. The need of preaching pictorially is a psychological necessity in our picture-minded generation.

To preach in pictures is to follow the example of the Master-Preacher. As much as 75 percent of Christ's recorded teaching is in pictorial form."[3]

J. Daniel Baumann is convinced of their importance. "The mark which most often distinguishes average preaching from excellent preaching is the use of illustrations. Reflect for a moment. What sermons stick with you? What made them particularly meaningful? Very likely it was an illustration(s) that made them memorable."[4]

John R. Stott considers himself bad at using illustrations, but agrees "that a Christian preacher has no possible excuse for neglecting illustrations. There is ample divine precedence to encourage him…The Bible teems with illustrations, particularly similes. Above

1. Arthur Wentworth Hewitt, *Highland Shepherds*, p.153
2. Faris D. Whitesell, *Power in Expository Preaching*, p. 75ff
3. James D. Robertson in *Baker's Dictionary of Practical Theology*, p. 62
4. J. Daniel Baumann, *An Introduction to Contemporary Preaching*, p. 171

all, there are the parables of Jesus...The use of illustrations has a long and honorable record in the history of the church...Also add human psychology as another part of the foundation on which the practice of illustration rests...In order to see, we need light. Illustrate means to illumine, to throw light upon an otherwise dark object."[1]

David James Burrell states that "if a sermon be a thrust, then a dull sermon is no sermon at all."[2] He then calls for the use of illustrations.

Andrew W. Blackwood, famous as a homiletics professor, claims that illustrations have four purposes:

1. To make an obscure matter clear,
2. To regain the hearer's attention and to increase his interest,
3. To lend variety,
4. Splendor

Blackwood concludes that the all inclusive reason for using any illustration is to increase the effectiveness of the sermon.[3]

Other writers point out the values and the misuse of illustrations. Clarence E. Macartney, himself a master illustrator, wrote: "There are sermons which are solid, substantial, and orderly, but which have no window of illustration. Then there are sermons which consist almost entirely of illustrations and lack the solid substance of truth. In between these extremes lies the golden mean of preaching."[4] Macartney calls for imagination in preaching and concludes that "the preacher of imagination is the prince of the pulpit."[5]

David R. Breed describes the purpose of illustration: "Illustration must convey more truth than may be expressed without it. It should add somewhat to the abstract term. An illustration is not to be used for its own sake, no matter how fine it may appear in itself, and

1. John R. Stott, *Between Two Worlds*, p. 236ff
2. David J. Burrell, *The Sermon*, p. 217
3. Andrew W. Blackwood, *The Fine Art of Preaching*, pp. 113-15
4. Clarence E. Macartney, *Preaching Without Notes*, p. 31
5. Ibid., p. 75

it is exceeding doubtful if it is ever to be used for the purpose of ornamentation."[1]

James Daane seeks for a definition: "A sermon illustration is not an end in itself. It must throw light on some aspect of the sermon and thereby clarify it. What constitutes an illustration? A story, a poem, a real-life happening, a reference to a current event, a quotation aptly put, a citation from a novelist—but always something which illustrates an aspect of the sermon. They are not injected into sermons to entertain the congregation or to display the minister's erudition. They should not be added to extend an overly brief sermon nor serve as a sort of seventh-inning sermonic stretch in one that is too long."[2]

H. Grady Davis says three things about illustrations.[3] 1) To be effective it must be an example clarifying or supporting some definite point that is being made. Illustrate is a transitive verb. We do not simply illustrate. We illustrate something. 2) An illustration is valuable only to the degree in which it centers attention on the point being made, not on itself, and 3) The more specific and the more concrete an illustration is, the more powerful it is.

David Martyn Lloyd-Jones is somewhat fearful of illustrations. "They are only meant to illustrate truth, not to call attention to themselves." He decries using an illustration to build a sermon. "Use them sparsely and carefully."…"When you use them you should make sure of your facts."[4]

Illustrations certainly have a real place in our preaching. They must be wisely and judiciously chosen. An illustration beyond the bounds of good taste can spoil a whole sermon. There is good balance between using too many illustrations and too few. Theodore P. Ferris put it well when he said: "On the one hand, one picture is worth ten thousand words. A sermon that is entirely without pictures, without illustrations, is likely to reach only those whose intellectual discipline makes it possible for them to appreciate abstractions. On

---

1.   David R. Breed, *Preparing to Preach*, p. 235
2.   James Daane, *Preaching With Confidence*, pp. 74-75
3.   H. Grady Davis, *Design for Preaching*, pp. 255-6
4.   D. Martyn Lloyd-Jones, *Preaching and Preachers*, p. 230ff

the other hand, a sermon with too many illustrations is like a woman with too many jewels. The jewels which are originally intended to enhance the figure, hide it."[1]

# Chapter 8
# The Use of Hymns in Preaching

Hymns can be used like poetry to enhance and enlarge what you are attempting to impart to your people. Hymns are a type of poetry which can be grasped more easily than other poetry because they are usually more familiar to the hearers. When quoting hymns in sermons to Korean audiences, I sang them. Since they knew the same hymns in their language, translation was hardly necessary. People tend to rejoice in hearing hymns quoted which have real meaning to them.

Learn to know your hymnbook. Use it in worship, not only for singing, but also in your sermons.

Hymns can throw light on many truths which you will be preaching about. We give some examples:

| | |
|---|---|
| The Church | —"Christ Is Made The Sure Foundation" |
| | —"I Love Your Kingdom Lord" |
| | —"Onward Christian Soldiers" |
| | —"The Church's One Foundation" |
| The Cross of Calvary | —"Beneath the Cross of Jesus" |
| | —"Blessed Calvary" |

---

1.    Theodore P. Ferris, *Go Tell the People*, p. 93, Scribner, 1951

—"O Sacred Head Surrounded"
—"There Is A Green Hill Far Away"
—"When I Survey the Wondrous Cross"

God's Guidance
—"All The Way My Saviour Leads Me"
—"Guide Me, O My Great Jehovah"
—"Lead On, O King Eternal"

Grace of God
—"Amazing Grace"
—"Marvelous Grace of Our Loving Lord"
—"Only A Sinner Saved By Grace"
—"Saved By Grace"
—"Wonderful Grace of Jesus"

The Incarnation
—"Angels From the Realms of Glory"
—"Hark, The Herald Angels Sing"
—"Joy to the World"
—"O Come All You Faithful"
—"O Little Town of Bethlehem"
—"Silent Night"

Love
—"Immortal Love, Forever Full"
—"Love Divine, All Loves Excelling"
—"My Jesus, I Love You"
—"O Love That Will Not Let Me Go"

Prayer
—"Come, My Soul, Your Suit Prepare"
—"Prayer Is The Soul's Sincere Desire"
—"Sweet Hour of Prayer"
—"The Beautiful Garden of Prayer"

Security
—"A Shelter In The Time of Storm"
—"In The Secret of His Presence"
—"O Safe to The Rock"
—"Rock of Ages"
—"Safe In The Arms of Jesus"

The Trinity
—"Come, Thou Almighty King"
—"Glory Be To God The Father"
—"Holy, Holy, Holy"

Some hymns are illustrative of Bible experiences, and can shed light on them:

"In the Garden" illustrates Mary's experience with Christ following the resurrection.

"Nearer My God to Thee" is illustrative of Jacob's experience with God at Bethel.

# Chapter 9
# Expository Sermons

Expository preaching is an organized sermonic form of making clear a passage of Scripture. It is not a running commentary without unity or outline. It is not pure exegesis. Various preachers and writers have given us a variety of definitions of expository preaching. W. M. Taylor says: "By expository preaching, I mean that method of pulpit discourse which consists in the consecutive interpretation and practical enforcement of a book of the sacred canon."[1] F. B. Meyer states: "Expository preaching is the consecutive treatment of some book or extended portion of Scripture."[2] A. W. Blackwood writes: "Expository preaching means that the light for any sermon comes mainly from a Bible passage longer than two or three consecutive verses."[3] I. T. Jones defines expository preaching as interpreting a chapter, a portion of a chapter, or a whole book of the Bible.[4] Broadus states that it may be devoted to a long passage, or a very short one. It may be one of a series or stand by itself.[5]

1.  William M. Taylor, *The Ministry of the Word*, p. 155
2.  F. B. Meyer, *Expository Preaching Plans and Methods*, p. 29
3.  Andrew W. Blackwood, *Expository Preaching for Today*, p. 13
4.  Ilion T. Jones, *Principles and Practice of Preaching*, p. 59
5.  John A. Broadus, *A Treatise on the Preparation and Delivery of Sermons*, p. 303

D. G. Barnhouse wrote: "Expository preaching is the art of explaining the text of the Word of God, using all the experience of life and learning to illuminate the exposition."[1] D. R. Breed says: "The expository sermon is the product of exegesis, but it is in no sense its exhibition. It is not a running commentary upon some passage of Scripture in which its separate parts are taken up seriatim and explained, but, as its name implies, it is a piece of rhetoric: a sermon."[2] M. F. Unger states: "Expository preaching must be biblical, biblically instructive, challenging, consistent with the whole of biblical truth, and must come to grips with the human will and conscience."[3] D. M. Lloyd-Jones does not consider exposition or running commentary to be expository preaching. He says: The sermon matter should always be derived from the Scriptures. It should always be expository. This will help you to cover all aspects of the truth.[4] F. D. Whitesell compares various methods to a tree. The topical approach takes one part of the tree as the subject. In the textual method, you take the whole tree. In the expository method you seek a comprehensive, detailed, and thorough knowledge of the tree.[5]

The importance of expository preaching should be obvious to us as evangelicals. The Bible is our only rule of faith and life. Bible exposition is the preacher's main business. It puts us in a class with names like Matthew Henry, Joseph Parker, Marcus Dods, G. Campbell Morgan, Alexander Maclaren, Paul S. Rees, Harold J. Ockenga, D. Martyn Lloyd-Jones, and F. B. Meyer.

If the pastor seeks to develop a working and witnessing church, he will go a long way toward achieving this goal by preaching expository sermons. Expository preaching will feed the saints, wean them from the world, and set their affection on things above. It makes for a well-rounded ministry. He never needs to worry about

1. Clarence S. Roddy, *We Prepare and Preach*, p. 29
2. David R. Breed, *Preparing to Preach*, p. 387
3. Merrill F. Unger, *Principles of Expository Preaching*, p. 48
4. David Martyn Lloyd-Jones, *Preaching and Preachers*, p. 196
5. Faris D. Whitesell, *Power in Expository Preaching*, p. XIV

having enough material to preach about. There is all you need for years to come.

## Example of a Whole Book Sermon

Book            —Hosea
Key Verse       —Hosea 13:9
Theme           —Man's rebellion against God involves him in ruin, but God is always present to redeem.

    I. Man's Rebellion
   II. Sin's Ruin
  III. God's Redemption

In each division you can develop three parts, beginning with the Hosea-Gomer story, then applying it to the nation of Israel, and, finally to us.

## Example of a Whole Chapter Sermon

Read Romans 8 and condense the great truths into a theme. Don't give a running commentary. This would compel you to read all 39 verses, which would leave you little time left for exposition. It would give a grasshopper effect, or a jet plane effect—500 miles an hour to observe the beautiful scenery. Study Charles Hodge's commentary on Romans[1] and discover that he finds seven reasons for Christian security in Chapter eight.

Now work on a theme:

> A Christian is eternally secure.
>
> > or
>
> One who puts his trust in Christ is forever safe in Him.
>
> > or
>
> Those who turn from self to Christ are forever secure in Him.

Hymns come to your mind: "Rock of Ages," "In the Secret of His Presence," "O Safe to The Rock," "The Lord's Our Rock—A Shelter in The Time of Storm."

Don't attempt to detail all of the chapter—only those truths relating to Christian security.

---

1.    Charles Hodge, *Hodge on Romans*, pp. 38-39

Find a *key verse*—Verse 35 is suggested. It is not a *text*. Points:
1. The Christian is delivered from condemnation—vs. 1-4.
2. The Christian possesses God's Holy Spirit—vs. 5-11.
3. The Christian is a member of God's family—vs. 12-17.
4. God sees the believer through troubles—vs. 18-28.
5. It is God's sovereign purpose to save us—vs. 29-30.
6. God's Son is our Savior—vs. 31-34.
7. God's love lasts forever—vs. 35-39.

Begin with the emphasis on security, and conclude with the importance of being *in* Christ in order to know this security.

### Example of a Shorter Passage Sermon[1]

| | |
|---|---|
| Passage | —I Peter 4:12-16 |
| Subject | —The Fiery Trial |
| Theme | —Trials and testings become a proving ground for the reality of our faith |

1. The fact of trials—vs. 12.
2. The purpose of trials—vs. 13a.
3. The results of trials—vs. 13b, 14a, 16.

# Chapter 10
# Textual Sermons

A textual sermon is one that draws topic, theme, and divisions out of a single text of Scripture. A sermon on a single verse of Scripture, explaining the truth of that verse, doing it completely to the extent of making the development of the sermon the unfolding of the text, is a textual sermon. The subject, the theme, and outline of the

---

1.    John H. Muller, *Exciting Christianity*, pp. 68-72

body of the sermon, all come from the teaching of the text. It is usually quite possible to expound the meaning of a single verse of Scripture in one sermon.[1]

The textual sermon differs from the topical sermon in that it sticks to the one text and does not venture abroad in search of divisions. It takes a selected text as the measure and blueprint of the truth to be presented.

Textual preaching differs from expository preaching in its exhaustive treatment of a text. The expository preacher has to select from several possible topics and themes, choosing one to be treated. The textual sermon is limited to one verse, but the verse has to be big enough to furnish divisions as well as topic and theme.

A sermon is called textual because its divisions stick to the text. It falls short if it has less divisions than the verse calls for, or adds divisions not found in the verse. This does not mean that a textual preacher is barred from explaining the Scriptural setting of his text, or from quoting other Bible verses. Blocker puts it this way: "In textual preaching the text is commander-in-chief, the text being a single verse of Scripture with enough content to qualify for the office; and the preacher's theme song in making his thematic outline is, 'Where it leads me, I will follow.' "[2]

Blackwood argues for the use of a text. Some of his points can be true of expository sermons as well as textual sermons. 1) It assures the speaker of a message from God, 2) A text sets up a goal for every sermon, 3) Using a text leads the man in the study to pray, and 4) to work.[3]

Dabney does not like the classification of a textual sermon. "I acknowledge that I am not careful to invent a more exact name for this species of discourse upon insulated fragments of Scripture, which should never have had place in the Church at all."[4] He is really arguing for expository preaching.

---

1. See Simon Blocker, *The Secret of Pulpit Power*, p. 113
2. Ibid., p. 115
3. Andrew W. Blackwood, *The Preparation of Sermons*, pp. 44-5
4. Robert L. Dabney, *Sacred Rhetoric*, p. 76

In a sense Breed writes in a similar vein to Dabney. He states that "the textual method is closely allied to the expository and the line of demarkation cannot be sharply drawn."[1] He does argue for the use of a text. "It is not proper at any time to preach without its use."[2]

Some samples of textual sermon outlines are offered below:

### Old Testament

Text            —Psalm 139:23-24
Subject      —The Sinner's Prayer to God
Theme        —Sinners must desire God's searching and cleansing if they would be led in the way everlasting.

    I. A Prayer for Searching
   II. A Desire for Cleansing
  III. A New Way of Life

---

Text            —Isaiah 55:1
Subject      —God's Free Offer *or* God's Bargain Counter
Theme        —God freely offers His grace and salvation to all sinners who will come to receive it.

    I. Candidates for the offer
   II. Contents of the offer
  III. Cost of the offer

---

Texts          —Proverbs 11:30 and Daniel 12:3 (Two texts combined)
Subject      —The Christian Duty of Soul Winning
Theme        —Winners of souls are wise and blessed Christians.

    I. The Reason for Soul Winning
   II. The Reward for Soul Winning

---

1.    David R. Breed, *Preparing to Preach*, p. 21
2.    Ibid., p. 23

## New Testament

| | |
|---|---|
| Text | —I Thessalonians 2:13 |
| Subject | —The Church and The Scriptures |
| Theme | —The Church receives and believes the Bible as God's truth. |
| Introduction | —The importance of the Bible to the life of the church. |

Divisions:

    I.  The Word of Revelation
       "Received it as the Word of God"
    II.  The Word of Preaching
       "Which you heard from us"
    III.  The Word of Faith
       "Received it in truth as the Word of God"

| | |
|---|---|
| Conclusion | —Entrance to the Kingdom is contingent upon believing. We are born again by the Word of God. |
| Closing Hymn | —"O Word of God Incarnate" |

---

| | |
|---|---|
| Text | —Hebrews 2:3 |
| Subject | —"Don't Neglect Salvation" |
| Theme | —Salvation possessed but neglected means inescapable penalty. |

Divisions:

    I.  The Meaning of Salvation
    II.  The Greatness of Salvation
    III.  The Neglect of Salvation
    IV.  The Penalty of Neglecting Salvation

### OR

| | |
|---|---|
| Theme | —A Christian must show his colors or face the consequences. |

    I.  Reasons for showing your colors as a Christian
    II.  Failures to show your colors as a Christian
    III.  Consequences of not showing your colors as a Christian[1]

---

1.    Simon Blocker, op. cit., p. 119

# Chapter 11
# Topical Sermons

A topical sermon is the development in sermonic form of a Bible truth. It can also bring Bible truth to bear on present day issues. Choose a topic and relate it to the Scripture. Condense the results of thought and prayerful study into a theme. Do your best to have a target, and shoot at it.

A weakness of topical preaching is the inherent danger of getting away from the Bible. The topical preacher is tempted to become a problem preacher, dealing with present-day problems and issues. It can stress adjustment more than redemption, and prescribe techniques rather than union with Christ.

It is also difficult to observe the principle of unity in topical preaching. The preacher is apt to bite off more than either he or his people can chew or swallow![1]

Skinner speaks of the problems involved in this way. "Topical preaching has the inherent tendency to be somewhat shallow and untrue to the total perspective of truth. There is also the temptation to express the preacher's personal views without a complete Biblical frame of reference. Nevertheless this approach has been used by some of the most effective preachers of history, and should form a part of every pulpit program!"[2]

Baumann writes rather favorably for topical sermons. "The topical sermon is built around a subject, an idea that bears no analytical relation to any one particular passage of Scripture. It is frequently the easiest type of preaching because it requires the least amount of background and Biblical research. It grants greater freedom to the

---

1.   See Simon Blocker, *The Secret of Pulpit Power*, Chapter X
2.   Craig Skinner, *The Teaching Ministry of the Pulpit*, pp. 141-2

preacher without the restriction of a text…Problems reside in this form of preaching, namely, the tendency on the part of the preacher to play topical favorites and the tendency toward unbiblical preaching…It lacks the safeguard of a text."[1]

Let us take an example of this approach to sermons. We'll work on the subject of "Confessing Christ." A good text is found in Matthew 10:32. You check out the topic in the Bible dictionary, and in commentaries. You can come up with various questions about the subject of Confessing Christ—What it means. Why is it important? Why is it difficult? Why is it necessary? What does it cost? What does it do for you? What does it mean to others? What it means to God.

As you begin to try to construct a theme with all the divisions in it, you soon begin to appraise the points already considered. Perhaps they can be boiled down to three or four divisions with the promise of unity for the sermon. Preaching on the topic of Confessing Christ certainly calls for an explanation of what it means to confess Christ. That is properly a first division. Secondly, it ought to be pointed out what it costs to confess Christ. That makes a second division. Third, it is well to explain the benefits or rewards of confessing Christ. Now we have division three. There still is no theme. Sometimes the divisions come before the theme. Here are some tries at it— 1) Confessing Christ has such importance and confers such benefits, that whatever the cost, it is a Christian's most urgent and imperative challenge—22 words. 2) Nothing is more significant or important or rewarding, however costly, than confessing personal faith in Jesus Christ as Saviour and Lord—21 words. 3) Confessing Christ means so much and has such far-reaching consequences that whatever the cost, it has to be done—20 words.

These themes are too long and are too hard to remember. Try a shorter one—Confessing Christ is the costly road to the grandest results. It's good, and it only has 10 words. BUT—"the costly road"

---

1.  J. Daniel Baumann, *An Introduction to Contemporary Preaching*, p. 101

in the middle of the theme stands in the middle, making it look like a hunchback.

Here it comes—Confessing Christ is worth all it costs. Now we're down to 7 words, and "worth" is now the center and summit of our theme. The divisions are in the theme. Now you can close with the hymn, "Ashamed of Jesus."[1]

# Chapter 12
# Doctrinal Sermons

"The English word doctrine is derived, as is the word doctor, from the Latin *docere*, meaning "to teach." Doctrine, presumably, is what is taught by a doctor, or learned man. Doctrine is the ordered arrangement of those truths by which the church lives."[2]

Breed states that "the doctrinal sermon is the culmination and crown of all sermonizing...It is of the very highest rank: there is nothing beyond it...It has to do with those sublime revelations which God has made to man...It is the result of the profound study of the mysteries of the kingdom of heaven as set forth in the Word of God."[3]

Blocker says that "doctrinal preaching is by its very nature the most basic form of preaching because it is always based on Bible truth rather than counsel or exhortation. It is the preaching or proclamation of the foundations of the Christian faith. Broad streams of revelation run through the Scripture...Countless

1.  Simon Blocker, op. cit., pp. 98-102
2.  J. Carter Swaim, in *Baker's Dictionary of Practical Theology*, p. 27
3.  David R. Breed, *Preparing to Preach*, p. 427

tributaries flow from these mighty streams, revealing duty and practical implications. Doctrinal preaching is the big steamer that does business on the main streams."[1]

Doctrinal sermons are not necessarily in a class by themselves. They can overlap with topical, textual, or expository categories. Either of these three types can also be doctrinal in nature.

Doctrinal preaching is the source of the church's life. Christians cannot survive spiritually unless they are fed on great doctrines, the "meat of the Word." Unfortunately, many Christian people react unfavorably to it. They often regard it as dry and uninteresting. It is up to us to see to it that this is not true. I can remember preaching in my first church on the Heidelberg Catechism. Following the sermon a well-versed deacon came up to me and said: "I always thought before that catechism sermons were dry!" Without a doubt doctrinal truth has often been presented in an uninteresting manner. The great truths have to be real to us if we are to make them real to our people. It is the proclamation of great doctrinal truths that enables Christians to "grow in grace, and in the knowledge of our Lord and Saviour, Jesus Christ."[2]

Doctrinal sermons should be textually based. They may also draw on other areas of the Bible in order to verify and back up the truth being considered. An attempt should be made to make one basic doctrine clear. This need not preclude reference to other related doctrines. It is better not to use an apologetic or a polemic approach. Instruction in the faith should be your aim.

We present a sermon on the Ascension of Christ as illustrative of thematic doctrinal messages.

| | |
|---|---|
| Subject | —THE ASCENSION OF CHRIST |
| Text | —Luke 24:50-51 |
| Theme | —Christ left earth for heaven to be crowned as our Divine Redeemer. |

Divisions:

---

1.   Simon Blocker, *The Secret of Pulpit Power, p. 122*
2.   II Peter 3:18

I. The ascension from earth
II. The reception in heaven
III. The fruits of the ascension

(Sanctified imagination can be used in division two, and using Psalm 24 and Revelation passages.)

# Chapter 13
# Narrative Sermons

"The Bible is the story of a Divine crusade of redemption. It is a history of God's interposition in human affairs. It is a record of events which have to do with God's introduction of His kingdom among men. It therefore treats of persons individually, in groups, and in the larger units of nations. As an historical record the Bible is full of narratives, stories of persons, families, nations and events. The narrative element is a rich harvest field for the preacher. The stories of the Bible have conspicuous preaching values. One of the most interesting types of sermon is the narrative sermon, the presentation of a story of the Bible in sermon form."[1]

"In the narrative sermon instruction is conveyed by means of example. It deals with some Biblical character or some Biblical scene. In structure and method it is the simplest form of sermonizing, but even so it is often the most interesting and the most profitable."[2]

Different types of narrative sermons can be noted. One style became prominent by an outstanding British and American preacher of the 1800s, William M. Taylor. He preached series of messages on Bible characters, and on the parables and miracles of Jesus. His

---

1.    Simon Blocker, *The Secret of Pulpit Power*, p. 131
2.    David R. Breed, *Preparing to Preach*, p. 375

method was to tell the narrative first. Taylor had unusual gifts of realistic portrayal. Then he added a number of lessons which were apparent in the narrative, for which he also had real competence. It is of interest that his book on preaching does not make any specific mention of the narrative sermon. It is possible that he would include narrative under expository preaching,[1] but it is not clearly stated as such. Surely this approach to narrative sermons has a real value.

However, a better method is to obtain a theme, and plan the divisions in a universal form. The divisions would have a timeless form, and then the varied aspects of the narrative would be fitted under them.

The narrative should be told during the sermon, but not at any one point, or all at once. The divisions can have to do with stages of the story.

In order to introduce your narrative sermon you can speak some timeless, arresting remarks about what you plan to say. Then you can state that you intend to build your remarks around a Scriptural narrative.

Be sure at all times that you keep the message contemporary. Let the story of Abraham, or Joseph, or Moses, or David be illustrative of a present day truth. Do not let the story stand alone without application to life today.

"Narrative preaching has much to commend it. If ably done, it is very interesting. In a day when general ignorance of the Bible over wide areas is nothing short of appalling, narrative sermons are fine techniques for spreading Biblical knowledge and inducing people to become habitual Bible readers. A thematic narrative sermon is an effective vehicle for interpretation of Bible narratives."[2]

The following narrative sermon outlines are based on the Luke 15 passage:

---

1.    William M. Taylor, *The Ministry of the Word*, Lecture VII
2.    Simon Blocker, op. cit., pp. 136-7

Subject     —"CHRIST, THE SEEKING SHEPHERD"

or

"CHRIST WANTS THE LOST"

Text        —Luke 15:3-7

Theme    —Christ's diligent search for the lost ends in rejoicing over finding of the sinner.

Divisions:

    I.   The lost condition of mankind

   II.   Christ's search for the lost

  III.   The rejoicing over finding of the sinner.

---

Subject     —"GOD'S WONDERFUL LOVE"

Text        —Luke 15:11-24

Theme    —God's wonderful love forgives a man who has run his own life and come to grief, if he repents.

Divisions:

    I.   Man by nature insists on running his own life.

   II.   When man runs his own life, he is sure to come to grief.

  III.   Man must repent and turn to God.

  IV.   When man comes to God, he is gladly received.

---

Subject     —"AT HOME, BUT WITHOUT GOD"

Text        —Luke 15:25-32

Theme    —Although one may have the outward form of religion, he may be far from God.

Divisions:

    I.   The outward form of religion

   II.   The lack of real religion

  III.   Real religion for all

# Chapter 14

# Children's Talks

In many of our churches it is expected that you will speak to the children during the morning worship service. If the Sunday School meets separately, then you can slot this talk into the service at almost any spot. If the children leave the church service for Sunday School classes or Junior Church, then it will need to come early in the service so that the children can leave in time for their classes or activity. The children's talk is usually followed by a children's hymn. In some churches the children are used to coming to the pulpit area, and in others they come to a front seat.

No matter the approach to the children's talk, there are several things which are vital to remember whenever you talk to children. The first is—don't make it too long. Five minutes is ordinarily enough. Their attention span is short. The second is—don't talk over their heads. Don't use big words unless you explain them. Your effort should be to bring spiritual truths down to the simplest levels, and to make them understandable to a child. Make sure the content is evangelical and has a biblical base.

There are many different ways to approach speaking to children. Frequently object lessons can be used to illustrate a point. Also, you can speak about ordinary experiences from daily life. Bible stories lend themselves for adaptation to children's talks and can be most meaningful. Other stories from life or from the mission fields can be used illustratively for the children. Your own activities during the week can also be adapted for the children, as long as you do it wisely. It is seldom effective to speak to them with notes—just talk directly to them.

It is possible to buy books of children's talks or object lessons. They certainly will need to be adapted. Generally you will not want to use them except to give you ideas. Then you take off on the idea and develop it your own way. Often the books lack in spiritual depth, or, on the other hand, they are too deep into spiritual truth for children to follow.

Ofttimes you will be surprised that your children's talks will be much appreciated by the adults.

# Chapter 15
# Sermon Series

When we decide to deliver a number of sermons under one general title we commonly speak of a sermon series, or a series of sermons.

Some series are closely related sermons, while others hang together quite loosely. Series can be a very important part of your preaching ministry. It is amazing that more is not written about them. I have gone through many books on Practical Theology, and have found only three of them touching on series of sermons—a short chapter on "Sermons in Courses"[1] at the end of David Breed's book, *"Preparing to Preach,"* a section on "Serial Preaching" in Clarence Macartney's *"Preaching Without Notes,"*[2] and five pages in James Stewart's *"Heralds of God."*[3]

I have found that series can be very meaningful in the ministry. Expository series have been done on the Psalms, Isaiah, Daniel, the Beatitudes, John, Acts, Romans, I Corinthians, II Corinthians, Galatians, Ephesians, Philippians, Colossians, I Thessalonians, II Thessalonians, I Timothy, II Timothy, Titus, Hebrews, James,

1.    David R. Breed, *Preparing to Preach*, chapter 7
2.    Clarence Macartney, *Preaching Without Notes*, pp. 93-106
3.    James S. Stewart, *Heralds of God*, p. 167 ff

I Peter,[1] II Peter, I John, the 7 churches of Revelation, and Unusual Books of the Bible.

Doctrinal series have included those on The Apostles' Creed, The Lord's Prayer, and our Calvinistic Faith. Textual or topical series on Bible kings, Bible marriages, Bible mountains, Bible queens, Bible questions, Bible tombstones, God's exceptions, great Bible texts, great Bible interviews, guess the Bible character, life questions, the highway of life, parables of Jesus, perplexing problems, questions about Jesus, questions of Jesus, The I AMs of Jesus, unusual Bible characters, and unusual Bible texts. Then there has been a series of dialog sermons, a Lenten series, and several series on the Cross.

Generally it is best not to let a series run too long. Most of mine have run six to eight sermons in length. The expository series on books can run much longer. Macartney, who has produced numerous books of series of sermons, speaks of preaching fifteen sermons on a doctrinal series, and twenty-one on "Peter and His Lord." "The advantage of a long series on a life such as that of Peter, or David, or Paul is that it compels one to continuous and consecutive Bible study. When the preacher finishes such a series, he feels that he knows every detail on his character's face."[2]

One of the dangers to avoid in series is the problem of repetition. It is not unusual for some preachers to rehash the previous sermon in the first third of the sermon which follows. Keep that to a *minimum*.

Breed lays out several qualities of series of sermons, or courses, as he calls them.[3]

1.   There must be unity. There should be a real relation between the separate subjects and the general subject. The single sermons must be a part of the whole.

2.   There must be progress. The second sermon must be a positive advance on the first and so on.

---

1.   John H. Muller, *Exciting Christianity*
2.   Clarence Macartney, op. cit., pp. 93-94
3.   David R. Breed, op. cit., pp. 451-3

3.  Each separate sermon must be in a measure complete in itself. It is a part of a whole, yet it is a whole part. A series of sermons is not one long sermon divided into separate portions, like a serial story in a magazine—to be continued next month. Each sermon must be complete, and able to stand by itself. Breed states that it is twice as hard to prepare a course of sermons as to prepare a single one. Plan out your entire series before you start it.

Preaching series of sermons can be a very interesting approach to sermonizing, and it can be a distinct challenge to the preacher. TRY IT!

# Chapter 16

# The Problem
# of Special Days

In the planning and preparing of sermons for the parish you will soon find that it will become a problem to provide variety in sermonizing for special days. It develops into a larger problem when you stay in one parish for an extended period of time.

Christmas and Easter come every year, and call for two or more sermons each year. These are great festival days, and many passages of Scripture can be drawn on for these messages. But Pentecost and Ascension also come every year, and for these days Scripture passages are much more limited. Other days such as Harvest Festival, Mother's Day and Father's Day also call for some real ingenuity to provide variety in your messages.

One of the ways I have sought to vary the approach has been to use first-person sermons at Christmas and Easter. In such a message the speaker always poses as another person throughout the sermon.

Everything is presented from that person's viewpoint. For instance, Christmas can be viewed from the vantage point of the shepherds, the wise men, the Innkeeper, the people of Bethlehem, Mary, Joseph, and Herod. Easter can be discussed from the observations of Nicodemus, Joseph of Arimathea, Mary Magdalene, Peter, John and Thomas. It can give interesting variety to well-known stories and experiences. Such an approach calls for a sanctified imagination to fill in details that aren't given in the Scriptures. First-person sermons take a lot of planning and need to be presented dramatically and carefully. They are not everybody's "cup of tea."

Start right away, during school days, to take note of any material that might fit into special days. Prepare a file folder for each day. You can never have too much material for the steady need of Special Day sermons.

# Chapter 17

# The Whole Counsel of God

As Paul was giving his farewell message to the Ephesian elders he spoke these significant words: "I have not shunned to declare unto you all the counsel of God."[1]

The RSV translates it "the whole counsel of God," "the complete will of God" is in Phillips, and "the whole will of God" is in the NIV. In other words, Paul rode no hobby horse. He was faithful in making known to those believers everything that God wanted them to know. Under his ministry they had heard the complete will and purpose of God for their lives. We should strive for the same end in our preaching and teaching ministry.

---

1.    Acts 20:27

We need to lay stress on all the major doctrines of our faith—from the truths of creation to the wonders of redemption. We need to speak of God the Father, God the Son, and God the Spirit. We need to emphasize the importance of the practical outworking of these doctrines in our daily living.

It is easy for some preachers to ride a hobby horse on one doctrine or one idea. Some are always into the second coming. Others dwell constantly on the Holy Spirit. To some baptism is a favorite subject. Still others stay on the practical side of the Christian life all the time without laying the necessary doctrinal foundation. Some talk about healing so much that you would think our bodies were more important than our spirits. Some will preach 40 or 50 sermons on one or two Bible chapters.

We have a full-orbed Gospel. It is our responsibility before God to present the whole counsel of God, so that our people can grow in faith as God's people, be well-informed and "be thoroughly equipped for every good work."[1]

---

1. II Timothy 3:17, NIV

# Part 2

# SERMON
# DELIVERY

# Chapter 18

# The Importance of Good Delivery

The gospel of Jesus Christ must be proclaimed. A sermon is not really a sermon until it is shared. A minister is not really a preacher until he communicates his message to others. The most polished manuscript is not a sermon until it is delivered. It was Phillips Brooks who defined preaching as both truth and personality. Truth which is contained in a manuscript becomes a sermon when it is mixed with the personality of the preacher and communicated to his listeners.

The sermon is not finished until it reaches its destination, and has been delivered. Its effectiveness depends a great deal on the way the preacher delivers it. "The end crowns the work."

Clovis Chappell heads his chapter on delivery as "Our Finest Hour." James Black names his "The Day of Action" and "The Day of Unburdening."

The tenth chapter of Acts gives us the record of a victorious service of worship. In street language, it "went over." It was a high hour for the soul. Those privileged to take part in it were so changed that they were able to make a significant contribution to their day. One of the biggest events that took place in the Roman Empire of that day was surely this service that Simon Peter conducted in the home of Cornelius.

The wonderful truth is that a worship experience of this kind is not the privilege of a Bible-time generation only. It is possible in our twentieth century as well as in the first. It is certainly possible in our churches today.

Generally speaking the biggest event of the week in your community is when you lead people in the worship of God and in the proclamation of His Word. It should always be a thrill. To preach with the consciousness that the Holy Spirit is taking your message and blessing it to the hearts of your congregation is one of the most thrilling experiences that a person may know this side of heaven.

Adams points out that sometimes theological students think that giving attention to pulpit speech is unimportant or "unspiritual." However, the facts about delivery demonstrate the vital importance of this study. Attention must be given to pulpit speech not in order to turn a preacher into a Demosthenes of the pulpit, but rather to keep him from distorting the Word of God. It is important to emphasize that we must learn to preach the Bible truthfully and effectively.[1]

It is very difficult to separate content and delivery. They are so closely entwined. Content clearly affects delivery. Ofttimes preachers reverse the order with dire results. Some have worked on the idea that you should always smile and look pleasant while preaching. Generally this is a good practice, but there are certainly times when it would be most inappropriate. For instance, to start talking about a death or a funeral with a broad grin could be disastrous. Then there are those who believe that every sermon should be shouted from beginning to end. To shout "GOD LOVES YOU" and then to augment the shout with a shaked fist could be tragic indeed. Adams asks: "Who would think of proposing to his fiancee by shaking his fist in her face and saying 'I love you' to the accompaniment of a shout or growl?"[2]

The preacher cannot speak effectively about hell while smiling, neither can he speak about the joys of heaven in a dull, lifeless, and unemotional way. Both the way that the voice is handled and the way that the body functions, must grow out of and parallel the content so that the delivery assists rather than hinders the transmission of the content.

1.    Adams, Jay: *Pulpit Speech*, p. 35
2.    Adams, op. cit., p. 34

Adams also has a whole chapter on "Acquiring a Preaching Style."[1] This is important. Style, however, is more than self-expression. Good style must be balanced with the norms of custom. One's style may well be unique, but his style must always be *in* style and not out of style.

Style relates to language usage—the choice and use of words. It is wise to study and practice the use of vocabulary, grammar, and syntax. Style is concerned with words and how we put them together to communicate ideas. We who believe in the clear inspiration of the Scriptures are aware of the fact that the choice of a correct word to express a thought is of great importance. The sovereign God used the different personalities of the writers of Scripture as well as their distinct styles. Bible-minded Christians, of all people, should believe in cultivating a clear and effective style. Every effective preacher of the Word should himself become a student of words.

The goal of preaching style is to acquire full fluency. Fully fluent speech calls no attention to itself while it effectively communicates content. Style and delivery really exist for the sake of content. Style is a means, and not an end. Thus it must be adapted to and appropriate to the purpose, the speaker, the audience, and the occasion. If it is not appropriately adapted, it will call attention to itself rather than to God's message.[2]

Good speakers use a variety of language levels and are flexible in their style. No one wears the same clothes on every occasion. You dress differently when going to church, going fishing, or repairing the car. Language is the dress of your thought. You must speak differently when giving a children's address, when speaking to adults from a pulpit, when addressing a banquet of Rotarians, or when conducting a funeral. You must adapt your speaking to the audience and the occasion, and speak appropriately. Your language level is determined by the audience and the occasion as well as by the topic.

---

1.    Adams, op. cit., p. 110ff
2.    Adams, op. cit., p. 116

Paul sought for clarity of words when he told the Corinthian Church that "unless you speak intelligible words with your tongue, how will anyone know what you are saying? You will just be speaking into the air."[1] Preachers can very easily be guilty of this offense. It is possible to offend by becoming overly formal in your speech. Your words can be wearing a tuxedo while you're attending a bar-b-que. For example, you would hardly give an intimation (announcement) about a youth event with the same vocabulary and solemnity as you would use in preaching doctrines like election and atonement. What may be fitting and proper for one occasion can be ineffective, or even absurd, on another occasion. Wisdom in the use of words and judgment in the language level used are essential.

You operate from the every day level of today's society plus a heightening to which the subject matter of the Scriptures naturally elevates it.

We should ever be ready to ask ourselves: "How can we improve our delivery?" Adams gives several suggestions.[2] *First*—Patiently practice breaking old patterns and establish new ones. *Second*—Practice during day-by-day speaking situations, not during formal messages. *Third*—Practice in short sessions, averaging about ten minutes. *Fourth*—Practice daily. *Fifth*—Make sure you follow proper and correct practices. If you practice wrongly you would do yourself more harm than good.

In your practice you should not work directly for oratorical skills in themselves. Neither should you try to incorporate planned gestures. Your concern should be to learn to preach with the same bodily actions and with the same voice usage that you would use in normal conversation.

When the sermon is being delivered the preacher must think only of God, of his congregation, and of the content of God's Word which he is expounding. It is no time to think about methodology. It can become self-defeating to think about the delivery during preaching itself. With proper practice, new habits can be developed and old ones

---

1.    I Corinthians 14:9 NIV
2.    Adams, op. cit., p. 37

will disappear. Continued growth can be assured only by continued practice. "Speech improvement should be the life-long endeavor of every preacher."[1]

# Chapter 19
# The Voice in Delivery

Preaching can be described as animated conversation. There is no room for shouting or yelling. Preaching is proclamation, not declamation (pompous tirade). You should be easily audible all through the sermon. Do without shouting or strain. Give words their value. Stress the important ones. Take hold especially of final consonants. Audibility is largely a matter of enunciation. There are cadences in all good speaking. Do not lower your voice when you lower your tone. That is a vice that has ruined many a good sermon.

Spurgeon lamented the wrong use of the voice in sermons. He said: "There are brethren in the ministry whose speech is intolerable; either they rouse you to wrath, or else they send you to sleep. No narcotic can ever equal some discourses in sleep-giving properties; no human being, unless gifted with infinite patience, could long endure to listen to them, and nature does well to give the victim deliverance through sleep."[2]

The normal speaking rate is between 125 and 190 words per minute. When you use over 200 words per minute you tend to reduce the ability to listen. We should strive to be rapid enough to show vitality and still slow enough to be certain of articulating distinctly

---

1.    Adams, Jay: op. cit., p. 40
2.    Spurgeon, Charles H., *Lectures to His Students*, p. 199

and being comprehensive. Variety and reasonable rapidity will insure interest in the movement of the sermon.

Some people think that shouting adds emphasis. However, a sermon that becomes an extended shouting session has no emphasis at all. Volume should never be confused with unction. Any change in pattern or pace will help you to achieve a measure of emphasis.

Black emphasizes being heard as a first essential in public speaking.[1] Not being heard is as bad as not being understood, and both create a vacuum. Ordinary people (barring the deaf) have a right to expect that any professional speaker should be easily audible. Our message is important enough to be heard. Sometimes people are to blame, because they are not attendant to the spoken word. But our duty, as far as we can, is to be easily and naturally heard.

Voice training should not be treated casually or indifferently. Some students, Black suggests,[2] treat it with a sort of superior disdain. Later they may find their congregation treating them with a dose of the same medicine. Black testifies that he overcame a stutter and a thickness of speech by honest practice and self-control. In nothing more than in speech does practice induce perfection. Make good use of all sound counsel and do not be above taking hints from any quarter. To take offence at helpful criticism is a kind of disguised vanity.[3]

Training of the voice may work wonders. Practice may give power and elasticity to the voice we have. It may also improve the quality of our voice, giving it a depth, a tone, and a range that can bring untold gain. If our heart is in preaching, we will not consider this trivial, or something to be sneered at. If you train your mind, you should certainly train the vehicle of its expression.[4]

1.  Black, James, *The Mystery of Preaching*, p. 180
2.  Ibid., p. 181
3.  Ibid., p. 182
4.  Ibid., p. 183

There is a special type of speaking which often is used by men in the pulpit. It differs from normal speaking. The Dutch have a word for it—"Prek-tone," which means a preaching tone. It is unnatural and stilted. Adams speaks of ministerial whines, drones, tunes, and monotones. Luccock describes a synthetic voice, and also a "too perfect voice."[1] Skinner says that an evident professionalism in delivery is a barrier rather than an asset in communication.

The above are habits that one picks up and develops. Adams says that "they usually involve a combination of pitch-rate melody patterns. These are those intolerable sounds made by preachers that seem to be peculiar to the profession."[2] Doubtless these habits developed because it was felt that it added a note of sanctity or authority to what was spoken. Actually, such tones turn people off. The message of God is the virile Gospel of God the Father Who sent His Son to the cross for our salvation. Jesus was a man's man, who lived and died like a man. Do not speak of Him in tones which emasculate Him of all manly qualities. They seriously detract from the Christian message, and tend to misrepresent it.

Monotones involve an inflexibility in pitch or rate. It can be devastating to preaching. Adams states that this habit is usually connected with personality.[3] One must learn how to throw himself, including his emotions, into his speaking. He must learn to be more outgoing. "A preacher must be willing to allow the Word of God to grasp him inwardly and preach it to others with the same effectiveness and power that it has had upon him."[4]

Resonance, articulation, and pronunciation are also important factors in the use of the voice. Resonance is the reinforcement and prolongation of a sound by reflection or by sympathetic vibration of other parts of the body. It is affected by opening and closing the

1. Halford E. Luccock, *In the Minister's Workshop*, pp. 195-6
2. Adams, Jay, *Pulpit Speech*, p. 143
3. Ibid., p. 144
4. Ibid., p. 145

mouth, and by placing tension on other organs. Articulation is the shaping of sounds into words. Clear and exact utterance of sounds in our language is essential to proper understanding and communication. Articulation works through the mouth, the tongue, the teeth, and the lips. Faulty articulation can be simple to correct. Pronunciation is the sum of most of the audible characteristics in a word. A pronouncing dictionary is a standard reference to proper pronunciation of English. It can vary from Australia to the United Kingdom to the United States.

The force and distinctiveness of pronunciation will always need some enlargement in addressing an assembly. Some variation in pitch, inflection, volume, and emphasis will add color and strength to any message.[1]

Jefferson summarizes the rules for voice and style by saying: "Be natural. This is the sum of the whole matter. Do not push the voice into clerical cadences, but let it flow out of a open throat, breaking into syllables which tell truly what you think and feel. Do not push the language into inflated and bombastic forms, but let it flow as naturally as a brook through one of God's own green meadows. Do not shove the thought into artificial altitudes, but let it move along the level on which you do your ordinary thinking. If you are altogether natural, you will become invisible. Style is perfect when it cannot be seen."[2]

The perfection of Christ as a preacher was that he showed preaching and life to be one. This has also been true of His greatest followers. Jesus not only instructed people with facts, but communicated His own way of life. The preacher, more so than any other man, is called upon to practice what he preaches. "Beyond a technical brilliance which Whitefield, for instance, clearly had, was his saintly character. More of man's nature is revealed in his voice than in any other way. It therefore follows that a preacher's soul can and

---

1.    Skinner, Craig, *The Teaching Ministry of the Pulpit*, p. 192
2.    Jefferson, Charles E., *The Minister as Prophet*, pp. 143-44

should be revealed through his voice. Essentially, the concern of the preacher is not his sermon but his soul."[1]

# Chapter 20

# The Process of Delivery

The various methods of delivering sermons receive the lion's share of attention from most of the writers who deal with delivery. Most of them are agreed that there are four different approaches, although they may call them by various names.

**METHOD NO. 1** The preparation of a full manuscript and the reading of it. As a young man starting in the ministry, whether he reads or preaches freely, writing out most of his sermon is a clear necessity. Writing involves exactness in thinking and speech. There is a real discipline in careful writing which we dare not sacrifice. Without using our pen we can easily develop a style that is sloppy and loose. Unconsciously we can build thought and phrase patterns which will become grooves, and soon become repetitious. I can testify that I followed the plan of writing out sermons in full during my first five years of preaching, and it has stood me in good stead ever since. A pattern was developed which was a big help when the pressures of serving larger congregations became heavy.

Joseph Parker of London acquired a unique freedom and power, rich and pungent, in extempore speech. It is reported that a young student, who had admired his sermon, went round to the vestry and asked Parker whether he himself should not launch out boldly and try the same method. He is reported to have answered, "Young man,

---

1.     Turnbull, Ralph G., ed., *Dictionary of Practical Theology*, p. 57

I wrote every word I uttered for fifteen years. When you have done what I did, then you can try what I do now."

Apart from the angle of writing, there are things to be said for and against the read sermon. A read sermon has a chance of being as full and rounded a statement as one can give on a topic—well-balanced, well-divided, and well expressed. Certainly, we can count on the guidance of the Holy Spirit in the study as well as in the pulpit.

On the other hand, a sermon that is read can easily be cold or lukewarm. It may be too detached and too much like an essay. Not everybody can read well. Few people forget themselves enough when the manuscript is before them.

Burnet and Black, being rather representative of the Scottish point of view, speak with considerable favor on the reading of a manuscript. Burnet[1] says: "There was a time when reading a sermon was highly unpopular. But the strong prejudice against the read sermon is a thing of the past, save perhaps in remote parts of the country. You will even hear people say that they feel certain relief and security when a man is obviously reading. They are reasonably safe from what Stevenson called deblatteration. Many men, moreover, have not only reduced 'reading' to a fine art: it has become a powerful weapon in their hands. They have done more than justice to the lofty level of thought and feeling at which the sermon was composed."

We tend to feel that only a few can follow this method successfully. It is best not to read the sermon unless you have to. Your eyes should be on your hearers, and this is difficult if you read.

**METHOD NO. 2** Prepare the manuscript and memorize it. The danger of this method is that it can sound like you're reading off the back of your head. I have observed this happening. It need not be so, however. This was the method I used in my early years of writing out the full manuscript, and it was well received. Another problem with this method is that it allows no room for improvisation. It can sound

---

1.    Burnet, Adam, *Pleading with Men*, pp. 167-8

like a recitation. When unexpected problems develop in the audience (a baby cries, a door slams, someone is stricken) you can easily forget your sermon.

**METHOD NO. 3** The use of brief notes, giving you the main ideas—perhaps paragraph headings.

**METHOD NO. 4** Full preparation, and then speaking without notes. Two whole books have been written on "PREACHING WITHOUT NOTES," one by Clarence Macartney and the other by Richard Storrs. To use this method you must know your skeleton well.

Macartney[1] warns that this method is by all odds the hardest way. He quotes Whitefield as saying that "preaching without notes costs as much, if not more, close and solitary thought, as well as confidence in God, than with notes." It takes a lot out of a man. He sees an advantage in: 1) the power of a direct appeal, 2) the note of earnestness it gives to a preacher, 3) the full play it gives to the preacher's personality, 4) that the preacher may avail himself of a quick welling up and outbreak of imagination, 5) that it tends to avoid monotony of speech and utterance, and 6) that it can give the preacher himself a joy out of preaching that he can have in no other way. This joy is often shared by the congregation.

Certainly there is something to be said for each method, but our preference goes to 3 and 4. Only you can decide which of these ways is the best for you. There have been extempore preachers who ought to have been tied to a manuscript. On the other hand, there have been "readers" who only, after long years, discovered how well they could do without one. Try all the ways, and give each a fair trial. There is certainly a plus to leaving the manuscript behind. "There are great joys waiting for the man who, not tempting Providence after lazy days, but with his best work done, abandons himself to the Spirit of the Living God."[2]

---

1.    Macartney, Clarence, *Preaching Without Notes*, page 145ff
2.    Burnet, op. cit., page 172

Now that you have laid out your plan for a method of delivery, there are other important aspects to the process of delivery if you are to have authentic preaching.

First, the whole personality of the preacher must be involved. That is what Phillips Brooks meant when he defined preaching as truth mediated through personality. All our faculties must be engaged. The whole man should be involved. Jones suggests[1] that even the body is involved. He describes how Dr. John A. Hutton had all the draperies removed from the railings around the rostrum when he came to Westminster Chapel. He explained that he believed a preacher should preach with his whole body. This could be called into question, but certainly the whole person should be involved in preaching.

The preacher should demonstrate some confidence in his task. He should never be apologetic and should not be tentative in presenting his points. He speaks under authority, and has a commission from God.[2] He is God's ambassador.[3] He is a sent messenger.[4] This is not self-confidence. Our confidence is in God and His Word.

There should be an element of freedom in preaching. The sermon must be prepared, but there should be freedom in the delivery of the sermon. The preacher must be open to the inspiration of the moment. "One of the remarkable things about preaching is that often one finds that the best things one says are things that have not been premeditated, and were not even thought of in the preparation of the sermon, but are given while one is actually speaking and preaching."[5]

Seriousness should characterize our presentation. Never give the impression that preaching is something light or superficial or trivial. You are dealing with the most serious matters that men and women

1. Lloyd-Jones, D.M., *Preaching and Preachers*, p. 82
2. See Matthew 28:19
3. II Corinthians 5:20
4. Romans 10:15
5. Lloyd-Jones, op. cit., p. 84

can consider together. Our message is a vital matter for people to know. Without it, they are in the truest sense 'lost.' Woe to us if we do not preach the Gospel.[1] We are bearers of good tidings from God's heart to man's heart. This conviction will give us a moral passion. It will lead us to use our gifts wisely and well.

Lloyd-Jones[2] points out that seriousness does not mean solemnity, or sadness, or morbidity. The preacher must be lively. You can be lively and serious at the same time. Lloyd-Jones put it still another way: "The preacher must never be dull, he must never be boring; he should never be what is called 'heavy.' I belong to the Reformed tradition. I am disturbed, therefore, when I am often told by members of churches that many of the younger Reformed men are very good men, who have no doubt read a great deal, and are very learned men, but that they are very dull and boring preachers, and I am told this by people who themselves hold the Reformed position. This is to me a very serious matter, there is something radically wrong with dull and boring preachers. How can a man be dull when he is handling such themes? I would say that a dull preacher is a contradiction in terms. With the grand theme and message of the Bible dullness is impossible."[3]

Another aspect of the process of delivery is warmth. It must be living, not cold. It must be moving, showing evidence that you yourself have been moved. Paul reminded the Ephesian elders that he had preached "with tears."[4] Our hearts must be involved as well as our heads.

Urgency is also involved. Paul suggested to Timothy that we must "preach the Word, be instant in season and out of season."[5] The message of the Gospel is something that cannot be postponed. You never know whether your audience will be alive next week or not.

1.    See I Corinthians 9:16
2.    Lloyd-Jones, op. cit., p. 87
3.    Ibid., page 87
4.    Acts 20:19
5.    II Timothy 4:2

We speak between time and eternity. This sense of urgency should characterize our pulpit work.

Feeling and pathos arises from a love for the people. It is one thing to love to preach, but still another to love those to whom we preach. It involves compassion. Jesus looked out upon the multitude and felt this. "When He saw the crowds, He had compassion on them because they were harassed and helpless, like sheep without a shepherd."[1] If we possess this vital factor, we can get our message across to needy people. God will bless His Word thus presented.

# Chapter 21
# Important Elements in Delivery

1. POSTURE: Stand behind the pulpit with its open Bible before you. Some advocate moving from side to side. This has inherent problems. For instance, what if there is a loud-speaking system in the church? Also, it can create a real upset at times. Walking around can be dangerous, and serves little purpose. Fortunately, many of our pulpits limit the area where we can move about.

   Do not lean on the pulpit. It is made to hold a Bible and notes, not you. Do not spread yourself over it. Keep your physical organism in abeyance. Let there be nothing in your pulpit stance or behavior which can divert attention from your message. The idea of gowns and Prince Albert coats is to hide possible sources of distraction.

---

1. Matthew 9:36 NIV

No shabbiness of dress is tolerable in the Christian minister. Give priority to the Gospel. Man should not hinder putting over the message of salvation.

Appropriate posture means that the shoulders should be back, relaxed and dropped, and level. The head should not be pushed too far forward or backward or tilted sideways. The chest should be erect, without strain.[1]

Mechanical features such as microphone placement and pulpit height can be conducive to good posture. When you begin to preach, you ought to go to the pulpit, and pause a few seconds. Take a normal breath, establish eye contact, and then start with a catchy and prepared opening sentence.

2. APPEARANCE: Our appearance does matter. It can enhance our success. Undue carelessness in dress or excessive concern for fashion may detract attention from our message. If the listeners are drawn to the appearance of the preacher, it is likely that the dress is inappropriate. A robe simplifies this problem. Otherwise dress conservatively. It is not necessary to wear black in the pulpit, nor is it wise to wear bright reds or yellows. A suit and tie, clean and unwrinkled, is recommended.

Possible distractions for listeners are bulging pockets, crooked or loose ties, jewelry that glitters, droopy socks, and revealed hairy legs.

Dress and appearance should be in harmony with the situation, the listeners, the message, the personality and physique of the speaker. The hair should be kept attractive, combed, and washed frequently. With changing standards of hair fashion the style chosen should be appropriate to the community. If one is not sensitive to community standards, he hinders the communicative process.[2]

---

1.  Baumann, J. Daniel, *An Introduction to Contemporary Preaching,* p. 188
2.  Ibid., pp. 187-188

3. BE YOURSELF: This is a good motto because our personality and our gifts are our own. They are the only talents we can use, and are the only ones for which we are responsible. Our own garden offers us our one chance of raising fruits and flowers. It is all we have. Let us use what God has given us. A difficult decision is the decision to be yourself.[1]

The temptation to be somebody other than ourselves is not a respecter of persons. Even the greatly gifted fall into it. At times all of us may be tempted to strike a pose, assume an attitude, or use a tone of voice not our own. We may think that this makes a better impression than we would if we acted as our own selves. That is seldom ever the case. When we seek to be what we are not we tend to fall into certain practices that hurt rather than help. Chappell [2] lists three of them—we become self-conscious, we place ourselves under a strain, and we lose whatever natural charm we may possess.

4. EYE-CONTACT: When you talk to people, look at them, one by one. Observe what they are saying back to you. Keep in dialogue with your listeners. It was said of Spurgeon that when he addressed two thousand people it was as though he were speaking personally to one man.

Avoid looking downward, out the windows, or over the listeners heads. Too much concentration on certain sections, or individuals, while ignoring others, should be avoided. The spark which should leap between pulpit and pew does not occur when no eye contact is made. Give everyone the impression that they are important, and that you are interested in communicating with them.

5. GESTURES: Gestures speak an important language. Many distinct and meaningful signals may be sent via the gesture. It is generally best to omit them at the beginning of your message until people warm up to the message and the messenger. Once

---

1. Chappell, Clovis G., *Anointed to Preach*, p. 99
2. Ibid., pp. 99-100

everyone is involved in the sermon, gestures can be very appropriate.

Gestures are very easy for some and very difficult for others. Most important is that your gestures be natural. Certainly you would not record in your sermon when to gesture. It is good if it comes naturally, and it is all right if it doesn't come. It must flow from a full involvement with the message you are presenting.

Baumann[1] lists the qualities of good gestures: 1) They ought to be definite. Random fidgeting with hands or flailing with arms detracts. Half a gesture has no value. Pew sitters are also disturbed by the "face fondlers," the "tie tighteners," and the "pants hikers." 2) Gestures should be varied. Don't use the same gesture over and over. 3) They should be properly timed. If gestures are either premature or late they can confuse rather than confirm the truth.

Dr. Blocker lays down a rule—"Do not gesture if you can avoid it. If you are so filled and thrilled by the message that you simply have to make gestures, make them graceful but not excessive. A preacher does not gesture souls into the kingdom of God. It is the regenerating Word which is the Sword of the Spirit."[2]

6. COMMUNICATION: Jay Adams wrote an interesting booklet in 1979 entitled *"Communicating With 20th Century Man."* Although his major points are beyond the purview of this particular chapter, he says some things that are relevant to our subject: "The fundamental root idea of the word communicate is to make a message common to both the communicator and the communicatee...One textbook defines it as the art of getting your ideas into somebody else's head. The Christian would say that communication is the art of getting God's ideas into somebody's head...Perhaps Christians have erred seriously in

---

1.    Baumann, op. cit., pp. 189-190
2.    Blocker, Simon, *The Secret of Pulpit Power*, p. 144

placing narrow limits upon the media of communication...The spoken word is direct communication by word of mouth."[1]

When we understand our Christian message we can communicate it to others. "Clarity of output is directly proportionate to clarity of intake."[2] The church must be flexible in adjusting to new forms of communication. Adams calls for the use of contemporary language. He illustrates that the Koine Greek of the New Testament was the common language of the day. He warns against forgetting to use language adaptable to our day. He laments that conservative ministers don't make enough of their practical theology courses, and often regard them as necessary evils.[3] This department is concerned with communication and is not incidental to other disciplines. He even warns that if students graduate with inadequate practical training they run the danger of apostasy.[4] "Men ill-prepared to communicate the substance they believe, grope about, trying to communicate to the world and the church. When they fail, they may begin to wonder about the validity of the substance itself."[5]

Adams laments that liberal seminaries often recognize the importance of effective communication more than orthodox schools do. "We must outstrip them. If they work hard at communicating what they have to offer, how can we do less when we have the glorious Gospel of our Lord Jesus Christ?"[6]

7. THE IMAGE WE PROJECT: The preacher's reputation as to character is important. Paul felt it necessary to defend himself against character attacks in II Corinthians. Such attacks are also attacks against our message.

---

1.   Adams, Jay E., *Communicating With 20th Century Man*, pp. 12-13
2.   Ibid., p. 14
3.   Ibid., p. 30
4.   Ibid., p. 31
5.   Idem
6.   Ibid., p. 32

Our image is not only shaped by the content of the sermon, but by the attitude we depict in delivery. Whether you are apathetic or enthusiastic makes a big difference. If you demonstrate welfare and concern for your audience, you get a better reception. Personal integrity and sincerity help build the image.

Adams sums up the image thus: "Emotional persuasion has to do with the audience and the speaker in a more intimate relationship with each other. The Christian minister, therefore, must strive to be a godly and competent man, for the sake of the Gospel."[1]

8. POWER: Lloyd-Jones states that "if there is no power it is not preaching."[2] It is not just a man uttering words, it is God using him. He is under the influence of the Holy Spirit. Paul speaks of his preaching as "a demonstration of the Spirit's power."[3] He also put it this way: "Our gospel came to you not simply with words, but also with power, with the Holy Spirit, and with deep conviction."[4] Power is an essential element in true preaching.

9. TENSION AND FEAR: There are varieties of opinion on this element in preaching. Paul E. Sangster says: "The first essential of good speech is relaxation. While nervousness can be a positive help in that it keys up a preacher to give his best, fright can paralyze the organs of speech."[5] Burnet says: "Don't worry about anything. You may feel overcome with shyness: you may be anxious lest the prayers may distract your mind from what you have to preach. Give yourself altogether to the prayers and

---

1. Adams, Jay E., *Pulpit Speech*, p. 96
2. Lloyd-Jones, Martyn, *Preaching and Preachers*, p. 95
3. I Corinthians 2:4
4. I Thessalonians 1:5 NIV
5. Sangster, Paul E. in *Baker's Dictionary of Practical Theology*, p. 56

worship, leaving the rest with God. There is nothing worse for a preacher than fear, nothing better than worship."[1]

Baumann says: "A little nervousness is not only necessary, it is absolutely imperative. Without some sweating of the palms, without some fear, the preacher can go to the pulpit without the necessary adrenaline shooting through his system and the resultant excitement which allows his message to have the contagious quality necessary in all effective communication. When the minister goes to the pulpit completely relaxed, it may be that he is not so dependent on God, but that he is overly confident in his own ability."[2]

Adams describes tension as the key problem that a beginning speaker must overcome. "In tension situations, the body, by psychological impetus, prepares itself for an emergency. Wise speakers know this and they know also that it is good and necessary for the body to be so prepared for speaking. They know that good speaking is dependent upon bodily alertness, so they harness the tension for service. Tension often helps ideas to jell during delivery.[3]

If we place ourselves in God's hands, and are well prepared, there is little to fear when facing an audience of God's people.

10. ATMOSPHERE: Generally we as preachers have to create our own atmosphere. The people have usually heard us before. They usually are not expecting great things. Many are present because of custom.

On the other hand, there are in every evangelical church those who surround you with prayer. You can feel their prayers as you might smell incense. No other speaker has this kind of help.

---

1.  Burnet, Adam, *Pleading With Men*, p. 173
2.  Bauman, J. Daniel, *An Introduction to Contemporary Preaching*, pp. 196-7
3.  Adams, Jay E., *Pulpit Speech*, pp. 154-155

There are ways in which you can train your people that will create atmosphere. Occasional sermons on worship and frequent references in children's talks to worship attitudes will help. Suggestions to bow their heads in prayer when they enter the pew can be most meaningful. Black writes that when you sense a restlessness or an upset in the service it is good to suggest that the people join you in a few moments of silent prayer.[1]

11. LANGUAGE: In the hearing situation the language must communicate immediately or not at all. Sentences should be short and clear. Words should be plain and familiar.

Grady Davis has majored in a study of language, and comes up with the following points: 1) The preacher should learn to express himself in as few words as possible. Unneeded words are in the way. 2) He should learn to use words that sound well together. If he cannot make music, he must avoid making harsh dissonances (discords). Granting that we cannot all be Beethovens with words, we can still avoid sounds that make the difference between euphony (pleasing sounds) and cacophony (harsh, jarring sounds). 3) He should cultivate a preference for short, strong, clear, and familiar words. He should use plain words where they will serve, so that the hearer does not notice the words, but only what they say. 4) He should cultivate a preference for sensuous rather than abstract, and specific rather than general words. Sensuous words are words that are close to the five senses, suggesting pictures that the mind can see, sounds it can hear, things it can touch, taste, and smell. Specific words designate particular things rather than groups or classes of things, and 5) He should rely on strong nouns and verbs to carry the weight of his thought.[2]

Adams discusses the language of emotional appeal.[3] It is more highly colored and strongly connotative than didactic language. The use of words must be governed by the biblical ethic

---

1.     Black, James, *The Mystery of Preaching*, p. 170
2.     Davis, Henry G., *Design for Preaching*, pp. 268-273
3.     Adams, op. cit., p. 89

of truth. It is easy to go wrong in the choice of language. Words can be subtly slanted. It is possible to substitute words for what are seen to be difficult doctrines of the Bible.

12. BODY LANGUAGE: Delivery not only involves the use of the voice, but it also includes bodily action. Our behavior communicates our real feelings in a silent language. Laughing, crying, volume, intonation, gesturing, and speed of movement are all ways of imparting your message. The body delivery must fit with the content. At every point it should aid the content rather than call attention to itself. We can distort the truths of God's Word by the actions of our body. Actions can speak louder than words.

13. EMOTION: It is not possible to preach the Christian Gospel without emotion. Chalmers said of certain sermons in his day that they were like a winter's day, short, clear, and cold. "The brevity," he remarked, "is good and the clarity is better, but the coldness is fatal. Moonlight preaching ripens no harvest." It is not well for preachers to despise emotion, but it should always come as a by product. Burnet speaks strongly of the person whose main object is to rouse it.[1]

Emotion should come as a natural reaction of our soul to some great idea or vision. It should come as a response to truth. Big ideas should touch us as speakers to appropriate moods, which in turn, if they are genuine, will bring their own note into our voice, so that pity, anger, or sorrow will find their suitable expression and tone.

Black puts it well when he says: "A grand passion will atone for everything, on the stage or in the pulpit...Surface emotion, at best a tawdry thing, is particularly nauseating in the pulpit. But big ideas stir as deeply as high winds and are as real. Give your ideas their own emotional value, in your heart and with the people. If passion is sincere and controlled—and remember

---

1.    Burnet, op. cit., p. 176

control gives the impression of reserve power—to suppress it argues a narrow soul."[1]

Humor has been considered a phase of emotion. Certainly we can enjoy our religion. It is not a grim business. But humor can be dangerous. It can easily overstep bounds and wound a sensitive soul. Nothing can hurt like ridicule. Deliberate telling of jokes in the pulpit is out of keeping with the ministry. Humor which comes incidentally can add sparkle to a message. Discretion is the better part of valor.

CONCLUSION:

Seek with earnest naturalness to deliver the message that God has given you. Do this in the faith that God's Word will not return unto you void, but will accomplish the purpose for which it was sent.[2]

As ministers, always remember that we are not our own but God's men, not doing our own work, but God's work.

"If anyone speaks, he should do it as one speaking the very words of God. If anyone serves, he should do it with the strength God provides, so that in all things God may be praised through Jesus Christ. TO HIM BE THE GLORY AND THE POWER FOREVER AND EVER. Amen."[3]

---

1.    Black, op. cit., pp. 175-176
2.    See Isaiah 55:11
3.    I Peter 4:11 NIV

# Part 3

# PUBLIC
# WORSHIP

# Chapter 22

# The Theory and
# Meaning of Worship

Worship is an elemental experience of life, just as love is. The impulse to worship is beyond the reach of analysis. Even theologians find it elusive. Yet it is universal. With few exceptions, it may be said that no people or race has been found who do not worship. Most everyone has worshipped at some time. The object of worship may be the devil, a rabbit's foot, an ancestral head, an idol, a sacred cow, or luck, or a ruler, but it's still some kind of worship. Man is "incurably religious."

"The story is told of a well-meaning missionary in Africa who, out of compassion for the wretched economic condition of the people, brought them a splendid steel plow and showed them how to use it. Returning after an absence he found his gift greatly appreciated, but hardly in the manner intended. The natives had turned it upside down, covered it with garlands of flowers, and were worshiping it. Evidently these poor souls found some need in their heart more compelling than the utilities of scientific agriculture."[1]

Worship is man's everlasting reply to the mystery of existence. It is the instinctive response of the creature to the Creator. It has a reason for its own existence, apart from any benefits that may accrue to the worshipper. It does not have to be explained or justified.

Sometimes worship is not utilitarian at all. It has often been very costly. Men have delivered their bodies to cruel scourging, tortures and death as acts of worship. Whether worship is ethical or not depends on the kind of deity worshipped. The Greek god Hermes was the patron of thieves. Prostitution and human sacrifice have

---

1.    S. Arthur Devan, *Ascent to Zion*, p. 4

been required elements of worship during many times and in many parts of the world. In biblical times captured peoples were "devoted to Jehovah," meaning that they were put to the sword.

It is only as men grew in their conception of God, revelation progressed under the spiritual leadership of the Hebrew prophets, and the way was prepared for men to think of God as the One who could be the God and Father of our Lord Jesus Christ, that worship was really ready to become the greatest ethical force at work in mankind. People tend to live only as high and as moral as the objects or beings they worship.

The matter of whether worship should be objective or subjective becomes a matter of disagreement among writers on worship. S. Arthur Devan in *"Ascent to Zion"* leans heavily toward the objective. James B. Pratt in *"The Religious Consciousness"* calls for worship to be chiefly objective. Andrew Blackwood in *"The Fine Art of Public Worship"* believes in the objective approach but calls for a proper balance.

From our point of view the objective would be primary, but a blending of both would be important to a fulfilling worship experience. It is objective in that it is directed by man toward God as a reality outside of himself. It is to please and glorify God. "He that cometh to God must believe that He is."[1]

"Worship is man's response to God's revelation of Himself. Two or three times each week the children of God should worship Him in His house, publicly. Three times daily the members of every Christian family should give thanks to God before they eat together, and, if possible, they should tarry after the morning and evening meal to worship together. Night and morning every child of God should read the Bible and pray by himself. Such is the Christian ideal of worship."[2] Our present concern is with public worship.

---

1.    Hebrews 11:6
2.    Andrew W. Blackwood, *The Fine Art of Public Worship*, pp. 14-15

A biblical example of a worshipper is found in Isaiah 6, where Isaiah himself goes into the temple. Note four elements of worship here:

1. The feeling of awe and wonder in the presence of God
2. Confession of sins
3. God's cleansing grace
4. Dedication to service

A good combination of both the objective and the subjective elements of worship is observed here. The man in the pew should turn his heart and mind toward God first. Later he will experience the blessings and the effects of coming into close contact with God.

Theoretically it is possible to move so far toward objectivity that we risk the loss of the man we are anxious to help. Man never ceases to be human, with all sorts of human interests and desires. Purely objective worship can be as cold as a cathedral. However, subjective worship can be weak. The two should be blended. It is illustrated in Charles Wesley's "Love Divine." After picturing the greatness of God's love in Christ, the worshipper is then "lost in wonder, love, and praise," a superb combination.

Our emphasis should be on God's character, and His worthship. It is easy to get concerned with times and places, rites and ceremonies, rather than with Him. With the woman at the well, to whom the Lord explained the meaning of public worship, we need to learn that where anyone has the will to worship God, He is waiting to show that person how; and that where the will to worship is not present, all our human devices are but as sounding brass and tinkling cymbal. "God is a Spirit, and they that worship Him must worship Him in spirit and in truth."[1]

Worship must be sincere and real, and centered on Him.

"The moments spent in worship are moments spent in contact with the great Reality of the universe and of life. What that may mean in liberation from sins and fears, in the release of hidden energies, in clarified mental and spiritual vision, in rested nerves, in the

---

1.   John 4:24

exaltation and integration of personality, in challenge to social action, in cultural development, in identification with humanity of the ages past and those that are to be, in the increment of vital forces and the joy of salvation—all these constitute a story that cannot be adequately told but is written in the secret annals of myriads of human lives.

It is God that men need, more than they need bread, and worship brings man to God. True, the initiative is His. One cannot by thinking find out God. But God comes to men whispering in the subliminal consciousness, "Seek ye my face!" And our hearts reply to him, "Thy face, Lord, will I seek." And those who seek him with their whole heart, find him in the sanctuary, and going out of the sanctuary find him outside too—under the arching skies, in forest glades, amid the hum of factory wheels, in the sacramental life of the family, on the battlefield, and in the hour of death. They find there is no place in the broad universe where he is not, and know at last that it is their lot to "dwell in the house of the Lord forever."[1]

Chapter 23

# Worship in the Old Testament

The Bible is our source book. In regard to public worship the teachings there are usually indirect. The method is that of example rather than of precept. The Bible is saturated with the spirit of worship. It is filled with examples of how to sing and pray to God. It has strongly influenced our public worship. It is the sourcebook for all

---

1.    S. Arthur Devan, op. cit., p. 21

our liturgies, and the inspiration for the writing of our hymns. One might well say—If our worship is not biblically based, it is unworthy.

Looking into the Old Testament, worship is the oldest and most persistent element. Man ever cries out for God, and ways of worship are his cry. Genesis lays the emphasis upon family and individual worship, but in Exodus and Leviticus there is a great deal said about public worship. There, everything is closely prescribed. Yet the only prescribed prayer is the Aaronic benediction (Numbers 6:24-26). Almost everything else is carefully standardized. Sacrifice played a large part in Hebrew worship. Leviticus is full of it. Of the five sacrifices only the meal offering was free from blood. The burnt offering, the peace offering, the sin offering, and the trespass offering all involved blood. The priest played a very prominent part in Hebrew worship. So did the place of worship. At first everything centered on the Tabernacle, and then it gave way to the Temple. The Hebrew year also was prominent in worship. The Passover involved a week of preparatory services. Pentecost marked the completion of harvest. The Feast of Trumpets was similar to a New Year's Day, but more religious. The Day of Atonement was a fast day, while the Feast of Tabernacles was a recollection of the days when they lived in tents. Once every fifty years there was a Year of Jubilee, which brought freedom for slaves, rest for the soil, and restoration of the land to the descendants of the original owners. The Hebrew system of worship was closely tied to farming.

The Psalms speak of the growing emphasis upon sacred music. The sons of Korah were professional musicians. Even during hard times there was regular provision for the maintenance of these musicians (see Neh. 11:23 and 12:47). Choral singing was prominent, with some help from instruments. Often there was a choir, sometimes a large one. It often included women as well as men. At times the singing was antiphonal as in Psalm 24. The 121st Psalm was sung while in pilgrimage to Jerusalem. Eventually the five parts of their hymnal were assembled into the book of Psalms. It is a supreme book of praise, and ranks among the masterpieces of world literature. It is the most important book in the Old Testament in respect to public worship.

The prophets give their ideals about the proper way to worship God. Isaiah had his transforming experience in worship, and spent much time and energy attempting to reform the ways of public worship in Judah. His contemporary, Amos, spoke largely to his people when assembled for public worship at Bethel. Jeremiah also sought in vain to prevent the disintegration of the grand old Hebrew ideals concerning public worship. Malachi makes it clear that a revival of spiritual religion depends in large measure upon a reform in the area of public worship.

Ezekiel presents visions of an ideal social order in which everything is to center around the Temple. Putting all these ideas together, we find that the Old Testament presents lofty ideals about public worship. Two dominant notes in these ideals are the forgiveness of sins and joy in the Lord. They come in this order. When men get right with God, they can enjoy each other.[1]

# Chapter 24
# Worship in the New Testament

Many of the teachings about worship from the Old Testament are taken for granted in the New Testament. The sacrifices of the Old Testament and the mediating priesthood are clearly done away.

In the Gospels and Acts there is a good deal about the Temple. They tell us that Jesus loved and revered the Temple. He was

---

1.     Cf. Andrew W. Blackwood, op. cit., p. 38

presented there as a babe, and found there among the doctors of the law at twelve years of age. He joined with His countrymen in celebrating the festivals of the Hebrew year. He loved the Temple enough to cleanse it twice. The Apostles showed due regard for the Temple.

The synagogue was actually more important than the Temple in the New Testament. It had sprung up during the Exile. In Jesus' day the synagogue was almost everywhere in the world around the Mediterranean. Worship and teaching were a vital part of its activity. The early Christian Church took over the synagogue forms of worship to a large degree. The Shema, music, prayers, reading of the Law and the Prophets, and Scripture exposition made up the service. This furnished the background for our Christian worship.[1]

In John 4 Jesus explained the very heart of Christian worship. It was in the Temple that Jesus spoke of Himself as the Water of Life (John 7:37-39). Very precious chapters in this Gospel (13-17) tell about the Upper Room. It was there that Jesus taught His disciples to remember Him in the sacrament of the Lord's Supper.

The great Pentecostal experience came in the Upper Room, where one hundred and twenty believers were assembled for worship. At Philippi in a meeting for worship the Christian Church began its march into Europe. Evangelism and missions really rose out of public worship. As one reads the Epistles the impression is clear that worship was important to the early Christians. The Epistles themselves played a vital part in public worship. It was there that they were read and heard. First Corinthians has a large concern with guidance for proper behavior in worship. The book of Revelation contains messages to the seven churches, evidently to be read as they assembled for public worship. It is also thought that many of the more lyrical passages are the sort of songs that the Christian Church used towards the end of the first century. (Note the numerous indented passages in Rev. 4-21 in the NIV). Blackwood puts it this way: "The book of Revelation yields inspiration and power when we

---

1.    Cf. Robert E. Webber, *Worship Old and New*, pp. 27-29

think of it as reflecting the spirit in which the early Church engaged in the worship of the Living Lord."[1]

There are several conclusions which we can draw about New Testament worship. 1) There was a lack of emphasis upon externals. The Old Testament emphasis on certain times and places, rites and duties gives way to worship being a matter of the heart. Wherever God's people gather, there they can worship Him. Often they met in private homes. 2) There was a new sense of freedom to worship God without the use of fixed forms. In the New Testament there is nothing which prescribes or suggests the use of fixed forms, but neither is there anything which forbids or discourages such use. Under the Holy Spirit there was considerable freedom in worship. 3) The New Testament lays more stress upon the people than on the leader. After the death and resurrection of Christ the people became conscious of their privilege as priests. Even when worship leaders were Peter, or John, or Paul, they knew that all of them together were priests of God. It was a revolutionary idea! 4) The spirit of worship became radiant. It began on Easter Day, and came to a glorious expression on Pentecost. Jews thought they were intoxicated. They were, but not with wine. Paul warns not to be drunk with wine, but to be filled with the Spirit. When God is in us, worship is enthusiastic and inspiring.

Public worship played a large part in the religion of the Old Testament, and a much larger part in the New Testament times. Truth, inspiration and vision were derived from worship, and hence the Christians lived and served heroically, even unto death. Public worship became the fountainhead of those living waters which we know as evangelism and missions. It became the reason for the writing and the preservation of the books of the New Testament. The people of God needed such inspired guidance to know what they believed and what God required of them.

This is the sort of public worship which the reforming fathers sought to restore during the Reformation and following. This is the sort of public worship which will enable us to meet the needs of our

---

1.     Andrew W. Blackwood, op. cit., p. 45

day. "On to the Living Christ! We will find Him, where the reformers found Him, in the open pages of the Bible."[1]

# Chapter 25
# The Elements of Worship

Our worship is frequently described as a "free service." It delights in the simplicities. It need be neither bare nor barren, but can have a magnificence and stateliness all its own. The grandeur of worship does not depend on external aids—symbols, robes, music or processions—but in spiritual qualities and effects. It has been called the "march of God" through the service. It is quite independent of differing methods and practices of worship. There can be as much grandeur in the meeting of a thousand men on a hillside chanting a covenantal psalm, as in the most ornate service of a high cathedral. Grandeur is not in the method but in the spirit.[2]

Our problem is, how shall we make our free service as rich and as satisfying as possible? We can speak of governing principles which are involved in an ideal worship service. The first and greatest note in any service is the expression of gratitude. Public worship is the recognized means for exhibiting the gratitude of Christ's people for the known mercies of God. It should be a dominant note in all Christian worship, and generous room should be allotted for it in praise and in prayer. This will impart an adoration, a dignity, and a wonder to our worship that will be uplifting and cleansing. Any "familiar" note in worship that might imperil this sense of wonder and gratitude should be avoided. We can cheapen worship by taking

1.   Ibid., p. 50
2.   James Black, *The Mystery of Preaching*, pp. 215-16

things for granted. To take nature for granted: the daily miracle of life for granted: the providence of God for granted: that empties worship of any saving grace. Worship degenerates when this astonishment has been lost. "What gave the Calvinistic church its unfailing dignity and power was its prostrating sense of awe,— wonder at the decrees and sovereignty of God, and wonder at His mercy, so unmerited. This produced a dignity of Christian life and worship that has marked all Calvinistic creed."[1]

This sense of wonder in worship will save us from some of the failings we deplore. It will save us from cheap familiarity in language and methods. It will prevent us from talking to God in light and casual terms such as we would use to our neighbors. It will also rescue us from a sloppy sentimentalism which ruins true reverence. Worship cannot possess any dignity or exalting greatness if God's glory and Christ's sacrifice are thought of as trivial or accepted things.

We must train our people to bow their heads in prayer as they assemble for worship. This can set the atmosphere for the service. The worshipper gains a sense of expectancy, and is tuned to sympathy with the service and the preacher. We come to Christ's church to meet Christ Himself, not the Real Presence of the mass, but the spiritual presence of the Risen Lord. People may meet God anywhere, but they can meet Him in a unique sense among an assembly of Christians at worship. If we believe this, it can impart life and fervency to the whole service. We come to express gratitude to God; but more than that, we come to meet Jesus. Keep this in mind when you plan your worship service.

We come to worship to express our common need, and to receive God's promised grace. We confess our sin, and request pardon. The passionate longing of man is for a cleansed life. We quietly and faithfully, without excuse, confess our sin. In Christ's name we expect pardon and forgiveness from God.

---

1.    Ibid., p. 218

In worship we seek direction and help amid the moral puzzles of daily life. Many worshippers are looking for direction. Let the whole service reveal the message of our Lord for troubled souls.

The service, by its moral quality, should vitalize the will, and lead the worshippers in obedience to God. Worship is life.

We should be careful about emotionalism. Emotion can affect us like an intoxication and pass off in the same way, leaving us in a lower vein. If emotion is not translated into life or action, there can be a spiritual loss.

A note of joy should pervade worship. It should be in every Christian service, even in a funeral. Our religion is victorious, with a dream of redeemed mankind in a redeemed world. The first thing that the pagans noticed in the early disciples was a sheer joy that played over them like magic. We need it today in our worship. We have deep reason for joy—we are forgiven, we are saved and kept amid temptation, we can face tomorrow with the assurance of God's presence. Joy does not mean being loud or unrestrained. A deep joy brings serenity and confidence.

To this end choose triumphant praise and dwell on thanksgiving in your prayers. Don't overlook need and suffering, but look through them and see the dawn.

Seek for reverence and dignity in worship, a reverence that is consonant with Christian joy. Reverence is simply our method of approach to God. Choice souls who know the love of God in Christ Jesus approach God with a "holy boldness." There is no special reverent manner. Posture has nothing to do with it. Joel said: "Rend your hearts and not your garments."[1] Reverence is an attitude of soul, and adoration and praise of God.

Order your services. Study arrangement and progress. Order does not mean fixity. Whatever the order or arrangement, the service should reach a climax. The climax is simply this—that God in His pardoning and directing power should be plainly visible, so that the

---

1.    Joel 2:13

worshippers may depart eased of their burdens and encouraged in their faith.

"The unity of the service is often discussed. Unity can be a bare and narrow unity, by exclusion, or it can be a comprehensive unity, made so by inclusion."[1]

Our aim should be for the latter. If everything in the service is geared to one idea and to one mood, it cannot minister to a diverse congregation. The sermon may emphasize one note. Other parts of the service can supplement it with other notes. Praise can be broad and general. The Scripture readings can come from another angle. None of God's children need go home untended and unfed.

Our freedom in worship leaves us free to use various rituals and liturgies. We are free even to bind ourselves. This gives us adaptability such as strictly liturgical churches do not have.

The selection of hymns or psalms is important. Always begin with an objective hymn, which gives honor and glory to God. The taste of a congregation for good hymns and psalms can be cultivated. Avoid falsely pietistic or highly sentimental songs. Avoid hymns in a minor key for the most part. Choose the robust, strong and manly praise which the best Christian authors have given us, hymns that uplift and exalt.

The reading of the Word in public is an important part of worship. God speaks to us through His Word. Therefore such readings should not be done casually or carelessly. Such an approach does not speak to the people of the importance of what God has to say to them.

It cannot be regarded too seriously, especially when we think of it as a message from God and the source of our spiritual life. To hear the Word nobly read is both an education and a joy for our people. Choose and study your passages carefully. You can't convey the meaning if the meaning is not clear to you. Read naturally, with ordinary flexibility, modulation, and ease. Avoid anything stagey or rhetorical in Bible reading.

---

1.     James Black, op. cit., p. 228

Responsive readings allow audience participation. The Psalms are suitable for this. Many of them were written for responsive chanting.

"Congregational prayer is the offered prayer of the gathered people of God. In the early church it was often spontaneous, open to all who felt inspired. As the church grew, this lack of discipline became dangerous as a source of disorder. To prevent abuses, recognized leaders were chosen to control public worship."[1]

The duty of the leader is to gather up and interpret the needs and desires of his brethren, and intercede on their behalf. It is a priestly function.

The leader of prayer faces some peculiar difficulties. He has a two-fold duty— 1) to know and interpret the heart of his people aright, gathering up their joys and sorrows, and 2) while remembering his people he must only remember God. In other words, he has both to remember his people and to forget them at the same time. You fault if you go too far in either direction.

Our public prayers can be read from prescribed liturgies, or they can be offered up freely. Both approaches have their advocates. I favor the free prayers, except for special occasions such as communion and baptism. Liturgical prayers can be formal and impersonal. It perpetuates ancient forms and phrases no longer commonly used. It can become too mechanical, cold, and passionless, and discharged like a lesson. Free prayer has a spontaneity, a beautiful trust, and a simple dignity. If reverently used, a prepared pastor may employ free prayer so that it is capable of great heights, and a thing of power. It is also adjustable to immediate needs and situations.

Public prayer must be geared to the situation. Invocations, offering prayers, prayers following the sermons, and benedictions are special, and have definite purposes for them. The "long" prayer, or the congregational prayer, should include adoration, thanksgiving, pardon, petition, and intercession. Do not let them go on too long. Usually this prayer is concluded with the Lord's Prayer.

---

1.    Ibid., p. 241

Other elements enter into worship. The recitation of law and creeds, the giving of the offering, and the sermon all are a part of our worship. Every part of worship is important, and should be done well, with an eye to the glory of God.

# Chapter 26
# Types of Worship

Most writers on worship distinguish between types of worship. Frequently it is spoken of as liturgical versus non-liturgical, often as objective versus subjective, and Blackwood[1] describes it as a struggle between religion and art, to determine which shall prevail in public worship.

We started with the Bible, which is the fountainhead of Christian worship. From that point worship followed a strange course. It becomes our duty to keep our worship in the evangelical tradition, more or less in line with that of the Apostolic Church.

Worship in the first century gave prominence to the spiritual. Gradually artistic forms gained control. The change from the orderly freedom of the Apostolic Church to the artistic forms of what we know as the Roman Catholic Church seems to have begun in the second century, increased during the third, largely prevailed in the fourth, and so on into the Middle Ages, until the time of the Reformation. The development of the Mass became the supreme triumph of art in worship. This movement toward liturgics and artistic forms meant going back from New Testament liberty to Old Testament rites. There was a growing tendency to exalt the externals in public worship, with an appeal to the five senses. There were vestments and

---

1.    See Andrew W. Blackwood, op. cit., Chap. III

bells, ablutions, frequent changes in posture, processions with the cross, prayers for the dead, etc. added to worship. Centering in sacrifice, there was a call for a mediating priesthood, who strove to determine the eternal destinies of men.

The Protestant Reformation sought to restore a more biblical balance, with an aim to recovering the spirit of New Testament worship. Sometimes the reformers went a bit too far. Today we can speak of three trends in Protestant worship. On one side are those who follow Martin Luther's ideas about public worship. He strove to retain and use all that was worthy in the system of worship which he was striving to reform. He retained much of the artistic forms of the Mass, but insisted that it should be in the language of the people. Hence Lutheran worship today retains considerable liturgical formality.

In England the Reformation took a different course. The Book of Common Prayer became the norm for public worship. Both the Lutheran and the Anglican forms of worship tend to be liturgical.

On the other side among Protestants are some of the Baptists, the Quakers (Friends), the Churches of Christ, and the Pentecostalists. They emphasize freedom in worship, and seem to care little for artistic or liturgical forms.

The in-between group includes a large number of Protestants. This is where the Presbyterians and Reformed churches take their stand. We are semi-liturgical, believing in a blend of religion and art, of the liturgy and freedom, and of the objective and subjective. "John Calvin sought to put into effect the Pauline ideals about public worship. Where Luther wished to preserve the artistic forms of the Catholic Church in so far as they were not in conflict with the Scriptures, Calvin favored the rejection of all forms which were not clearly taught in the Scriptures. Under Calvin's leadership public worship in Geneva became noted for its emphasis upon the majesty of God, the sinfulness of man, and the wonders of redeeming grace. There was much stress laid on the singing of the Psalms and the exposition

of the Bible from the pulpit."[1] He preferred simple forms, with order
and dignity always evident in worship.

"Our form of worship will depend upon the kind of deity which
we worship. As Christians we worship 'the God and Father of our
Lord Jesus Christ.' It is to Him that our adoration is offered, our confessions are made, our petitions are asked, and our sacrifices yielded.
It is He whose word we reverence, whose will we seek, and on
whose revelation we place our trust. The question in respect to worship is whether we think of Him as beyond ourselves and our world,
or as within. Is God transcendent or immanent? If either thought is
carried too far it overreaches itself. Transcendence can become
deism, and immanence can become pantheism."[2] Both of these ends
are negations of the Gospel. The proper position for us to take is to
blend the two approaches to God, recognizing that He is both above
our understanding and within our hearts.

Ordinary Christian worship then must start from the assumption
that there is a difference and a separation between them. The sublime
record of revelation, the glorious good news of the Gospel, and the
long history of Christian experience, are chronicles recording those
transactions. Our worship today is a further transaction between God
and man. The Creator is dealing with His creatures, the King with
His subjects, the Father with His children.

Churches tend to fall into categories of liturgical and non-liturgical worship, with semi-liturgical falling in between the two. Even
the least ritualistic tend to have a certain amount of ritual. For instance, Pentecostalists generally raise their hands to God. They also
follow a regular pattern when they are "slain in the Spirit."

Claims for the advantage of liturgical worship are these: 1) The
congregation has a larger share in its worship. The people know
what to expect and hence make the appropriate responses, move-
ments and gestures. 2) If the form is old, it brings home to the worshipper a sense of union with the generations past. If it is in

1.    Ibid., p. 58-59
2.    S. Arthur Devan, op. cit., pp. 87-88

widespread use (like the Apostles' Creed and the Lord's Prayer) it can give the worshipper a tremendous sense of oneness with worshipping Christians everywhere. 3) The service of worship is not dependent on the ability, the powers of expression, and the spiritual mood of the man who happens to be the leader in worship. 4) The use of liturgy aids in orderliness and reverence, and 5) Dramatic values can more easily be introduced into worship.

On the other hand, advocates of a free, or non-liturgical service of worship claim the following advantages: 1) It is free from formalism and vain repetition, 2) There is always novelty, change, freshness, and contemporaneousness. It avoids monotony. 3) When the minister uses his own diction there is a greater sense of reality, and hence of vitality. It is natural and genuine, and 4) It has the advantage of flexible adjustment to the immediate needs of those present, and to the times in which they stand. Liturgy tends to be timeless and collective, blanket in form, and can be irrelevant.

The best form of worship tends to fall in between the various extremes, and therefore we can reap some of the advantages of both approaches in worship. It is not so much an either/or as a both/and. The two approaches can be regarded as complementary rather than contradictory. Both are rooted in human nature. Both are found in the record of God's dealings with men in the Scriptures. Both have been accorded the seal of divine blessing.

Although Devan agrees with the above, he finds that many services actually conducted on the semi-liturgic plan are awkward.[1] As I see it, this need not be the case. In our worship we can combine the best of the past and the best of the present. We can allow participation from the congregation, as well as leadership from the pulpit. We can use the best of Christian hymnology, and also use some of the newer music. We can maintain orderly worship and retain reverence, and still give evidence of reality. There is room for dramatic emphases in our services. We go beyond mere repetition. We can begin with objective hymns and end with subjective hymns. We can be

---

1.     Ibid., p. 98

flexible, and apply our worship to any given situation. We can be solemn and reverent, and also enter into joyous forms of worship. We never drag God down to our level in worship, but we do seek to lift men up to God. May our type of worship ever bring glory unto the great God of the universe, and also bring man into His presence. We enter to worship, and we depart to serve. We drink at the fountain of living water, and then give forth rivers of living water to a dry and thirsty earth.

Chapter 27

# The Conduct of Worship
# and
# The Worship Leader

Christian public worship is a social act. Something is happening, and it is a function of human society as a whole. Mankind is approaching its Creator, its Ruler, and its Redeemer. Even a dim realization of this cosmic significance of a simple gathering in an obscure little church brings incredible dignity and importance to the occasion. When the significance is felt by the leaders and the people there is an element of power in the service which lifts it above all commonplaces. Every Sunday a great celebration is going on—a celebration of life, a celebration of redemption, a celebration of God Himself.[1]

The leader of public worship should be trained. In private worship and in small groups untutored men can function, but when

---

1.    Ibid., pp. 213-14

scores or hundreds of people come together to worship God in His house, they should have expert leadership.

"In one sense the worship leader is a prophet. A prophet is one who speaks for another. That Other for whom we speak is God. The heart of the message has to do with God. First in the reading from the Word, and then in the preaching of the Gospel, the constant endeavor is to make the truth as it is in God, or in Christ, both clear and luminous. While the truth may be very old, the prophet of God seeks to make it as new as the sunlight which streams through the stained-glass windows."[1]

In another sense the worship leader is a priest. If it is the prophet's mission to speak for God to men, it is the priest's privilege to speak for men to God. As in the case of Jeremiah or Ezekiel, the man of God today can be both a prophet and a priest. In the higher New Testament sense, every Christian is a priest, with direct and immediate access to the mercy seat. But when the people come together for public worship, they need someone to represent them before God. As the father speaks for the household at family prayers, so does the pastor speak for the entire congregation in their corporate prayers to God.[2]

The minister leads his flock in worship. The figure is like that of a shepherd, or perhaps like that of a conductor leading a symphony orchestra. These leaders tend to use persuasiveness rather than force. So in public worship the ideal leader would be the one whom the people could follow without thinking that they were being led. His chief desire is to bring the people, one by one, into right relations with God, and then into right relations with men, withal having a new determination to do God's holy will on earth as it is done in heaven.

There are several difficulties in leading public worship. First is the difficulty of making God seem real. How does one find words to make the supreme truths appear to be real and practical? Modern

1.    Andrew W. Blackwood, op. cit., p. 21
2.    Ibid., p. 22

people may be dissatisfied with the husks which the world has to offer, and are groping after something to satisfy the hunger of the heart. It is necessary to appeal to such people on their present level of thought and feeling, and then gradually lead up to the place where God will become the most real fact in their lives. In the final analysis it depends on the work of the Holy Spirit in regeneration, but our human leadership can be used of God in the process.

A second difficulty is to make public worship interesting. It is at this point that approaches to worship can be inserted that may well be debated. Is it wise, for instance, for the leader to take a microphone in hand, and speak as he walks down the aisle? Should a leader sit on a stool during his sermon? Are talkbacks in place? Does sacred dance have a place in our worship? Does hand clapping fit the idea of reverence in worship? Is there a standard for the quality of hymns and spiritual songs beyond which we should not go? How can we appeal to self-centered people, or to people who come to be entertained, without robbing Christian worship of its God-centeredness? What men need above all else is a personal experience of Christ's redeeming and transforming grace.

A final difficulty is that of making every part of the worship hour distinctly Christian. In Christ, God and man find each other. The secret of Christ-centered leadership is to have a personal relationship with Him renewed day by day. You cannot lead others into the holy mount unless you have been there yourself. The Holy Spirit is ready to bless consecrated leadership.

Blackwood lists five aspects of leadership, as he discusses the personality of the leader. "Not every lover of God and men is able to lead effectively in public worship."[1] 1)The true leader is careful about externals. He should avoid stiffness and insincerity, but always seek to be dignified. He should remember that the voice is an index of a person's culture. Keep it pleasing, clear, and resonant, never loud or strident (grating, rasping, harsh). A good wife can be helpful at this point. 2) A good leader should have strong intellectual

---

1.    Ibid., p. 25

powers, developed in school and training. You have to be able to size up a situation, devise practical ways of doing what needs to be done, and then lead others in your plan. The schools can only direct and guide, whereas each person must use his intellect properly. 3) A leader must have a breadth and depth of emotional powers. You cannot express feeling in worship unless you can feel yourself. This is involved in nearly all the aspects of public worship. The call is for sympathy, or Christian love in action. You become effective when you are able to put yourself in the place of the man in the pew and look at the world through his eyes. 4) The worship leader should be a man of strong willpower. The will is another name for the entire personality in action. A person may possess the first three qualities and still lack that dynamic quality known as "drive," which makes a person an effective leader. He has a strong sense of purpose and direction, with the ability to keep the service moving steadily. Without becoming nervous or excited, he must be able to impart enthusiasm. Without losing self-control, he must have the ability to express strong and deep emotions. He needs the ability to awaken the conscience and move the will of the worshipper Godward.

What does one do when a baby screams, or a child is left to run down to the pulpit, or a person faints, or one has a heart attack? Circumstances vary. Ordinarily the leader remains in the pulpit, leads in prayer or in a song, and lets the church officers care for the situation. 5) The leader of worship needs imagination. It often is the quality most lacking. It is a gift which can be developed through proper use.

Negatively, leadership should never draw attention to itself. Every minister who does his best in the leadership of worship is good in the eyes of God.

At Cairo in the Museum of Egyptian Antiquities, the curator pointed out an earthen vessel which seemed without beauty or worth. Then he turned on a light within it, and it proved to be a vase of alabaster, shining with beauty. So when the light of God's indwelling presence shines out through the leader in worship, he becomes a radiant Christian personality. Such leadership is sought for our parishes today.

# Chapter 28
# The Sacraments as Worship and Midweek Worship

The meaning and the place of the sacraments are not within our purview in this chapter. Our concern is with the worship element of them, and the manner in which they are celebrated.

A minister's standing in his own community depends largely upon his ability to lead on special occasions. One of these is the time of baptism. The man with the shepherd heart rejoices when Christian parents bring their babies or small children to the font for baptism, or for a service of dedication. Normally these ceremonies should be conducted in the church in the presence of the congregation as a part of the worship service. It should be a very meaningful and sacred time.

In special cases when the baptism is performed in a home, or in another place, proper care should be given to carry on the sacrament reverently and in good order.

In churches which baptize adults by immersion great care should be exercised to carry out the ordinance with real meaning.

The sacrament of the Lord's Supper should be the crowning service in the church. As one writer suggested, it should be earth's nearest approach to heaven. The hearts of the Emmaus road disciples burned within them when the living Christ made Himself known in the breaking of the bread. When we as worship leaders serve the Lord's Supper our vital concern should be with the Christ, to be presented as the Bread of Life.

Before the Lord's Supper is celebrated there should be adequate preparation. It can involve a preparatory Sunday with sermon. It

93

should include a planning meeting with the elders to make sure that all things are done decently and in order. There should also be a conference between the organist, the choir leader (if there is one), and the pastor to make sure all the music for the service is correlated.

The message on communion Sunday would necessarily be shorter than usual. I always call it a meditation. Of course it would relate to the sacrament, with emphasis on the cross or the truths of the atonement. The appeal should be to the heart. During the hymn which follows the message the pastor and the elders usually gather around the communion table. The elders remove the cloth.

The Lord's Supper itself is a sermon in action. The service should glow with a light from above. The main parts of the liturgical service should be held in the memory, so that we do not appear to be just reading.

When the time comes to bless the bread, then the elders (or deacons) should rise, and stand in proper position, after which the plates are given to them. When all the plates are in hand the elders should then serve the congregation. They return to the table with the plates and are seated. You then serve the elders, you can have your lay leader serve you, you make a statement about the meaning of the moment, and then all partake of the bread together. A similar procedure follows in the blessing and serving of the cup. There are some pastors who serve themselves and the elders first, and then the people partake as they are served. For my part, I see this method as less meaningful as well as less reverent. The togetherness of the participation is a live demonstration of the "one bread, one body" idea.

For background during the serving you can either have the organist play hymns quietly, or you can quote Scripture and/or hymns during this period. I find complete silence awkward, but there are pious souls who prefer it. The average person needs assistance in meditation, such as music, quoted hymns and Scripture provide.

Following the Supper, you can repeat or read Psalm 103:1-12. A closing hymn is sung, and the elders cover the table again. The pastor should return to the pulpit for the benediction. Make sure the service is conducted with deep and sincere reverence. I once participated in a union communion service when the guest speaker undertook to tell jokes and funny stories. This is out of place. The Lord's Supper should be held as a sacred time, a high point in the life of the church.

The midweek service can vary a great deal, depending on the situation. Special day services during the week such as Christmas, Good Friday, and Ascension would normally be conducted in a similar way to those on Sunday morning. Others would probably tend to be less formal. If it is a service given largely to Bible study and prayer, it would probably start with a hymn or two and an opening prayer. Then would follow the study, and conclude with a prayer time. This order can be reversed. A brief testimony time can be allowed, but it needs to be closely guarded against misuse. It can very easily revert to the same ones saying the same thing every week.

The main purpose of such services should be devotional and inspirational, with instruction playing a part as well. Today there are Bible studies frequently held in homes. It is important that they be under proper supervision, lest they veer in wrong directions. The pastor should either lead the studies, or at least keep close contact with them.

## Chapter 29

# Opportunities for Worship Experiences at Weddings and Funerals and Other Occasions

Our opportunities to conduct public worship are not confined to our own church building, or to the normal Sunday morning, evening and midweek services.

Union services provide such occasions. There are Christmas candlelight carol sings, union community services, and evangelistic crusades. At these times you probably will only be asked to read Scripture, or sing, or pray, or speak. The quality of worship and music may not meet your standards. Do what you can to influence it to higher levels. At one Christmas carol sing I was asked to sing "O Holy Night." The next year I was invited to read the Christmas Scriptures. This was a challenge, so I took the passages in Isaiah 7 and 9, Luke 2, Matthew 1, John 1, and Galatians 4. They totaled 50 verses. I memorized them, and gave them without a Bible. This made them stand out with meaning. At union services I have been asked to pray or read the Scripture, or give the message. These are times when we can let our light shine. I have also made known my dissatisfaction with the raucous type of music used on some of these occasions. Some ministers will dominate union services if you don't watch out. Always be "wise as serpents and harmless as doves."

You also may be asked to pray at various meetings, such as city and county (shire) councils, service clubs, etc. You can lift the level of prayer for such meetings. The level of the opening prayers at some of our service clubs is often low, and sometimes can hardly be called prayer. On special occasions you may be asked to pray. Make sure it is well done. At community levels we have to make sure we are not offensive, and at the same time hold to the things that we believe. If there are Jews present, closing your prayer in "our Lord's Name," will cover them and us without offence. Public prayer is much more common in the United States than in Australia.

Funerals came our way often in Australia, and gave us opportunities to lead people in worship who never otherwise worshiped. My records show that I only averaged slightly more than five funerals a year while serving churches in the United States, even though several of the churches were sizeable. During my years of service in Australia I averaged twenty-one funerals each year, while pastoring churches with smaller constituencies. These statistics seem to underline the fact that there are large opportunities in the Australian community to conduct funerals if you make an effort to carry them out with meaning and purpose. My personal approach is to do as much of the service as possible without benefit of a book or a Bible. At a graveside service recently I gave the 23rd Psalm, parts of Romans 8, John 11:25, Job 1:21, and parts of I Corinthians 15, the committal, the committal prayer and benediction all from memory. Comments which followed showed that this was greatly appreciated. Fiddling through pages, trying to find your place, etc. detracts much from the worship of the occasion.

In his book on "The Funeral" Andrew Blackwood states "there are two kinds of ministers: the one knows how to conduct a funeral; the other does not."[1] Our aim is to produce ministers who know how to do it. On occasion you will be called to conduct a funeral at a moment's notice. Gather yourself together, ask God to help you, and don't let on that you had no notice. The promise to Paul is also ours: "My grace is sufficient for thee."[2]

Don't try to use a funeral to tell people off. It is not a time to scold, or to judge. Give your witness with wisdom and discretion,

1.    Andrew W. Blackwood, *The Funeral*, p. 14
2.    II Corinthians 12:9a

and always seek to be comforting and uplifting. Do what you can to personalize the service for the deceased and his/her family, even though you have not known him/her in life.

Weddings are most meaningful times in the lives of our people. We can help to give them special meaning. The ceremony itself is a time of worship. It includes prayer and Scripture reading, and involves solemn vows. Solemnity should mark the occasion, even though a light word can break a tension at times. Efforts are made by most brides and their families to do every detail up nicely. See to it that the service is planned well, practiced properly, and carried out with dignity. It will be much appreciated, and not soon forgotten.

Make the most of every opportunity you have to lead people in the worship of our God and Heavenly Father.

# Chapter 30

# Music in Worship

Music is the finest of the arts, and sacred music is the best. No secular music has ever surpassed the spiritual harmonies of Johann Sebastian Bach. In many parishes we have to think of our music on a lower level.

Christianity is certainly a singing religion. Music had a notable place among the Hebrews also. The Old Testament is full of the song of the Lord. The Psalter was its hymnbook. Companies of pilgrims on their way to Mount Zion raised their voices in sacred song. Music and worship are clearly related.

Music can be a great aid to prepare us for worship. It can transfer attention from the ordinary concerns of life to spiritual things.

We sing together. Our common song of praise takes us out of spiritual isolation. Group singing has a unifying effect. Devan says: "A few well-played notes on an organ, a well-handled song service, or the hearty congregational singing of a single hymn can weld jarring personalities and prepare the way for spiritual impression and action."[1]

The singing of hymns is the most important part of the music of the church. It falls on the minister to choose the proper hymns. Unwise selection can create havoc for the singing. The choice involves proper planning for the service. Always choose objective hymns of worship to begin the service, ones which center on God. During worship you will probably use a hymn geared to the children. At the close a subjective hymn, which personalizes the truth proclaimed, is in order. Always study carefully the hymn before you choose it. Hewitt tells of a time when he as a boy preacher announced an opening hymn which turned out to be a hymn to close the service.[2]

Generally it is better to stand when we sing. It is wise to be careful about suggesting radical changes in the local church music. Also one should be careful about hymns which are loved. Blackwood warns that "the wise minister never voices any criticism of a hymn or a tune which other people love. He knows that there is a place for the gospel songs."[3]

Choirs can add greatly to the quality of music in worship. Pastors should work hand in hand with the choir director. The choir anthems should not supercede the singing of the hymns by the congregation, but the choir can give good leadership in the singing.

When organists are faithful and efficient at their task, the minister should make sure that proper appreciation is expressed. Ministerial thoughtfulness to his musicians will pay rich dividends.

1.    S. Arthur Devan, op. cit., pp. 155-6
2.    Arthur W. Hewitt, *Highland Shepherds*, p. 27
3.    Andrew W. Blackwood, *The Fine Art of Public Worship*, p. 119

# Part 4

# PASTORING

# Chapter 31

# The Importance of the Pastoral Aspect of the Ministry

Heretofore in this book we have been discussing preaching and public worship. Now we approach the pastoral ministry. In our opinion, they go hand in hand. One cannot be a successful and helpful preacher without being a good pastor. A large part of the minister's labor lies outside the pulpit. The pastor must go where the people are, with a heart that loves and solaces and heals. The pastor must live with his people, think with their mind, feel with their feelings, see with their eyes, hear with their ears, suffer with their spirit, bear their griefs, and carry their sorrows.

Books are of great importance to us in the ministry, but they tend to speak to us in a theoretical and abstract way. Contact with people teaches us in concrete and in reality. We must learn to understand human nature. Such a knowledge is second only to a knowledge and understanding of the Word of God. Pastoral work is learned only by practice. It was the famous Thomas Chalmers who made the statement: "A house-going minister makes a church-going people." This is as true today as it ever was.

Charles E. Jefferson wrote a book on preaching, "*The Minister as Prophet*," and followed it with a book on pastoring, "*The Minister as Shepherd*." He makes some interesting points in the latter book which we will summarize, and then add our own emphases.

Shepherd is one of the best titles for the minister. It has a wealth of meaning, and is free from stain. It drives us straight back to Jesus, who spoke of Himself as "the Good Shepherd."[1] As He looked out

---

1.    John 10:11

over the crowds who followed Him, "He was moved with compassion toward them, because they were as sheep not having a shepherd."[1] Jesus instructed Peter to "feed my sheep."[2] In other words, He was telling Peter to do the work of a shepherd. When giving instructions to church leaders Peter said: "Feed the flock of God...and when the Chief Shepherd shall appear, ye shall receive a crown of glory that fadeth not away."[3] Paul likewise had a shepherd's heart for his converts. He instructed the leaders of the Ephesian Church to "Take heed unto yourselves, and to all the flock, to feed the Church of the Lord, which He purchased with His own blood."[4]

The famous benediction from the New Testament over Christian workers is this: "And now the God of peace, Who brought again from the dead our Lord Jesus, that Great Shepherd of the sheep, through the blood of the everlasting covenant, make you perfect in every good work to do His will, working in you that which is well-pleasing in His sight, through Jesus Christ, to Whom be glory forever and ever. Amen."[5] If our aim in life is to be Christlike, then we are to do the work of a shepherd.

"When church leaders began to lose the vision of the Good Shepherd, they at the same time began to drift away from the New Testament ideal of ministerial service."[6]

The work of a shepherd is humble. A shepherd cannot shine... His work is often unheralded. It is a form of service which costs him something. It seldom brings the applause of the crowd. The satisfactions come from within. If souls are built up in righteousness, the work is lasting.

"A minister can scamp his pastoral work and still retain his position as the shepherd of the flock, but he cannot retain his position in

1.    Mark 6:34
2.    John 21:16, 17
3.    I Peter 5:2, 4-5
4.    Acts 20:28
5.    Hebrews 13:20-21
6.    Charles E. Jefferson, *The Minister as Shepherd*, p. 19

God's kingdom."[1] It is the weak who shirk pastoral service. *Never* be guilty of saying that you hate pastoral work.

"It is an encouraging thought that the humblest minister may become a faithful and successful pastor. God never intended that this world should be saved by pulpit geniuses, or else He would create more of them...Every herald of the Gospel who loves his Master, loves his Bible, loves his fellowmen, and who hungers to win souls to the Saviour, can be a good pastor, if he honestly aims to become one."[2]

The world is in need of real shepherds of the flock. This is our task. At the last we shall be judged by whether or not we have fed and nurtured the flock of God.

# Chapter 32
# First Days in a New Field

"Well begun is half done." In a new pastorate, as in a honeymoon, be sure to make a good beginning. First impressions are very important.

As the leader in worship and the preacher of the Word, seek to be at your very best from the beginning of your ministry. Concentrate on being a good shepherd. Meanwhile, seek to size up your community and your congregation. Then you can begin making a general plan.

1. Determine to learn to know the people in their homes. Seek to cover every home as soon as possible. This can be a great help in learning to know names and faces. Seeing the family together in

---

1.  op. cit., p. 41
2.  Theodore L. Cuyler, *How to be a Pastor*, p. 20

their home can put them in place in your mind. At church they may sit in different sections, or be working in various departments. Often you haven't connected sons or daughters with their parents until you see them at home.

Make notes of what you learn. Work on knowing and remembering names. Make this your working motto: "I can recall the name of every person whom I wish to know. By God's grace I shall learn to love everybody. I can do all things through Christ who strengthens me." Work on it with help from your wife. One pastor who excelled with names gave these rules:

* Be sure to get the name. Ask for it to be repeated if you don't understand it right away, or have them spell it distinctly.
* Write it down. Say it aloud, more than once.
* Associate it with something fixed, facially.
* Visualize the other person, with a 'camera eye.'
* Use the name whenever you meet the person.
* Talk over at night every new name or face.
* Take time. Use all your senses. Will to know.
* Determine by God's grace to excel in this art.

2. Seek to win the hearts of all the people. Simply be yourself. Always appear friendly. Learn how to shake hands. Be concerned about the other person. They will trust you and confide in you if they like you personally. Be careful not to betray their confidence in you.

3. Learn the facts about the parish. With open eyes and ears you can size up the local situation in a few months. Unless the preceding regime has been a disaster, give deference to what has been done. Go easy on criticism.

4. Gladly accept parish customs. Of course, that does not mean to allow bingo in the parish hall. Otherwise, don't ask for changes immediately in the existing way of doing things. Conform to the best local ideals and traditions. If they need changing, seek to do it wisely and carefully. Don't come in "like a bull into a china shop."

In short, study the new field, and then plan the work. BEGIN WITH THE PEOPLE, AND NOT YOUR BOOKS.[1]

---

1. See Andrew W. Blackwood, *Pastoral Work*, pp. 35-38, for the four headings above.

# Chapter 33

# **Pastoral Calling**

The importance of pastoral calling can hardly be overestimated. It is not an easy task, nor should it be taken lightly. I know of one minister who stated that he would drive around the block three times before he could muster up enough courage to call in a home. J. H. Jowett states that a sermon is easier than a conversation. He goes on to tell how he shrank from the personal home contact early in his ministry.[1]

"Let a pastor make himself at home in everybody's home, let him come often and visit their sick room, and kneel beside their empty cribs, and their broken hearts, and pray with them; let him go to the businessmen in his congregation when they have suffered reverses and give them a word of cheer; let him be quick to recognize the poor, and the children—and he will weave a cord around the hearts of his people that will withstand tremendous pressure. He will have won their hearts to himself, and that is a great step toward drawing them to the house of God, and winning their souls to the Saviour."[2]

It is difficult to suggest a plan for pastoral calling, and even harder to devise a plan that will work out in practice. What will suit one minister's personality will not fit another's. What can prove successful in one parish situation may be ineffective in another. The time and season of the year can make considerable difference in one's approach.

Make it a matter of habit to be a good pastor. It is best if you can develop a pattern of calling for your parish during your first year of

---

1.  James H. Jowett, *The Preacher—His Life and Work*, pp. 180-181
2.  Theodore L. Cuyler, *How to be a Pastor*, p. 10

service there. Perhaps you can draw up that plan on your first holiday. It will not take long for you to gain a good overview of your parish.

Be sure your plan includes all your people. Beware of "special" friends, or prejudicing yourself against certain of the flock. The sick and the sorrowing will have a primary claim on your time. Then the aged and infirm have some priority. Newcomers, visitors, and potential members call for attention. Never cease to look out for the unchurched. Don't forget the regular members. I have found a card system to be helpful to keep track of calls on the families. This is a way to keep anyone from being neglected.

Take notice of the local area. Obtain a map of your community soon after you arrive. If your parish is large, you can use pinpoints on a wall map to determine where every family lives. In our Australian parishes we published geographical directories as part of our alphabetical directories. This not only helps the minister, but also gets people acquainted with their neighbors in the parish, and is an aid to the elders for their contacts. Blackwood points out that the pastor "should be able to find his way over the parish with as much economy of time and effort as a mail carrier or a family physician. Each of these busy men plans his work."[1]

You need to consider the time factor. It is well to set a goal of visiting every home in your parish once a year. As numbers increase and duties multiply, it may not be feasible to go that often. In our last parish in Australia, which listed 120 homes in the directory, we tried to make regular calls at every home every year, and then make brief contacts with all of them more often. When we served a church of over 300 homes in Chicago, and of over 400 homes in California we made the initial calls in all of the homes, and then had to seek further help from assistants and elders.

One needs to be careful about calling at meal times and at odd hours of the day or night. Older people often retire at very early hours. If you discover that the lady of the house has a Tupperware or

---

1.   Andrew W. Blackwood, *Pastoral Work*, p. 44

jewelry party in progress, or a committee meeting for her club or the Guild, excuse yourself and promise a return visit.

Announcement of your calls in the weekly bulletin (newssheet) can work in two directions. It allows the families to plan on your coming. On the other hand, it ties you to a plan which doesn't always work.

It is often a wise thing to use the telephone to make a convenient time for a call. There are other times when this gives some families on the outer edge of the church a chance to avoid your visit.

Keep most of your calls short, but don't give an impression of being hurried. Make a plan for your own pastoral calling that will work for you. Always keep it flexible, since unusual conditions are bound to develop in your ministry.

There will be times when you and your people will become involved in religious surveys of the community, or in inviting folk to evangelistic campaigns. These are usually short calls, but some fruitful results often occur.

If you start a new church, or if you are reaching out into a developing neighborhood, you may want to do door-to-door calling. When we started a new field in Orlando, Florida we made over 3,000 door-to-door contacts as a family. When we returned to serve the same church twenty years later we were amazed to discover that not only those who joined the church, but also many in the community remembered that contact at the door many years before. Some even recalled exact words and conversation that took place. You never know how far or how long your influence extends when you call as a faithful pastor to your people and your community.

# Chapter 34
# Calling On the Sick

One of the very specific types of calling that falls to the lot of the shepherd-pastor is that of visiting the sick. This particular task is our bounden Christian duty. One of the commendatory statements that our Lord will give in the judgment day is this: "I was sick, and you visited me."[1] In the book of James the elders of the church are to be called in when there is sickness.[2] Pastors have an obligation to shepherd the sheep in their times of need, which calls for both home and hospital visitation of the sick. Blackwood states that "nothing that the clergyman does provides a more searching test of his pastoral skill and intellectual acumen than his care of the sick."[3]

Train your people to notify you whenever an illness or a hospital stay is involved. As soon as you are notified, seek to determine the nature of the illness and the seriousness thereof. Sometimes the issue is touchy. Don't push for information. Then make the call as soon as possible. When you enter the sick room, you cannot be sure of what to expect. The Lord knows all, however, and He will guide you in what to say and do. You enter the room as the physician of the soul. In times of illness patients and their families are usually very open and responsive to spiritual truth. Do not stress the sickness or the related problems. Show concern for them, but don't emphasize problems.

If you use Scripture at the bedside, quote it rather than reading it, if possible. To walk into a sick room auspiciously with a Bible in your hand can create strange impressions, and tends to frighten the sick one. You should seek to store various passages from the Psalms

1.   Matthew 25:36
2.   James 5:14, 15
3.   Andrew W. Blackwood, *Pastoral Work*, p. 102

and the New Testament in your mind, ready for use at any time. If this proves too difficult for you, slip a New Testament with the Psalms in your coat pocket. Offer a prayer if you possibly can fit it in. It is usually expected, but there are times when it is difficult to work it in. Normally you would not force the issue of prayer. The only time I have made an issue of it is when the patient is being wheeled to the operating room (theater) and there has been no opportunity or time to pray with him/her previously. Most attendants will give you a brief moment to pray with the patient, if you identify yourself as the pastor. There is no fixed technique in these matters for a Protestant minister. He just has to adjust to the circumstances he finds at the time.

There are other suggestions in visiting the sick:

1) You can use hymns as well as Scripture. If you are unable to sing them, quote them. I have had hundreds of experiences when singing a familiar hymn got through to a patient in a semi-conscious state when nothing else could provoke a response. In case other patients are in a hospital room, you can seek to do this quietly and unobtrusively.

2) Listen to the patient's story. Don't talk about yourself, or about your own aches and pains. Don't crepe-hang, or suggest negative thoughts to the sick one.

3) Don't tell them that they're about to die, unless the family specifically requests it. Many a "dying" patient recovers. Be careful of your conversation with others in the room when you think the patient is "out of it." They may be more aware of what is being said than you think. Don't talk in whispers, or do so just outside the door. The patient will think the worst of such goings-on.

4) In case the illness calls for an operation, try to call and pray before it happens. If you can arrange to sit with the family during the operation, it can prove most helpful and meaningful. Then follow through afterward.

5) Don't *ever dare* to tell a patient who is a Christian that the reason they are ill is because they didn't trust God, or failed to believe in His ability to heal. This is not for you to say.

6) *Never* say to the sick one or their family that it is *always* God's
will to heal illness. The Bible doesn't say so. Paul, a man of great
faith, didn't get healing when he prayed for it.[1]

7) There certainly is a great deal of difference between dealing with
a patient and a family who are committed Christians, than with
those who are outside of Christ. You can use an entirely different
approach when helping Christians. If they are not people of faith,
it is a "different ball of wax."

8) When you leave a sick room, leave the problem there. Don't take
it with you. While you're there, be concerned and sympathetic.
When you leave, you must leave it behind, or it can get you
down.

Our personal testimony, after having made nearly 30,000 calls in
more than 200 different hospitals and convalescent homes, is that the
visitation of the sick is one of the great opportunities to bring the
blessings of the Christian Gospel to those who are in a time of need.

# Chapter 35

# Visiting the Aged

The number of people in our society today who are past sixty
years of age has increased dramatically. Life expectancy for both
men and women is far greater today than it was fifty to one-hundred
years ago. We must gear our pastoral work to these facts.

The most neglected folk in our parishes may well be the aged.
They may not have any family nearby, or their family may neglect
them. If they are in retirement homes, convalescent facilities, or
geriatric wards, they may well need special attention.

---

1. See II Corinthians 12:7-10

Be cheerful when you visit older folk. Let your countenance be radiant. Although you go with an aim to cheer them up, there are times that they will cheer you up.

When you drop in on the aged ones, bring them a fresh morsel from heaven. It is your privilege to minister the things of God to them. Develop a regularity about your visits. In one California convalescent home where I ministered two or three times each week, one of the elderly bedridden ladies would perch her head in her hand, and watch for me to come. In a Victoria geriatric ward which I visited weekly, a ninety-year old blind lady would always inform me if I came on a different day than usual, or if I had missed calling the previous week. In my first student charge in Michigan there was a man who had been bedridden for over twenty years. Every Monday I called and read one of the Sunday sermons to him. He was a truly converted person, and deeply appreciated hearing the Gospel messages which he missed at church. In each case they were examples of how the aged can come to expect you, and really appreciate your visits.

There are some problems that are typical of old age which you will face. Some just sit day after day and do little else but brood. Others are senile, and you just have to overlook it. Some are forgetful. The degree of forgetfulness varies. Often it is minor, and other times it is major. One lady in Victoria, whose husband had been active as an elder in the church before his death, was usually expecting him to bring her to church the next Sunday. Occasionally I would say that her daughter would do that, but most of the time it was better not to correct her. It is seldom wise to argue with them if they are mixed up. You have to learn to put up with their foibles. Accept their infirmities. Don't always believe everything they tell you about being neglected by their children. It might be true, but often the aged forget what has been done for them. In fact, they may well forget that you have called.

Listen to the experiences the aged love to relate to you. They have much which they can teach us. Never mind if you have heard the story before. Most of the aged are ready to receive pastoral care.

Encourage them in the faith. If they are confessing Christians, you can arrange to have them receive the Lord's Supper at home or in the hospital if they desire it.

There are some of the aged who need to get out of themselves, and start doing for others. One elderly lady living in a Chicago convalescent home was very depressed. On each weekly visit we attempted to cheer her. Soon she was pushing people about in their wheelchairs, which caused her to forget her own problems. The effect upon her was remarkable. Other older ladies love to knit, crochet, and sew for others. Some of our ladies in their late eighties do a remarkable job, and produce lovely things. It makes them feel useful.

As you call on the aged, there are those who can really *lift you* up. Their healthy attitude and their expressions of appreciation can cause you to walk with a lighter step when you leave them.

As you give, you will receive. As you counsel, you will be enlightened. While you lift another's burden, your own burden will be lighter. Jesus' words apply here: "He that loses his life for My sake shall find it."[1]

# Chapter 36

# Ministering to the Dying

When death comes, the pastor indeed has a call to serve. This is normally a time of severe crisis—it may be for the dying one—it may be even more for the living.

There has been a new interest in the subject of death and dying in recent years. Many books have appeared dealing with the approach to

---

1.   Matthew 16:35

death. Special studies have been made with those facing death, and with their families, such as that made by Elizabeth Kubler-Ross.[1] Her analysis of those who know that they have terminal illness is that they go through certain stages: 1) Denial and isolation, 2) Anger, 3) Bargaining, 4) Depression, 5) Acceptance, and 6) Hope. She summarizes these stages in a later book.[2]

"The dying patient has to pass through many stages in his struggle to come to grips with his illness and his ultimate death. He may deny the bad news for a while and continue to work as if he were as well and strong as before. He may desperately visit one physician after the other in the hope that the diagnosis was not correct. He may wish to shield his family from the truth.

Sooner or later he will have to face the grim reality, and he often reacts with an angry 'why me?' to his illness...If we assist this patient he will then be able to pass to the stage of bargaining. He may bargain with God for an extension of life, or he may promise good behavior and religious dedication if he is spared more suffering.

In the depression stage he mourns past losses first and then begins to lose interest in the outside world. If he is allowed to grieve, if his life is not artificially prolonged and if his family has learned 'to let go,' he will be able to die with peace and in a stage of acceptance."

The wonderful part about our ministry to the dying is that we can hold out the hope of eternal life through Jesus Christ our Lord. The glory of the Gospel shines through in moments like these. Families too need the assurance that comes to those whose loved ones have belonged to the Lord but have gone on before.

There are times when it becomes the pastor's task to notify the one who is ill that there is no evident hope of recovery. This should

1.    Elizabeth Kubler-Ross, *On Death and Dying*, (New York: Macmillan, 1969) Chapters 3 through 8

2.    E. Kubler-Ross, *Questions and Answers on Death and Dying* (New York: Macmillan, 1974) pp. 1-2

be done with the concurrence of the doctor and the family. There is an increasing desire today on the part of many people to "lay the cards on the table" and face the facts. Families have often thought that they have kept the dire truth from their sick loved ones when they really have not. If death is not faced squarely, then the ability of the pastor to minister to the terminally ill is severely hampered.

Many a time the consciousness that death is imminent has given us as pastors an opportunity to witness to the patient concerning their soul's salvation. Some of the greatest experiences of my ministry have been at deathbeds of those who have failed to believe during their active lives but acknowledged Christ as Saviour while on their bed. After the death occurs, we have always used the story of the bedside conversion at the funeral. Often this has multiplied the blessing.

It is good if the shepherd can be with his sheep when death comes. It is a time when a staying hand can be a great help. It is a time when a prayer or a psalm can lift the sights beyond the physical body, now lifeless, to the heavenly home and eternal life. If the shepherd has been close during those crucial hours, it is not quickly forgotten. When we left our pastorate in Redlands, California in 1958, after the last service, and after all the tearful good-byes had been said, we noted five women standing near who just didn't want to leave. Then it came over us that we had ministered closely to each of them during their husband's last illness, and had laid all of them to rest. They hadn't forgotten.[1]

---

1.    John H. Muller, *A Plan for the Building Up of the Body of Christ*, (doctoral dissertation) pp. 102-103

## Chapter 37

# Comforting Those in Sorrow

When you are notified that there has been a death in your church family, go to the bereaved family in their home or in the hospital immediately.

Sometimes a nurse (called Sisters in Australia) will notify you that a person listed under your denomination has passed away. The expectation is that you will come to the hospital and pray before they take the body away. Oblige, even though it isn't our Protestant custom. Just commit the deceased to the Heavenly Father.

When you get to the family of the deceased church member, be kind and understanding. One Aussie pastor came to a home where a second death occurred only a few months after a previous one. His opening comment was: "You must be getting used to it by now." The wife and mother involved was horrified with this remark.

Be comforting. Use passages of Scripture if you can work it in. Be sure to pray. If the sorrowing ones are believers, you can draw on all the verities that follow the resurrection and the hope of eternal life.

Offer to help in any way that you can. In certain American communities we made a practice of going with the family to consult with the funeral director and plan for the service. This can be especially helpful to a widow who has no family. In Australian communities the director may call you to his office to meet the family, or give you a home address where you can meet them. Of course, if it involves your regular church attenders, you will know where to go to console the bereaved.

Follow-up after death is important. As Adams puts it: "Grief tears life to shreds, and shakes one from top to bottom."[1] During

---

1.    Jay E. Adams, *Shepherding God's Flock*, p. 136 (3 volumes in 1)

116

grief other emotions such as anger, guilt, and fear often get involved. Considerable care has to be given to counseling in situations such as this.

It is well to remember that sorrow is a proper emotion and it is not wise to hold it back at the time of death. Tears can be a wholesome therapy to a grieving person.

There are times when all that the pastor needs to do is to sit and "hold the hand" (literally or figuratively) of the sorrowing one. There are some occasions when we need to "weep with them that weep."[1]

Think of the church as a depository of comfort, with you the minister as its agent to dispense it. Hearts desperately need comfort when there is an empty place in the home. If pastors don't move in, representatives of sects and strange groups are likely to try to take over.

Despair over death is neither right or necessary for the Christian. When we walk through the valleys of dense darkness, God is with us.[2] Heaven is the Christian's final home, and Christian loved ones have the hope of reunion with those who have gone on before. It is possible for us, under God, to lead our people to a real and triumphant victory over sorrow. "Blessed are they that mourn, for they *shall* be comforted."[3]

Don't miss out on opportunities to serve, to witness, to comfort, and to heal broken hearts. Ask God to guide you, and you can be a channel of blessing.

---

1. Romans 12:15
2. See Psalm 23:4
3. Matthew 5:4

# Chapter 38
# Ministering
# the Sacraments

In most of our Protestant churches we observe two sacraments, baptism and the Lord's Supper. The Baptists speak of them as ordinances. We speak of them as a means of grace, and look at them as objective channels for God's blessing which Christ has instituted for the Church. They should be combined with the Word, and become effective through the operation of the Holy Spirit. The Word is adapted to the ear, and the sacraments to the eye.

The Reformed view of the sacraments is that they do not of themselves confer grace. They have no magical power to produce holiness. God has appointed them as the ordinary means through which He works His grace in the hearts of sinners, and their willful neglect can only result in spiritual loss. The Word of God must accompany the Sacraments, and never be separated from them.

Hodge lists three points on the sacraments found in the various confessions and catechisms of the Reformed faith: 1) The sacraments are real means of grace, that is, means appointed and employed by Christ for conveying the benefits of His redemption to His people, 2) There is no source of virtue in the sacraments, in the sense of power or efficiency. The efficacy of the sacraments is due largely to the blessing of Christ and the working of His Spirit, and 3) The sacraments are effectual as means of grace only, so far as adults are concerned, to those who by faith receive them. Their saving or sanctifying influence is experienced only by believers.[1]

The first sacrament we are called upon to administer is baptism. The theology of baptism is well covered by Berkhof in his chapter

---

1.     Charles Hodge, *Systematic Theology*, Vol. III, pp. 499-500

on "Christian Baptism."[1] There are also many booklets about the baptism of children.[2]

Since we follow the practice of child baptism, the matter of who is a candidate for baptism becomes an important one. In my experience in the Reformed Church in America we usually expected one parent at least to be a member or a baptized member of the church in order to present their child for baptism. There is a similar rule in the Presbyterian Church of Australia.

Other churches will have different rules to go by. In many U.S. communities people will request baptism who seldom darken the doors of the church. In Australia, where a "state-church mentality" prevails, there will be those who have an affinity for Catholicism, Anglicanism, Presbyterianism, or the Uniting Church who will request baptism (often termed christening) for their children, even though they have little more than a nodding acquaintance with the church. This matter has to be handled with great wisdom and discretion. Parents can be "turned off" permanently from the church by a flat refusal. In any case, counseling about the meaning and purpose of baptism is essential. It may well be an evangelistic opportunity for you.

Most denominations present an order for baptism, which should be followed.

1. Louis Berkhof, *Systematic Theology*, p. 622ff
2. Herman Hoeksema, *The Biblical Ground for the Baptism of Infants*,
   John Scott Johnson, *Baptism*,
   Arthur Gunn, *Biblical Baptism*,
   M. Eugene Osterhaven, *What is Christian Baptism?*,
   John Murray, *Christian Baptism*,
   Jay E. Adams, *Meaning and Mode of Baptism*,
   Albertus Pieters, *Why We Baptize Infants*

The Lord's Supper has its origins in the Passover feast of the Old Testament.[1] Jesus followed the observance of the Passover with His disciples in Jerusalem with the institution of the Lord's Supper.[2]

Today we celebrate the Lord's Supper regularly in obedience to our Lord's command to remember Him. We do not hold to a sacramental view, which sees the Lord's physical presence in the elements (the bread and the cup) but our Reformed view sees the spiritual presence of Christ. It has been stated this way—The spiritual presence of Christ spiritually discerned.

Communion in the home or hospital should be served by the pastor and an elder, when it is requested. Usually there is prayer, a summary statement of the meaning and purpose of the sacrament is given, and the elements are served by the elder. Prayer concludes the occasion.

At the second service of the day, a similar plan can be offered to those who missed communion earlier in the day.

# Chapter 39

# Funerals

Blackwood introduced a book on funerals by illustrating from two well-known men's last request: "When William James died, his widow sent a note to George A. Gordon of the New Old South Church in Boston: 'I want you to officiate at the funeral, as one of William's friends, and also as a man of faith.' What an ideal for any pastor!...Conversely, when Robert Burns lay dying he spoke about his obsequies. Referring to a company of ill-trained volunteer soldiers, he said: 'Don't let the awkward squad fire a salute over my

1. See Exodus 12
2. See Luke 22:7-20

grave.' While the poet was not thinking of any clergyman, every minister should take those words to heart."[1]

The above illustrations point out the importance for the minister to do a good job at funerals. They deserve our best efforts.

Today in the U.S. most funerals are held in funeral chapels, unless the deceased was an active church person. The trend is the same in Australian large cities, but in "country" Australia, which includes smaller cities, nearly all the funerals are held in churches.

Start the service on time, as long as the family has been seated. Quote something like John 11:25 and offer a brief prayer, asking God's blessing. In Australia nearly every funeral service includes one or two hymns, sung by the congregation. Special music is not as common as in the U.S. The inevitable hymns in Aussie funerals are: "Abide With Me," "Amazing Grace," "Nearer My God to Thee," "Rock of Ages," "The Lord is My Shepherd," and "What A Friend We Have in Jesus."

Next comes the reading of various Scripture passages. Suggestions for use are: Psalm 1, Psalm 23, Psalm 90, Psalm 103, John 14:1-6 and 27, Romans 8:28, 35-39, I Corinthians 15:19-22, II Corinthians 5:1, and Revelation 14:13. Variations can be used for children. Some passages are especially appropriate for Christians. Quote them, if possible, or read them with real meaning. Don't treat this portion of the service as a formality.

Then you can turn to the obituary and message. Be sure of your facts concerning the life which is past, and get the family names correct. Bring in what you can about the deceased. If you know about the last moments of life, share them. Personalize as much as you can. Impersonal funerals seem so cold and without feeling. Preach to the living, but do it carefully and exercise careful judgment. Do not condemn anyone. Leave the final decision to God.

The message can be concluded with the main prayer of the service, followed by the Lord's Prayer. During the singing of the last hymn, you can go over to the coffin. When the funeral director is

---

1.    Andrew W. Blackwood, *The Funeral*, pp. 13-14

ready to move, then march ahead of the coffin and the pallbearers to the hearse, and stand aside as the coffin is placed in the hearse. It is preferable to ride in the hearse to the cemetery, rather than to drive your own car behind the hearse or the family cars.

At the cemetery you precede the pallbearers and the coffin to the graveside. When the people have gathered near (you often have to motion to them, or speak to them, to come closer), and the funeral director gives you the nod, you then proceed with the committal. It is good if you can do this without a book in hand. I begin with a hymn like "Peace, Perfect Peace" or "Abide With Me" (If it wasn't used in the service). If you can't sing it, quote it. During the words of committal (Earth to earth, etc.) many funeral directors will have a vial of earth which they will pour on the coffin. I always have two flowers, and toss petals toward the coffin during the whole committal. At this same point the coffin will be lowered into the ground (not the custom in the U.S.A.). My first experience of seeing this was my first Aussie funeral. I was so shocked that I nearly fell into the grave with the coffin. Gradually I got used to it.

After the benediction you can sing or quote the last verse of the hymn you used before.

There may be an R.S.L. (American Legion) team or a Masonic contingent present. Step aside, and let them do their thing.

Be sure to shake the hands of the immediate family, and express your sympathy to them. Stand aside respectfully until people begin to leave.

In case there is only a graveside service, be sure to add some Scripture and comments which you would normally make in the church or chapel service. If there is only a crematorium service, do something similar.

If an emergency or crisis situation develops (such as the coffin slipping into the grave or the collapse of the grave) it is very essential that you maintain your "cool" throughout lest you upset the mourners who are gathered.

Usually you will be invited to a home or hall where the family and close friends gather. It gives you an opportunity to meet people, and to make contacts.

Don't forget to follow-up with the sorrowing ones. They need you more after everyone else has gone.

We now present a summary of the pastor's role which we have gleaned from several funeral directors, elaborating on how clergy should conduct themselves at the time of a death:

A preacher should make himself fully available whether the people are practising Christians or not. The clergy are seen by the family as being able to help in counseling and it is imperative that they do so. Larger funeral chapels employ retired clergy as bereavement counsellors. Counseling is as important as the service delivered. After the funeral itself clergy and funeral directors can work closely together in follow-up. Some families don't want any counseling because they don't go to church. They feel embarrassed using clergy at this time.

It is very important for clergy to make themselves available as soon as possible (and not tomorrow at 2 p.m.) after being notified of a death.

The clergyman should get as much information as possible for a eulogy because eulogies are important to the family, i.e., the person's family history and his/her personality. Using no eulogy makes for a very impersonal funeral.

Funeral services should not be too long. However, don't hurry it—speak slowly and clearly.

Don't be afraid to speak in the direction of the coffin and of the family, as necessary. This gives the service more feeling and personal touch.

The clergyman should not follow the hearse in preference to the family. If he doesn't ride in the hearse he should make his own way ahead of the procession.

The clergyman should not leave the graveside without giving suitable condolence and respects to the families.

Never try to discredit Lodge or R.S.L. (Returned Servicemen's League) or American Legion services. They are very important to the bereaved family.

Treat all families with respect whether they are black or white.

If the family requests, try to be available to assist with counseling at viewings of the deceased in the funeral home. Make sure you are prepared for this role. You should have seen the body of a deceased person prior to this time, or you can be a liability on that occasion.

Your appearance is important—please be neat and tidy.

Be prepared to alter your service, as required. Don't think it can only be done one way.

Be your own personal self. Don't look morbid.

In small towns and country areas especially it is very essential for there to be a good relationship between the funeral director and preacher to make everything work smoothly, i.e., you know what each other is going to do next. They should discuss what they are going to do before the service so that no mistakes are made. An excellent idea is for the minister to hand the funeral director an order of service.

If the family requests a non-religious service it is up to you as a minister to stand for your beliefs.

In tragic circumstances, try to be even more perceptive to the family's wishes about when the funeral should be conducted, even if this means cancelling prior engagements.

One director stressed that the minister should *never* say that he didn't know the deceased. Instead, work around this by finding out what you can about the deceased person.

———

The above comments from funeral directors should be of benefit to all those who conduct funerals. Generally you will find that funeral directors are good people to work with.

# Chapter 40
# Weddings

The role of the pastor in weddings in the U.S.A. is different than in Australia. In the U.S. the couple presents their blood tests and birth certificates at the County Courthouse, and obtain a marriage license. When the minister has performed the marriage, he just has to sign the license, have the witnesses sign it, and he sends it in. In Australia you actually act for the State.

There you must first get qualified as a marriage celebrant. Then you give a "Notice of Intended Marriage" form to the couple to fill out, observe their birth certificates and other pertinent materials such as divorce or consent papers.

The next step in either country is premarital counseling. It can take various forms. It can be done in one long session (by prearrangement), or it can be accomplished in several sessions. The amount of counseling will vary depending on your assessment of the need for it. A very young couple, for instance, might need much more counseling than a mature couple.

The counseling should include the basic ideas of marriage. There should be an emphasis on the major aspects of sharing, concern, and communication. Of course, you will suggest the importance of a common faith, and the part that the church can play in their lives. Do *not* use pressure for a commitment to Christ. I have a minister friend who always prays with his counselees to receive Christ. I sense that they do so because he wants them to, and it is often superficial. I've found little results from these efforts.

You must also determine the details of their plans for the wedding. Make notes of them. Find out what organist, soloist and music they intend to use (make sure it's not something "way-out" and inappropriate.) Discover how many attendants will be a part of the ceremony. Make clear to them that you will be in charge of the practice in consultation with the bride. Set the time for the practice, preferably the night before the ceremony.

At the time of the practice, explain to the assembled participants exactly what they will be expected to do. Tell them to be *ahead* of time, certainly not late for the appointed hour. This prevalent idea that it's the bride's prerogative to be late is nonsense. She sets the time, and she should observe it. Place your wife (or a wedding hostess who will understand your plan for the ceremony) at the door, so that the bridesmaids, the maid or matron of honor, the flower girl, and then the bride on her father's arm, will enter the church in proper order. Then have the organist play the wedding march and bring each member of the party in in proper order, beginning with the men. Make sure that they stand in symmetrical positions to each other (shoulder to shoulder). Don't let the wedding party look hodge-podge. Have them all sit down again and find out if they have any questions. If necessary, go through the marching again. It is important that you stress walking slowly. If a step is used, it is essential to do it well.

Other thoughts for the practice—The bride should come in on the father's right arm. The groom stands at the left of the minister, and the bride at the right of the minister. Check with the couple whether they wish to kneel during the prayer and the Lord's Prayer. The kiss is usually given following the benediction. After this, the minister usually introduces the couple as Mr. and Mrs._____ .

There is a strong trend in the U.S. to light a unity candle. Three candles are used for this ceremony. The outer two candles are lit ahead of the service. Each party takes a candle from the outer candles and together they light the center candle, then blowing out their own, signifying that the two have become one.

Before the wedding, make sure that the necessary documents are properly filled out. In Australia the documents are signed during the wedding ceremony, although most of them can be signed before or after. In the U.S. they can be signed before or after the service.

Try to keep photographers from taking pictures (especially with flash) during the actual ceremony. You can always pose any part of it afterward. Keep the ceremony itself as sacred as possible.

You will usually be invited to the reception. Avoid the punch if it's spiked. Most hosts offer an alternative. You will most likely be asked to give an invocation before the wedding meal. (In Australia the first meal after marriage is called the wedding breakfast, no matter the time of day.) You may even be asked to emcee the reception. If so, accept gladly. You at least can avoid questionable jokes and can easily improve on the sad incompetence of many of the emcees I have heard.

Some plan for fees for the pastor, the organist and the use of the church should be set. This avoids misunderstanding.

May you have many happy experiences at weddings and may the results be lasting marriages.

# Chapter 41
# Church Administration

When you are called to serve a parish you will become an administrator, whether you like it or not. Some Christian ministers seem to have a blindspot when it comes to serving Him through Church administration. Some even decry planning and organization as a worldly activity, and others see it as a wearisome necessity. It is not unusual to hear ministers crying the blues over the load that administration lays on them. Some consider church management a waste of time, and others see it as a necessary evil, keeping them from the "real world" of the ministry.

It is well to note that in I Timothy 3 Paul sees the work of administration as inherent in the ministerial office. It is not a "worldly" activity, but a biblical one. It is dishonoring to God to carry on His work in a careless, sloppy, and confused manner. A messy and un-kempt desk or study is not a credit to the Lord's workman.

Good administration is not a waste of a pastor's time. "It is no less spiritual to plan a series of meetings well so that the Gospel may be preached than to do the preaching...The Holy Spirit freely uses human leadership as the principal means of achieving His pur-poses."[1]

Adams illustrates this by means of a general and his army. The general does not consider his army to be a liability, but rather the principal asset that he has for winning the war. A well organized army can achieve his goals and purposes. Therefore he sees to it that every unit is well-disciplined. He sets up networks of rapid com-munication. He expects not only every division, but every soldier in it, to be fully skilled and equipped for every task to which he is called. He is deeply involved not only in strategy and command, but also in organizing. He is concerned with all these matters because he cannot fight his battles alone. He knows the importance of clear communication, good training, and excellent discipline.

As a shepherd of the flock the pastor too must have his people well trained and disciplined, and under properly delegated leader-ship. He cannot do his work alone. The Chief Shepherd of the sheep wants his undershepherds to nourish, train, mobilize, and deploy the flock in ways that serve Him, and bring honor to His Name.[2]

I remember reading a whole book on Church Administration years ago.[3] It is a field we must understand. When you take over a parish, you are the leader. You head up the organization in most churches. A smooth running church depends to a large extent on you. The worship services, the Bible studies, the youth activities,

1.  Jay E. Adams, *Shepherding God's Flock*, Vol. 3. p. 2
2.  Ibid., pp. 3-4
3.  William H. Leach, *Church Administration*, Geo. H. Doran Co., 1928

the outreach and calling program, the bulletins and newssheets, the financial planning, the musical program, services to the community, congregational meetings, Board and Session (Elders) meetings, custodian's work, plans for your absence and—to a lesser degree—the women's activities, all depend on your guidance and leadership. Obviously, there is much that can be delegated as responsibility to others, but you are still the "spark" that keeps things functioning, you still need to use the oil can on the machinery to keep it running efficiently.

Assess your parish as to its potential and its proper direction, and start working on a plan. Remember that what is effective in one city or area is not necessarily effective in another. Each parish has its distinctives.

The church is not a business, nor a human organization, but it can still learn from the business world. Any techniques must be subjected to biblical scrutiny.

Your first administrative responsibility is to see to it that the worship services are properly and reverently conducted, and that the sermons are well prepared and effectively delivered. As you plan the weekly bulletin, you work out all the details for the worship services. You check with the choir director and the organists concerning the hymns and tunes to be used as well as the anthems. If any lay participation is expected it should be planned ahead. The meetings of the week ahead should be properly announced in the calendar. If placed in the bulletin (called intimations in Australia) repetition will not be necessary in the worship services. You have to correlate Bible studies, youth activities, and the women's meetings so that they function in proper relation to each other. Sunday School needs to be under proper leadership, and so do the other activities. If you work in Australia you should be involved in the C.R.E. program at the local state school, and you should attempt to get some of your people involved.

You should be aware of the budget and the financial commitments of the church. When it comes to congregational meetings, you will need to be conscious of the finances and other matters to be discussed. Tact is often needed to keep order, and to keep the discussion

in hand. The same is also true for Session and Board meetings. Keep
the unity of the church in mind in your attitude and spirit. Don't let
one or two people dominate the meeting. Seek for a general participation. If you demonstrate real Christian leadership, you will
usually be treated with respect.

# Chapter 42
# Sharing of Leadership

A minister may be an eloquent pulpiteer, and yet have an inactive
church. It is an art to get people to work, and to keep them at it.

You must be wide-awake and industrious yourself, in order to inspire others to work. There is considerable latent power in most of
our churches. Try to discover what a person is best fitted for, and
then set them to work at it. When new members come, find them a
task. If they are not set to work, they can easily become a drone in
the hive.

The fundamental principle for developing leadership is found in
God's Word. "And He gave some as apostles, and some as prophets,
and some as evangelists, and some as pastors and teachers, for the
equipping of the saints for the work of service, to the building up of
the body of Christ."[1]

Thus our position as leaders lends to our equipping of the saints
for leadership. This enables the whole body to build itself up in
love.[2] The early church grew because of the involvement in witnessing of every member. When they were scattered by persecution, they

1.    Ephesians 4:11-12
2.    Ephesians 4:16

went everywhere preaching the Word.[1] They presented the Gospel to everyone they met.

The leader delegates responsibilities even though he is still accountable. He shares his managerial task. To this end the Presbyterian and Reformed churches have elders (called deacons in the Baptist church). While leading the people of Israel Moses' work became too heavy for him, and elders were appointed to share in it.[2] Together they shared the work. The continuity of this eldership runs throughout the Old Testament, and continues right into the book of Acts. All the New Testament congregations seem to have a plurality of elders, who appear to share in the management of the churches. No minister of the Gospel can bear up under the burden of governing the church alone.

In Acts 6 the biblical picture of sharing leadership appears again under the appointment of deacons, who relieved the apostles of numerous administrative details. They realized that they couldn't do everything. They chose to delegate the task of the distribution of funds to men of high quality. The diaconate in the Presbyterian Church of Australia is a part of the Board of Management. Delegation should also extend beyond the Board to qualified members of the congregation, who have special skills and talents.

Committee planning is very important in the church's life. Committees can be responsible in financing, education, building care and improvement, pulpit supply, sacraments, ushering, permission for building use, custodial supervision, and music in all of its aspects.

Guidelines should be laid out for committees and their responsibilities. Chairpersons should usually be from the Session or the Board, but others from the congregation who have talents and capabilities should be utilized. For instance, a builder who is a member of the congregation should certainly be tapped for service on a building committee. Committees should not be too large, or they become unwieldy. Committee chairpersons should be cautioned

---

1.  Acts 8:4
2.  Exodus 18:13-26

against making decisions without consulting their committee members. Limits should be placed on spending by a committee, without higher permission.

Be sure to be a good delegator of responsibility.

# Chapter 43

# The Keeping of Records

Andrew Blackwood states that "the dreariest part of pastoral work may consist in trying to keep adequate records."[1] Such drudgery would increase if one was a physician or in various aspects of the chaplaincy. A book on keeping records by Dr. Louis Tucker says: "The growth of any Protestant Congregation depends on the personality of the minister, and on the excellence of his pastoral bookkeeping...None of these things are taught in the seminaries. There is a course in pastoral theology, but it deals with grand matters, like converting atheists, and says nothing about practical matters like making lists of calls...No seminary I ever heard of had a course in pastoral bookkeeping."[2]

There are certain musts in record keeping. 1) A record of weddings, 2) A record of funerals, 3) A record of baptisms, and 4) A record of your communicant members and adherents (those who participate but are not full members).

In Australia the State requires you to keep records of weddings. Most churches require records of baptisms, as well as of members and adherents. There should also be a church funeral book. Keep dates of birth and names of parents in your baptism records.

1.    Andrew W. Blackwood, *Pastoral Work,* p. 125
2.    Louis Tucker, *Clerical Errors,* pp. 150-151

You should also have your own records of baptisms, weddings, and funerals which you keep with you from parish to parish.

A church directory is something you should strive for in every parish you serve, every year. If you have the facilities to make them, and you're in a changing parish, you may want to publish them as often as every quarter. We have done this in new and growing churches.

Then you need to keep a record of your sermons. The sermons themselves (or your notes) should be filed either by number or by subject. Then you need a record chronologically done, and textually done. Also, you need a record of series, special days, and special subjects. As the years go by, the records become more important!!! Who wants to repeat himself in the same church?

If you make weekly bulletins and/or monthly newssheets, these should be filed for reference.

Now, beyond these records, comes the question of a filing system. There is a great variety of opinion on this subject. One of our Seminary (Theological College in Australia) professors rode a hobby horse on this subject. My wife, as the Seminary secretary in those days, typed over 2,000 stencils to be mimeographed for him alone, over a two-year period. He had an elaborate filing system. When he died, his wife had to hire a truck to haul the accumulation out of his attic. Then there are those, on the other hand, who have practically no filing system. There is some happy medium between these extremes. You need some method of keeping items of information which you clip from the papers and magazines, and gather from your reading. Manila folders on various subjects are the best method to keep them. Then when you wish to speak on a given subject you have material readily available.

It is also helpful to file your books of sermons by texts so that you can refer to them when using a certain text.

Finally, copies of the letters you write, which relate to church matters should be kept on file. Personal letters are important to *you only* for filing, but letters of an official nature are most important for filing.

HAPPY RECORD-KEEPING!!!

# Chapter 44

# **Conducting Meetings**

It is normally a part of a minister's task to conduct meetings in his parish. In most churches the minister usually presides.

There are several important things to remember:

1) Keep good order.
2) Keep things moving. It is easy to get bogged down on one issue—often an unimportant one at that. There is seldom a need for late meetings.
3) Don't allow irrelevancies, or matters unrelated to the subject under discussion.
4) Don't allow unkindnesses. Insist on Christian conduct in church meetings.
5) Follow a planned agenda. Have it printed for all, if possible.
6) The general order of a meeting is as follows:
Opening prayer
Note those present (Aussies receive apologies at this point from those who are absent.)
Minutes of previous meeting/s read and approved.
Treasurer's report and approval of bills to be paid
Inward and outward correspondence
Committee reports
Old and new business
Adjournment. Time of next meeting stated.
Closing prayer and benediction
7) The putting of motions:
Motions must be clearly stated. Avoid omnibus motions—those trying to say too much.
Motions must be seconded before discussion ensues.

Allow discussion on the motion. One should not speak to a motion a second time unless others have had their opportunity. Keep the discussion to the issue at hand.

Put the motion to a vote. Announce its passing or failure to pass. You cast the deciding vote if the vote is tied.

8) The privacy of church meetings. Some hang heavy on this matter, while others are careless. The issues to be kept confidential are personal and private matters, revealing how people voted on controversial issues, etc.

There are a number of types of meetings you may be called upon to lead:

1) Consistory (Board of Management)
2) Elders (Session)
3) Classis (Presbytery)
4) Synod (Assembly)
5) Congregational meetings. Guard against the congregational meeting becoming a time for rebellion and protest. Be well prepared.
6) Community functions.

You also can be asked to be the moderator of a vacant parish. In Australian Presbyterian Churches this is called "interim moderator." It is a very responsible position. Some become very jealous of their prerogatives. This is not necessary. Christian grace should always prevail.

## Chapter 45

# Community Involvement

Sometimes the local pastor has been called "The Servant of the Community." Blackwood states that there are two extremes in this attitude.—"A clergyman of a certain type makes three hundred addresses a year outside his parish. Needless to say, he neglects the flock. Another pastor acts as though he were not concerned about the community. Even in a downtown church, he may have no influence beyond his congregation...That way of living seems shortsighted and selfish, if not unchristian."[1] I believe it was John Wesley who said: "I look upon all the world as my parish."

The Bible states that elders "must have a good reputation with outsiders."[2] Since ministers are (or will be) preaching elders, this is a requirement for us too. Paul made a much-quoted statement: "I have become all things to all men so that by all possible means I might save some."[3] These Bible statements give us a base for our thinking about a pastor's involvement in the community where he serves.

Our church people usually learn to know us well. The people of the community don't always get to know us intimately. They can only judge us by our actions and attitudes which we show as we walk down the street, or which we demonstrate in public meetings. Our reputation with them can easily be affected by our friendliness (or lack of it) as we pass them on the street or in the store. This may well be the only sermon of yours that they will ever hear. This is particularly true in smaller communities.

You may not be directly responsible for the church or manse yard, but if you are, the way you keep it will speak volumes about

1.    Andrew W. Blackwood, *Pastoral Work*, p. 202
2.    I Timothy 3:7 NIV
3.    I Corinthians 9:22 NIV

you. We once went to see a new church and manse that was built in a growing community. We were unbelieving as we found the manse. It was totally unkempt. The church yard was no better!!! What kind of a testimony would this give to a community about a new church??? From nearby neighbors we discovered that they had made complaints to the city about these conditions. Tragic indeed!!!

Surely the pastor would want to set an example as a good neighbor, with all that that word implies. After all, Jesus placed a strong emphasis on loving your neighbor. A pastor must practice it!

Clearly, ministers should be involved in local pastor's associations—usually known as Minister's Fraternal in Australia. Evangelicals should let their voice be heard in ministers' groups. Don't let the liberals dominate! Many programs will be worked through your ministers' fellowships such as hospital services, radio devotionals, Christmas sings, union services, religious instruction in the schools, etc. By participating in these programs you become known in the community, and are able to exert an influence. If Council of Churches people are in control, you may find it difficult to participate. In one city in California we found it necessary to organize an Evangelical Ministers' Fellowship, which, in time, grew larger than the other Council.

In larger cities you may be able to involve your church in a Billy Graham Crusade, or a Bill Newman Crusade (Aus.) or some type of evangelistic campaign. It can prove a blessing to unite with other churches in presenting the Gospel to your community. Be sure you don't get involved with off-color groups which would compromise your position as an evangelical or relate you to the wrong people in the public mind.

Now there are many avenues of service to the community. There are some principles that can be brought to bear on your decision as to what to do, who to join, what projects to back, etc. They can be put in question form.—1) Will the contemplated effort or membership compromise the Gospel? 2) Can I justify the amount of time it will take? 3) Will it fit into my priorities? 4) What will it indicate to the community? When it comes to business, economic, social, and political activities in the community, the minister of Christ must conduct himself with great wisdom.

Some pastors are involved in lodges. This is open to a lot of question and can take a lot of time. I do not advise it.

During the latter half of my ministry I have been involved in service clubs such as Civitan, Kiwanis, Rotary and Lions. Generally their principles are good, and allow you a real opportunity to become acquainted with local leaders and to become known in the community. Quietly, but surely, make it known that you will not drink liquor or participate in either gambling or Sunday activities. They will respect you for it. I felt honored to be invited to fill the minister slot in Swan Hill's Rotary Club, the first one to do so in twelve years. It gave me an opportunity to know many local leaders personally. This also held true elsewhere. They make use of you as a speaker, as one who gives invocations, and even to lead Sunday services at large district conventions. These are certainly opportunities to extend our witness. You can debate the service club issue, but I find it a profitable association in my ministry.

Certainly a minister would want to be involved in efforts to make his community a better place in which to live. The size of the community will make quite a difference in your approach. For instance, when I lived and worked in Bellflower, a city of 55,000 in Los Angeles County, I was a part of the large Kiwanis Club, prayed in Council meetings, School Board meetings, took leadership in community activities, knew the various mayors personally, and was presented a plaque by the mayor at our farewell. Then we moved into the Los Angeles inner-city. In that large city you would be fortunate to get within 500 feet of the mayor at a city function. The only ministers' associations and Kiwanis clubs available were in the downtown area. I discovered that our District 77 (which had 250,000 residents) had a Clergy-Police Council. This was made up of leading black clergymen of the area who worked with the police to rapport between them and the people of that district. I joined it, found the group meaningful, and was made second vice-president, and then first vice-president. When we left L.A. nine black ministers and the white police chief lined up across the front of the church to express their appreciation and gave me a plaque of community recognition. Then each one of the black pastors gave us a hug. These two experiences show how different communities can be approached in vastly different ways, and still obtain good results.

In Australia they kept me busy giving patriotic speeches on ANZAC Day (similar to the U.S. Memorial Day), especially when they learned that I had no leftist leanings. This gives you a wide community exposure.

In larger cities you will discover a multiplicity of meetings and seminars to attend. In some cases you will want to send laymen to represent you, and delegate tasks. In other cases, you will want to go yourself, but you must be selective. There are only 24 hours in each day, six to eight hours of which are spent resting our tired bodies.

Newspaper, radio and TV stations are other ways to make community contacts. Get to know you local editor and the manager of your radio (wireless) station. During my student years I wrote a Christian Endeavor article for the paper in Holland, Michigan for five years. This was a weekly message in a daily paper. In Clymer, New York a few ministers took turns writing articles. In Miami, Florida I wrote a Minute Sermon for a weekly newspaper every week for eight years. In Kerang and in Colac, Victoria the ministers take turns writing a weekly article for the local paper. Other papers will sometimes use sermons or extracts of them. In Redlands, California we broadcast thirty-five minutes of our evening service for five years. In Orlando, Florida we gave daily devotional talks over a Christian radio station. In Swan Hill, Victoria the ministers took turns doing a week of short morning devotional talks on the local station. The radio and television give you a wide community coverage.

Always concentrate on your local church, but reach out as much as you can to let the light of the Gospel shine in your community.

# Chapter 46
# Youth Work

The future of the church lies with the youth. In Australia they seem to have lost a generation for the church. It is not good. We must win the youth. No pastor can afford to slight his youth program.

If you are fortunate enough to have a full-time youth worker, you can be thankful. Then your main concern should be to show your face at their activities from time to time, and maintain a friendly rapport with them. If this isn't the case, you may have a couple or a single person who lead the youth activities. As long as they understand youth, they can do a great deal to carry the brunt of the program. Supervision in all cases is vital. Make sure that standards of program and activities fit with the position of an evangelical church.

If neither of the above situations prevail in your case, you and your wife will be obliged to lead the youth program, regardless of your age. Keeping up with the youth may wear you down, but do the best and the most you can. In our own ministry we carried the youth program 61% of the time, shared it with others 22%, and turned it over to others 17%. This can vary with circumstances in your parish.

There are various programs available. We grew up with Christian Endeavor, and worked heartily with it for many years on the local, area, and state levels. The emphasis is on participation by the youth, and training in leadership. This type of program pays off in developing the youth in areas such as speaking, prayer, devotional life, and tithing. It also stresses a good relationship with young people of other evangelical denominations.

Other parachurch youth programs include Youth for Christ, Young Life, Campus Crusade for Christ, and Inter-Varsity, any of which can be helpful.

There are many and varied approaches to programming for your youth. Ingenuity is necessary. To some, age-grouping is of great importance. To others, the age spread doesn't seem to make any difference.

Topics led by the youth themselves are good. Speakers can be brought in. Films and videos can be used. Fun nights can make it clear that Christians can have a good time in a wholesome way, without things like alcohol and drugs. Meetings can be held with other youth groups. Food festivals such as progressive dinners and hall-crawls (Aus.) can make for pleasant variety evenings. There is something to be learned from visits to Jewish, Catholic, and Orthodox services, provided that proper instruction is given beforehand, and discussion follows. Occasionally the youth can participate in a Sunday service. Also, youth choirs can be developed.

Snow trips, overnighters, and weekend retreats can be meaningful events, if properly planned and supervised. Youth camps have been major events in the life of our youth in the U.S. From them have come decisions and commitments which have made lasting contributions to individuals and to the total life of the church.

Adams makes a strong case of the need for the pastor to be involved in seeing that active and meaningful programs for the young people are available to provide weekday Christian fun and fellowship as well as Sunday meetings. During the years when friendship and peer pressure are so important, the pastor must be vigilant for his youth.[1]

Always remember that the youth in our churches today are the churches of tomorrow.

1.    Jay E. Adams, *Shepherding God's Flock*, Vol. III, p. 123

# Chapter 47
# The Sunday School

In most of our churches where you work there will be a Sunday School. If not, you'll want to start one as soon as possible.

Although catechizing and educating in the Christian faith has been a part of the program of the Church through the years, Sunday School (or church School) as we know it today is comparatively modern. Its history is usually traced to Robert Raikes (1735-1811). He was a wealthy English businessman and editor of *The Gloucester Journal*. He was interested in prison reform and in ministering to the families of criminals in the slums of that great manufacturing city, and was deeply impressed by the lack of education among them. He learned of four women who kept private schools for reading and writing, and made arrangements with them to teach such children as he might send them on Sundays for instruction in these simple arts and also in the catechism of the Anglican Church. He paid them each a shilling a day for their trouble. Later, he interested Rev. Thomas Stock in his philanthropy and engaged him to make the round of the schools on Sunday afternoon to examine the progress being made and to enforce order and discipline. Such was the beginning.

It should be noted here that Raikes' idea was quite different from that of the modern Sunday School. In his mind it was a charitable venture for the purpose of reform. It was not under church auspices and for many years was vigorously opposed by the clergy. The curriculum was more secular than religious. The schools met on Sunday because that was the only day in the week when the children were not employed. As is often the case, the events growing out of Raikes' commendable effort conferred upon him the credit of being the founder of the modern Sunday School.

Col. Richard Townley, of Lancashire, was inspired by Raikes' example to introduce similar schools in the manufacturing counties of York and Lancaster. Then the idea began to spread. The Bishop of Rochester denounced it. The Archbishop of Canterbury called the bishops together to see whether something might be done to stop it. But soon the wiser heads of the church saw it was best to take the idea under their wings and advance it as a church enterprise. The Methodists were already organizing Sunday Schools at every crossroad. Soon all religious denominations throughout the United Kingdom had accepted the principle. It became the fad for ladies of fashion to teach in Sunday Schools. Finally, the Queen herself gave the movement the stamp of her royal favor. Sending for Robert Raikes she learned the story from his own lips, and, as he reports it, "Her Majesty most graciously said that she envied those who had the power of doing good by thus personally promoting the welfare of society, in giving instruction and morality to the general mass of the common people; a pleasure from which, by her situation, she was debarred." This reintroduction into church activities of the divinely appointed method of Christian education by the Sunday-School movement marked the final step in the renaissance period.

In 1786, six years after the founding of the first Sunday School by Robert Raikes in Gloucester, England, we hear of the first Sunday School in America. By 1791, the First-Day School Society was formed for the purpose of securing religious instruction for poor children on Sunday.

The opposition to the movement on the part of the churches was pronounced. The following incident is representative of the spirit of the times. In old First Church in Norwich Town, Connecticut, a young lady who had learned something of Sunday School work from Divie Bethune of New York City organized a little school to meet in the gallery of the church. The church authorities pronounced her work to be a desecration of the Lord's Day, and forbade further meetings. Withdrawing her little charge to a neighboring school-house, the pastor is reported to have shaken his ivory-cane at them and shouted with righteous indignation, "You imps of satan, doing the devil's work. I'll have you set in the street!" And so he did. Nothing daunted, the Sunday School met the following week on the steps of the church, and kept it up until public sentiment demanded they be readmitted to the gallery. In more enlightened communities the church officials rented their buildings to the Sunday schools until they came to realize the value of the movement in educating the religiously illiterate and in promoting the cause of Christ in general.

The movement naturally found its way from these countries into Australia, and has become a major part of the movement to educate in the Christian faith throughout the world.

At the local church level, it is best to have Sunday School at a separate hour. If classes are held during the church worship hour, you won't be able to do much more than teach a lesson. If Sunday School meets at a separate hour, either before or after church, you can accomplish much more. The first part of the hour can then be used for group singing, prayer, memory work, competition, etc.

The Sunday School should be properly organized, with an elected superintendent in charge. If there are enough students, there should be various departments, especially for the very young children. Classes should be provided for all ages. The number of classes would depend on the number of pupils and the available teachers.

Teachers must be selected with great care. They certainly should be committed Christians, who love to teach the Bible. They also must know how to handle those in the various age groups they expect to teach. It is good if teachers' training classes can be arranged, either regularly or periodically.

In the present approaches to child education, we need to be challenged to good teaching in our Sunday Schools. Here are some stereotypes:

Mrs. W. is teaching the book of Zephaniah to 4 and 5 year olds. They are memorizing one verse from each chapter, verses with words like "wrought" and "righteousness" and "meekness," which the children cannot understand. When they get unruly, she has them sing songs with cute motions. Of course, at the end of each class she gives an invitation.

Miss F. is an "activity" teacher. She keeps the children busy coloring Bible pictures most of the hour, hurries through her weekly

Bible story, and chats with her teenage helper while the children go back to coloring and cutting.

These are teachers who go to the extremes. On the other hand, Mr. C. feels that moral training needs to begin early, and that there is no better way than by coming to understand God's Word. He uses both Old and New Testament stories that point up acceptable behaviors and good Christian attitudes. He makes sure the children master Bible facts first, then he makes sure they understand the values of truth, sharing, helping, honesty, consideration, kindness, etc., which the Bible teaches. This approach is much better.[1]

The curriculum needs your careful scrutiny. Australia offers Scripture Union and Mission Publications. Both are sound, and have Baptist leanings. The Sydney Anglican Diocese also has material which is reputed to be good.

On the American scene we can recommend Great Commission Publications of the Orthodox Presbyterian Church, Bible Way materials of the Christian Reformed Church, and David C. Cook of Elgin, Illinois. Also well-known are Gospel Light of Glendale, California and Scripture Press of Wheaton, Illinois.

The Sunday School should have record books of attendance, and can well provide incentives such as awards for faithful attendance.

Offerings can be used for the curriculum costs. Once a month offerings can be designated for missions, and missionary stories can be told, or missionary letters read.

Cultivate your Sunday School. It is the breeding ground for future church members. It can also be a place for your adults to grow in grace and in knowledge of God's Word.

---

1.     Above stereotypes suggested in Lawrence O. Richards, *A Theology of Christian Education*, pp. 165-166

# Chapter 48

# Evangelism

Nothing should crowd evangelism out of your church's program. We should always be alert to presenting Christ—the Evangel—to needy men and women. Evangelism is the winning of men and women to a personal knowledge of Jesus Christ as Lord and Saviour. We can't keep Christ for ourselves. W must share Him with others.

Too often ministers come out of our seminaries (Theological Colleges) without a passion for winning souls. Hence the average church is not trying to evangelize its community. "The spirit of evangelism ought to pervade all our worship and teaching, as well as our other activities, much as the salt permeates the sea."[1]

"This big business of evangelism clamors for the primal place in the Christian enterprise. Christ's commission commands it. Present conditions demand it...'Make disciples' is the imperative of Christ yesterday, today, and until He comes again. That means evangelism. That means giving the Good News of the saving grace of God in Christ to lost men."[2]

"Thank God the message of evangelism—the Gospel—is still 'the power of God unto salvation to every one that believeth.' This message is the power of God (the dynamite) which smashes to bits the citadel of sin that satan has established in the human heart. This message is the only answer to man's real needs."[3]

"Before evangelism is a program, it is a passion—a passion of the heart which issues in saving action. Evangelism is the passion of Moses, 'Oh, this people have sinned...yet now, if Thou wilt forgive their sin—if not, blot me, I pray Thee, out of the book which Thou

1.     Andrew W. Blackwood, *Evangelism in the Home Church*, p. 17
2.     Roland Q. Leavell, *The Romance of Evangelism*, p. 9
3.     Bill Newman, *Called to Proclaim*, p. 7

hast written.' It is the passion of Paul, 'Woe is me if I preach not the Gospel.' It is the anguished cry of Jesus as He weeps over a doomed city, 'Oh Jerusalem, how oft would I have gathered thee.' Evangelism is the cry of Knox, 'Give me Scotland or I die,' and of Wesley, 'The world is my parish.' Evangelism is Henry Martyn landing on the shores of India and crying, 'Here let me burn out for God!' It is David Brainerd coughing up blood from his tubercular lungs as he prays in the snow for the Indians. It is George Whitefield crossing the Atlantic thirteen times in a small boat to preach in the American colonies...It is Jim Elliot and his young friends staining the sands of a little river in Ecuador with their blood to reach an obscure band of Auca Indians for Christ...Evangelism is a cross in the heart of God."[1]

Our concern as pastors, after we are convinced of the urgency of evangelism, is to implement a program on the local church level. The role of the pastor is crucial. He must himself set the example. Then he needs to train his elders and other believers in the church who have gifts. All the members of the church need to get involved in praying and working for church growth and evangelism.

There are many programs available which can be used on the local level. There is the approach which D. J. Kennedy used to build the Coral Ridge Presbyterian Church in Fort Lauderdale, Florida from zero to over 5,000 members. It has become worldwide and is known as Evangelism Explosion. It confronts an individual with the question: If you should die tonight, what answer would you give as to why you should enter heaven? Campus Crusade for Christ uses the Four Spiritual Laws in their evangelistic approach. The World Home Bible League has its Project Philip, which presents Christ to those who know Him not. Quite a list could be given of plans and approaches to use.

Each local church must determine what strategy to use to spread the Gospel in its community. A very important point to remember is

---

1.    Leighton Ford, *The Christian Persuader*, pp. 13-14

that no program should be taught so that it is used in parrot fashion. This can sound so artificial, and often doesn't bring the desired results. Each individual must adapt whatever program is used to himself, and then to the person or persons to whom he is witnessing. If we earnestly desire to witness and evangelize, God will bless our feeble efforts to the salvation of souls, which in turn will glorify God.

# Chapter 49

# The Pastor's Wife

The subject of the pastor's wife has received attention in recent years from a number of writers. "*I Married a Minister*," edited by Jesse Bader's wife appeared in 1942, and Hewitt's "*The Shepherdess*" in 1943. Blackwood included a chapter in his "*Pastoral Work*" on "The Place of the Pastor's Wife," in 1945 and Lora Lee Parrott wrote "*How to be a Preacher's Wife and Like It*" in 1956. Previous to these books, it was a subject seldom mentioned except in parish talk.

Certainly the kind of a wife a minister has is of crucial importance. A good wife can double a pastor's usefulness. If she falls short, she can wreck his ministry.

In choosing a wife, you should seek a sincere and committed Christian, one who is dedicated to Christian service, and one who is willing to go where God leads.

The pastor's wife will be called to take an active part in the church and its activities. The ideal is for her to work indirectly. Your people will not always let it be so. When we arrived at a city church in Chicago late in the year, we discovered that my wife had already been elected to head all the women's work of the church for the new year.

Generally it is better to work behind the
others to lead. The amount of involvement in c
tempered by the family situation. It is good if sh
your get-acquainted calls so that she can learn          ..e whole
congregation as soon as possible. As the family grows up, she can
also go with you in your door-to-door contacts. If you do this, it is
best to stay close together, perhaps on opposite sides of the street.

Often the wife can be a personal counselor to the ladies and girls
of the church and community. She can discuss intimate problems
with them in a way that the pastor cannot.

Blackwood states that "the most immediate privilege of the
pastor's wife is to make her husband happy. The best place to let her
light shine is through the windows of a happy home. She can
help...in countless ways: by being cheerful...by keeping the house
neat and attractive, by making wholesome meals...by keeping him
from overindulgence of appetites, by rearing...children aright, by
talking over problems..., and by refraining from being the 'boss' of
the congregation. She may be the power behind the throne, but she
ought not to wield a big stick. Love works best by indirection."[1]

Hewitt starts his book with a chapter on "The Shepherdess As a
Lover." We note some of his comments: "The highest joy and the
first duty of a shepherdess is that of being a good wife to her chosen
mate."[2] "To be his perfect lover is her greatest and most sacred
duty."[3] "The romantic love of a husband is kept by the same means
through which it is attained...Woe be unto you if your husband must
love you in spite of what you are instead of because of what your
are!"[4] "Woe be to you if, while your lover is seeing all others at their
very best, he is compelled to see you daily at your worst."[5] He then

1.    Andrew W. Blackwood, *Pastoral Work*, p. 55
2.    Arthur W. Hewitt, *The Shepherdess*, p .2
3.    Idem
4.    Ibid., p. 7
5.    Ibid., p. 9

suggests four good habits to develop: 1) The habit of affection, 2) The habit of respect, 3) The habit of devotion to God, and 4) The habit of *sharing* all of life.[1]

Your wife can be your best critic. If there are faults in the sermon presentation she can point them out while praising the excellences in it. She will be able to pick up annoying mannerisms for you. All will need to be done tactfully, gently, and in love. And, at an appropriate time. Blackwood warns about the timing. "One of the worst things a pastor's wife can do is to find fault with his preaching before he has regained his equilibrium. He may feel wretched enough without having a shower of cold water administered by one whom he loves."[2]

The wisdom of her having a "mother confessor" can be debated. There are times when she will need one. At other times it can be most unwise.

The parsonage (manse) is the center of the life of the pastor and his wife. Ofttimes it is also a center of church life. Usually it is provided by the church. There is a trend today for ministers to own their own homes, and then the church provides an allowance for that purpose. This allows them to build up an equity, but it can also create problems when one moves from parish to parish.

Ofttimes the manse is a part of the church property. This can be helpful in many ways. You are close to the scene of activity. Also you become a watch dog for the buildings. It also can mean that you have little privacy.

We had the choice of living in a black community behind our Los Angeles church or commuting from the suburb. We chose to live in the community. I feel that it brought us closer to the people of the area, and gave us a greater opportunity to serve. It did create a few problems, such as two breakins, and an occasional tramp at the door.

1. Ibid, pp. 18-23
2. Andrew W. Blackwood, op. cit., p. 56

The setting of the home tends to mean more to the pastor's wife than it does to him. She will have to make some sacrifices, or she will not be worthy of her position in life. However unlovely the surroundings, she can do most good by living among the people, as one of them. She can afford every growing girl an example of queenly grace. She can set before every growing boy a pattern of womanly charm.

As she mingles with the people she can show them how to be friendly without becoming effusive, and how to love God without losing the common touch.[1]

Is it any wonder that many a strong pastor has said: "Under God, I owe everything to my wife." It has been said that "behind every successful man there is a good woman." May all our wives be that kind of person!!!

## Chapter 50

# Staff Ministries

There is an increasing use and development of staff ministries today. Assistant and associate pastors in the U.S. have proliferated tremendously in the last twenty-five years.

A large church almost requires a staff ministry. Blackwood suggests that with every five-hundred members in the congregation another staff member should be added.

While serving in Bellflower, California, with a church of 1,150 total membership, we had four on the staff. I was the Senior Pastor, there was a full-time Associate, a full-time Youth and/or Education

---

1.    Andrew W. Blackwood, op. cit., p. 60

Director, and a part-time Music Director. There were also two office secretaries.

In the United States considerable problems have developed with staff members remaining on after the Senior Pastor leaves. This helps for continuity of program, but can create a real problem when a new Senior Pastor is called. He does not have a choice in selecting his staff, and those who carry on often have an "in" with the congregation which puts the new arrival on a spot. To this end some denominations in the U.S. have required that the staff offer their resignations when the Senior Pastor leaves.

If a staff is the way the church chooses to go, then choosing the proper staff members becomes of prime importance. There must be a compatibility of personalities. The staff should complement one another, and have strengths in different areas in order to make a staff work well together.

If you are called to a staff ministry, make sure your tasks are clearly defined, and that you are of one mind in essential beliefs with your Senior Pastor. Division of duties should be clearly understood and agreed upon ahead of time.

Staff meetings are necessary if unity of spirit is to be maintained and for everyone to clearly understand what their functions are. Loyalty to each other's ministry must be stoutly maintained. There is no good cause to undercut each other's work. It must be seen to that members of the congregation are not allowed to divide one staff member from the other. The staff must determine to stand back to back.

Talent should be put to the best possible use. Don't let talent in certain fields go wasted. It would be wise to arrange beforehand how often each pastor is expected to preach.

Look out for overloading of staff members, and likewise, one must keep watch of the person who doesn't do enough.

It is not wise for one to become an assistant if his greatest desire is to preach. He will be obliged to give the priority in preaching to the Senior Pastor.

There is a tendency today to use competent lay people as part-time assistants in fields where they have proficiency. This works very well with those who retire early, and have skills which the church can use. This can be a most helpful trend for the church.

Many of our theological students have participated in the life of the church as internes, or in other ways. It has similarity to the apprentice program in the commercial and business world. Much can be learned from a strong, kind shepherd, who has maturity in the ministry.

# Chapter 51
# Working With Difficult Persons

You can take for granted that your ministry will lead you into working with people who are difficult to handle. Almost every group of people includes some who are cantankerous. Sometimes they bother you so much that you would consider fleeing the pastoral charge to get away from them.

Dr. David Cowie served his last church (Presbyterian) and died in the city of Bellflower, California when I was serving the Reformed Church there. He told of how when he was a young pastor he served a church in Los Angeles that was growing rapidly and doing well; but on the governing board he had a man who was both a negative thinker and a very cantankerous critic. Finally the situation grew so bad that he resigned and took another pastorate in Kansas City. "But," he lamented, "the week I arrived at my new church, I went to the board meeting to meet the leaders, and there, sitting at the conference table, was the same guy!"

The comment on this illustration in "*Bringing Out the Best in People*" is that "Cowie was right. They may have different faces and different names, but, no matter where we go, troublesome people are going to be waiting for us. It simply does not pay to flee from difficult interpersonal situations."[1]

Since we cannot flee them, the best way is to face the problem of difficult persons, and to seek to work with them. We will list some of the most typical problem people we shall have to deal with:

1. Fault finders.
2. Those who talk too much. They have to express their opinion at length on every issue.
3. Those who want to be in charge. They can't let others lead.
4. Those who sit with the rule book in their hands and insist on every detail of the letter of the law being observed.
5. Those who lack in spirituality. They can only look at church matters through business eyes. They have no vision for spiritual truth.
6. Those who are so spiritual-minded that they are no earthly good. They talk piously, but do not understand the realities of life.

In leading a board or session which includes such people, there are certain factors to consider. Develop a good esprit de corps. Make belonging to the group a thing to be desired. Face up to the difficult people when necessary, and by all means don't let them take over or give in to them.

Here are some good principles to observe—Hold to good order. Make sure everyone addresses you as chairman. Do not allow conversation between various members. Give everyone a chance to speak their mind on a given issue, but only once until others have been given their chance to express themselves. When a vote is taken, the majority rules, and the accepted position must be received. No further discussion should be allowed when an issue has been decided.

Know your rule book as well as the rules of conducting a meeting. However, insist on the spirit of the law rather than the letter.

---

1. Alan Loy McGinnis, *Bringing Out the Best in People*, p. 154

There are times when a rule can be set aside if everyone understands the reason for doing so.

Emphasize the spiritual. Never forget the basic reasons for the church's existence. On the other hand, don't let pious prattle stop the group from taking Christian action. Remember the time when Moses was praying to God for help that God told him to stop crying unto Him and to tell the Israelites to move on (into the Red Sea).[1]

Always express appreciation for services rendered and for kind and helpful words spoken. Don't be slow to compliment others.

When it comes to fault finders 1) don't let them get you down. Some seem to have this trait by nature, and always find fault rather than the good accomplished. Accept their comment for what it is worth, and let the rest dissipate. The talk-on-every-subject person 2) should be kept in tow. Everybody else probably wants them to shut up as much as you do. If they get out of line, tell them so as kindly as you can. 3) There are some who feel they must dictate policy, and are not willing to give in to proper leadership. There are some who have served long and seen churches through troubled times who find it difficult to give in to new and younger successors. They must be dealt with kindly but firmly. Always recognize the good they have accomplished, but gradually let others take positions of leadership. Those in categories 4, 5, and 6 have already been discussed.

Don't be quick to get into an argument. Seek to maintain peace. Don't try to build allegiance to yourself, but rather to the cause, to the organization, and one to the other.

Remember that you can't please everyone. At times you must listen to both sides of the problem. Try then for a compromise, and throw your weight behind the compromise. A good leader will try not to lose anyone, but at the same time he will not allow in-fighting to destroy his organization.

"Assume the best about people, and they will do everything to live up to those expectations."[2]

---

1.    Exodus 14:15-16
2.    Alan Loy McGinnis, op. cit., p. 160

A recent book has come out on ministering to problem people in the church. The emphasis is on illustrative cases.[1]

# Chapter 52
# Rewards of the Ministry

The happiest man in town may well be the pastor. Our song should be:

> "I am happy in the service of the King.
> I have peace and joy that nothing else can bring
> In the service of the King."

Pastors have the joy of healthy bodies. Life insurance experts report that there is no other calling which has such a record for longevity. They have no bad habits which shorten life, such as smoking, drinking alcoholic beverages, shooting drugs, or engaging in sexual promiscuity. "Their physical well-being is partly because of their varied activities, their long quiet hours of study, friendly contacts with people, and frequent opportunities for fellowship with groups of the best people in the community. What could do more to make a man happy and keep him well?"[2] He can say with the Psalmist, "The lines are fallen unto me in pleasant places".[3]

Health of soul ought always to be the experience of a pastor who breathes the fresh air of prayer and intakes the food of the Word of God. Health of soul and of body often go together.

---

1.  Marshall Shelley, *Well-Intentioned Dragons*
2.  Andrew W. Blackwood, *Pastoral Work, p. 225*
3.  Psalm 16:6

There is great joy in bringing Christ to hungry hearts. You can meet all kinds of human needs. The pastor becomes to many "a friend who sticks closer than a brother."[1]

"A minister who does his work with an eye single to God's glory...receives the best things the world affords. A multitude of people become his...friends. Fathers and mothers are as proud of him as though he were a member of their family. Old men look down on him lovingly as on a son. Young men look up to him reverently as a father. Men of his own age love him as a brother. He enjoys free access to many homes. Appreciation, gratitude, and affection are poured out like perfume before him. If love is the best thing in the world, then the faithful pastor gets much of this treasure."[2]

To be sure, he will not be loved by everybody. The Pharisee and Sadducee and Scribe type will always be against him. Men will misunderstand him and misrepresent him. The idler will gossip about him, and the ungrateful will return evil for good. All this is to be expected. Our Lord went through severe criticism. The servant is not above his master. Do your duty and you will stir up trouble, but you will never be left without faithful hearts to love you. The petty criticism one receives in public places counts for nothing in the long sweep of the years. When a pastor comes near the end of his career, he forgets all about the little gusts of bitterness which now and then blow across his path, and says with the Psalmist: "Goodness and mercy have followed me all the days of my life."[3]

If a pastor is permitted by the goodness of God to kindle a fire on an altar that was cold and recreate the world for a heart that had lost the joy of living, his reward is great. It is a great thing to win love for oneself, but it is a greater thing to win love for God. The pastor can do both. Men will love him as they love no other man because he has taught them to love God.

---

1.　Proverbs 18:24b
2.　Charles E. Jefferson, *The Minister as Shepherd*, pp. 180-181
3.　Psalm 23:6

The highest reward that comes to the pastor is an increase in spiritual stature. A minister's character is formed in the stream of parish life. His work as a shepherd enriches his heart and refines his spirit. The reward of the pastor-shepherd is that he becomes increasingly like the Good Shepherd, he is transformed into the same image from glory to glory.

The crowning reward is everlasting fellowship with Jesus Christ and unending participation in His glory. "And when the Chief Shepherd appears, you will receive the crown of glory that will never fade away."[1]

---

1.    I Peter 5:4 NIV

# Part 5

# COUNSELING

# Chapter 53

# The Importance
# of Counseling

Counseling has pushed to the fore in recent years until it has come to be regarded as a major task in our ministry today.

There are those who are not happy with this shift of emphasis. D. M. Lloyd-Jones expressed his fears concerning it. Jimmy Swaggert has ranted and raved against it on his TV programs, maintaining that answers to all of our problems are found in the Bible. Articles have been written by pastors which have said clearly that counseling is a waste of time.

There are reasons why we should be careful of laying too much stress on counseling in our ministry. I find them in three areas of concern:

1) It is possible to allow counseling to replace pastoral calling. The plan is for the pastor to make himself available for counseling in his office. Parishioners are then expected to come to him for counsel. This is as far as his parish contact goes. He does not intend to call in the homes of his people. This is the same trend as you observe in the realm of the family doctor.

2) Counseling can take large slices of your time and it often can involve just a few people of the parish.

3) There are inherent dangers in counseling for the pastor to get too closely involved with his counselees. The result has been either severe emotional strain or immoral conduct.

We need to be alert to the potential problems, and proceed into this field with proper understanding of the whole approach to counseling.

# Chapter 54

# Various Schools of Approach to Counseling

As we survey the broad field of counseling we discover that there are several quite different approaches to it. Before we try to determine the Christian approach, let us take note of three different schools of thought, represented by Rogers, Freud, and Skinner.

Carl Rogers is the dean of the encounter group movement. To him counseling is a matter of mirroring the client's feelings rather than responding conversationally. Any advice, direction, or persuasion on the part of the counselor is taboo. The counselor holds up a mirror to the counselee, and becomes the catalytic agent who enables the client to solve his own problems. All that is within man is good. Corruption enters from without. People have an inherent self-actualizing tendency, which, when freed from restriction or forced channeling, will lead to personal satisfaction and social harmony When this is applied to child upbringing, it would eliminate most discipline.

There is a basic presupposition that man has all of the resources that he needs to solve his problems within himself. He can realize his own potential. Hence the title often used of the movement—Human Potential. Man's problem is his failure to realize his own potential. Counseling then becomes the practice of midwifery. The counselor merely assists at the birth of ideas and solutions of which the client is delivered.

Adams sees the Rogerian assumption that each man possesses the answer to all of his problems as diametrically opposed to the Christian faith, since Christianity teaches that man is not self-sufficient, and needs redemptive help to enable him to live aright. He sees it as unfortunate that some Christian ministers have adopted Rogerian methodology in counseling, failing to recognize that their eclectic approach is inconsistent with their most basic convictions.

On the other hand, Crabb states that "the proper Christian response to Rogers is not to sneeringly reject all that he says as the ravings of a delusional optimist. Rogers has put his finger on a real problem among people, including many Christian people. Because Christians are supposed to love, we often do not admit it when we don't love—we fake it. Any hypocrisy separates a person from the reality of himself and reduces the new man in Christ to a fragmented phony. Rogers is profoundly correct in insisting that we acknowledge all that we are, including our gut feelings. He is tragically wrong in believing integration is best achieved by encouraging the expression of all that we are. To give in to my sinful feelings of hate is to separate me from my conscience and to grieve the indwelling Holy Spirit. Integration is wonderfully available to the person who honestly admits the hate, labels it as a fruit of the flesh, confesses it as sin, and learns to love in the power of God's spirit."[1]

Collins suggests that instead of the humanistic term—"self-actualization"—a term like "Christ-actualization" might be substituted to indicate that the goal in life is to be complete in Christ, developing our greatest potential through the power of the Holy Spirit who brings us to spiritual maturity.

Sigmund Freud emphasizes analysis. His method calls for a trip back into the counselee's past, attempting to unearth the persons, forces, and influences that led to the present "neurotic" or "psychotic" behavior of the counselee. Always persons out of the past are discovered who influenced and wrongly socialized the counselee. Internal conflict then arises which causes disturbing attitudes and/or behavior. After the analysis, one then proceeds to therapy. In therapy the superego is weakened, the conflict with the id

---

1.      Lawrence H. Crabb, *Basic Principles of Biblical Counseling*, pp. 33-34

(inner drive) is resolved, guilt is removed, and the counselee becomes well. The therapy is achieved by resocializing the counselee through siding with his wants against his oughts, thus bringing the latter into line with the former.

According to Freud's methodology, man is not responsible for what he does. His behavior, his attitudes, and his difficulties all stem from bad treatment by others. Freudian therapy essentially promotes living for oneself without the burden of a conscience. In promoting self-gratification within the bounds of reality and social acceptability he covers conscience-less behavior with the veneer of social acceptability. For instance, as a means of satisfying sexual urges, rape is inadvisable because it incurs society's wrath. Therefore, find a cooperative partner or pay for it. Questions of morality are irrelevant. Christians must completely reject Freud's solutions.

B. F. Skinner's approach to counseling can be described as behaviorism, or behavior modification. Man must allow science to control his human behavior. Man is the product of his environment—control the environment scientifically, and you can control man. Skinner thus would rob people of all significance. The entire concept of personal responsibility is absolutely emptied of meaning. The problem of crime is solved by defining it out of existence. We no longer have criminal people, we only have criminal involvements.

Christians must reject Skinner's teaching that man is no more than a complicated dog. Man is made in God's image, and Christ died for people as persons. Christian counselors should hold their counselees responsible for how they choose to live their lives. If they choose to ignore God's directions, they are blameworthy. Responsibility for one's actions cannot be shifted from the person to his environment.

Adams rejects Skinner categorically. Crabb, however, points out that "Christians are indebted to Skinner for specifying the manner in which behavior is influenced by circumstances. Knowledge must not be rejected as non-Christian just because it springs from a non-Christian source. Skinner's work on conditioning includes true knowledge about how I relate to my world, and can be used to advantage by a Christian counselor operating exclusively within a Christian framework."[1]

There are certainly many other approaches to counseling, but most of them are varieties of the Freudian, Rogerian, and Skinnerian theories.

In the next chapter we will seek to analyze the approaches of Adams, Collins and Crabb to Christian counseling.

# Chapter 55

# Counseling—Various Christian Approaches

We have noted the heavy emphasis on counseling today, talked about the potential dangers involved, and then briefly noted the approaches of Rogers, Freud, and Skinner. In this chapter we will note the Christian approach to counseling with special emphasis on the works of Jay Adams, Gary Collins, and Lawrence Crabb. These three are men of firm evangelical conviction.

Jay Adams has been with Westminster Seminary in Philadelphia and Escondido, California, and has had his own counseling center in the Philadelphia area. He has written numerous volumes on counseling. He chooses to call his method the nouthetic approach. Basically, it means confrontation. It comes from the Greek word—*nouthesia.* It is defined as admonition, warning, or counsel. The Scriptural references are Romans 15:14, Colossians 1:28, Colossians 3:16, Acts

1.    Ibid, p. 38

20:31, and I Corinthians 4:14, where the verb is used, and I Corinthians 10:11, Ephesians 6:4, and Titus 3:10, where it is used as a noun. Read and reread these passages in the Greek and in various versions. It certainly can be debated whether these passages say anything about a particular type of counseling which confronts people with the Scripture in an authoritative manner.

Adams' nouthetic approach incorporates three ideas:[1]

1) There is something wrong in the counselee (sin) that God says must be changed.
2) The counselor seeks to effect that change by biblically appropriate verbal confrontation.
3) The change is attempted for the benefit of the counselee.

Adams maintains that psychiatrists and psychologists have usurped the work of preachers, and are trying to change people's behavior and values in an ungodly manner. He states that "by studying the Word of God carefully, and observing how the biblical principles describe the people you counsel you can gain all the information and experience you need to become a competent, confident Christian counselor without a study of psychology."[2]

Adams asks lots of questions about the reality of mental illness. He objects to the concept, and finds the term used quite ambiguously. "Organic malfunctions affecting the brain that are caused by brain damage, tumors, gene inheritance, glandular or chemical disorders, validly may be termed mental illnesses. But at the same time a vast number of other human problems have been classified as mental illnesses for which there is no evidence that they have been engendered by disease or illness at all. As a description of many of these problems, the term mental illness is nothing more than a figure of speech, and in most cases a poor one at that."[3] He sees this as camouflage, intended to divert attention from one's otherwise deviate behavior.

---

1.   Jay Adams, *Competent to Counsel*, pp. 44-50
2.   Jay Adams, *The Big Umbrella*, pp. 23-24
3.   Jay Adams, *Competent to Counsel*, p. 28

I find Collins and Crabb to be more moderate in their approach to Christian counseling, and yet they are thoroughly committed to the biblical and evangelical position. Lawrence Crabb recognizes the need of integrating biblical truth into a psychological approach to counseling. "A solidly Biblical approach draws from secular psychology without betraying its scriptural premise."[1] He feels that Adams makes simplistic assumptions.[2]

Collins deals with Adams' rejection of all help from psychology as follows: "Was the Bible really written as a textbook on counseling? It deals with loneliness, discouragement, marriage problems, grief, parent-child relations, anger, fear and a host of other counseling situations. As the Word of God, it has great and lasting relevance to the counselor's work and the needs of his or her counselees, but it does not claim to be and neither is it meant to be God's sole revelation about people-helping. In medicine, teaching and other people-centered helping fields, mankind has been permitted to learn much about God's creation through science and academic study. Why, then, should psychology be singled out as the one field that has nothing to contribute to the work of the counselor?"[3]

"Of crucial importance is that the guides must be committed to the inspiration and authority of the Bible, both as the standard against which all psychology must be tested and as the written Word of God with which all valid counseling must agree."[4]

William T. Kirwan of Covenant Seminary has written a book entitled "Biblical Concepts for Christian Counseling" in which he makes a case for the integrating of psychology and theology. He states that "Biblical Christianity and psychology, when rightly understood, do not conflict but represent functionally cooperative positions. By taking both spheres into account, a mental-health

1.   Lawrence J. Crabb, Jr., *Basic Principles of Biblical Counseling*, p. 18
2.   Ibid., p. 50
3.   Gary R. Collins, *Christian Counselling*, p. 19
4.   Idem.

professional can help Christians avoid the inevitable results of violating psychological laws structured into human personality by God."[1]

# Chapter 56
# Counseling—Our Approach

Counseling is certainly an area of pastoral activity, a very special area. It can be considered a part of shepherding as it extends help to wandering, torn, defeated, and dispirited sheep. Helping people is a part of our task. The Bible makes this clear. Counseling is a way of helping people. It seeks to stimulate personality growth and development, helps individuals to cope more effectively with the problems of life, provides encouragement and guidance for those who are facing losses or disappointment, and assists persons whose life patterns are self-defeating. The Christian counselor has the ultimate goal of seeking to bring people into a personal relationship with Jesus Christ, or deepening it.

The Bible speaks of Jesus as being the "Counselor."[2] He is the best model of an effective counselor that we can follow. His "personality, knowledge and skills enabled Him effectively to assist those people who needed help. When one attempts to analyze the counseling of Jesus, there is always the tendency, unconscious or deliberate, to view Christ's ministry in a way which reinforces our own views about how people are helped. The directive-confrontational counselor recognizes that Jesus was confrontational at times; the

---

1.  William T. Kirwan, *Biblical Concepts for Christian Counseling*, p. 21
2.  Isaiah 9:6

non-directive client-centered counselor finds support for this approach in other examples of Christ's helping the needy. It is undoubtedly more accurate to state that Jesus used a variety of counseling techniques depending on the situation, the nature of the counselee, and the specific problem. At times he listened to people carefully and without giving much overt direction, but on other occasions he taught decisively. He encouraged and supported but he also confronted and challenged. He accepted people who were sinful and needy, but he also demanded repentance, obedience and action."[1]

At the heart of all our Christian counseling is the help and influence of the Holy Spirit. The Bible describes Him as a comforter, a helper, one who teaches us all things, brings back Christ's words, convicts of sin, and guides us into all truth.[2] It is the place of the counselor to make himself available to the Holy Spirit. With the Holy Spirit at work through him he can be used to comfort, help, teach, recall, convict and guide those who seek his aid.

Jesus promised believers that He came to give life, and to give it more abundantly.[3] It should be obvious that many Christians are not entering into the fulness of the abundant life. These people need our counseling. Collins speaks of the overarching goal of bringing people to discipleship, and then mentions self-understanding, healthy communication, change of behavior, self-actualization, and support as other goals.[4]

For a counselor to be effective in his task he should demonstrate certain qualities. Collins speaks of them as warmth, genuineness, and empathy.[5] Kirwan adds two more to the list of three—concreteness and self-exploration.[6]

---

1. Gary R. Collins, *Christian Counselling*, p. 15
2. John 14:16, 26; 15:7-14
3. See John 10:10
4. Collins, op. cit., pp. 23-24
5. Ibid., pp. 24-25
6. Kirwan, op. cit., pp. 137-141

Counseling techniques should include attentiveness to the needs of the counselee, a willingness to listen, then a response, and finally, teaching.

It is always well to remember that each counselee should be treated individually. They have unique problems of their own. Each individual must be approached a bit differently. Hence your counseling will vary from person to person. Counseling can be complicated, emotionally draining, and most demanding of our time and energy.

There are a number of things which a counselor would do well to avoid. We list a few of them: 1) Sharing bits of personal information, 2) Making the session a period of visiting instead of counseling, 3) Being disrespectful instead of sympathetic, 4) Trying to accomplish too much in one visit, 5) Being too directive, 6) Attempting to dominate the counselee, 7) Failing to remain objective—becoming emotionally involved, 8) Any sexual involvement of any kind whatsoever, 9) Losing your empathy, and 10) personal burnout.

God has chosen to work through human beings. He will work through you as a counselor if you are open to His leading and direction. It is not an easy task, but it can be very satisfying and fulfilling.

# Chapter 57

# Singleness

It is surprising how many persons are living as singles today. In the United States one out of three adults is living in an unmarried state. This proportion would be similar in Australia and other countries. The reasons are several: Some have never married and some have lost partners through death or divorce. The number of single parents (or parents without partners) is increasing at a substantial rate.

Singles are often misunderstood. Too often they are classed with those who want a swinging, free style of life. Many singles are not a part of this style.

One of the problems that singles face is how to meet other singles. In several of our churches we have had regular meetings for singles, which have been appreciated. This precludes the necessity for meeting other singles in bars and night spots. Churches should welcome unmarried people into their fellowship.

It is not fair to look down on singleness, as something less than good. Paul spoke of singleness as a gift, and he wrote in positive terms about a single lifestyle.[1] He sees the single life as being able to give a full devotion to the Lord. Jesus Himself illustrates the blessedness of the single life. When problems develop for singles, counseling can be most helpful.

Collins details some of the problems that can develop for singles.[2]

1) Some have not yet found a partner. In Australia many postpone marriage in order to travel about. Others want to prepare for and pursue a career first. The decision as to who to marry is put off until it becomes difficult.

2) Some choose not to marry. Their reasons may be very legitimate, but the single is often misunderstood. Pressures to marry are frequently placed on them.

3) Some have had marriages break up. Problems often follow. Loneliness, criticism, and a sense of failure are common problems.

4) Some have lost a partner. Hence a sense of loss, pain, and loneliness can ensue. Grief continues long after everyone else has resumed their normal routine. Living alone and making decisions brings pressures.

5) Illness and handicaps

---

1. See I Corinthians 7
2. Gary Collins, op.cit., p. 133ff

6) Fears of intimacy, immaturity, no sense of responsibility
7) Homosexuality

In counseling singles you have to deal with loneliness, self-worth, identity, direction, facing sex squarely, and emotions. We can help them with gaining acceptance, with life planning, by guiding their relations with other persons, and by encouraging them to trust God's providence. They must learn to recognize that to be single is not to be second class. Counselors can help them develop a meaningful life.

# Chapter 58

# Choosing a Partner

Next in importance to the decision to become a Christian is the choosing of a life partner. Although marriage is not considered to be as permanent a contract today as in the past, Christians look at it as a life-long decision.

Frequently Christian counselors will be called upon for advice on the choice of a partner. This is an important task. Christians should seek their partners from those of like Christian convictions. The passage in II Corinthians 6 is frequently quoted as referring to marriage, which it could include, but it is really a forbidding to associate with false teachers. I Corinthians 7:39 does state that a widow "may marry anyone she wishes, but he must belong to the Lord."

The guidance of the Lord should certainly be sought in one's choice. Love should be "felt" between the potential partners, although deeper love grows over the years. Similar backgrounds are also important.

Other traits to seek are adaptability and flexibility, empathy, emotional stability, and the willingness to have open communication.

A counselor can help those who are considering marriage from an outside perspective, whereas those involved are too close to the situation to be impartial.

## Chapter 59

# Preparation for Marriage

The seriousness of marriage calls for plenty of preparation. Since so many marriages fail today, this magnifies the need for thorough preparation.

Good counseling can serve as a preventative. It should help to build a union which can survive future attacks.

We must make pre-marriage counseling a requirement for those who request us to marry them. This is not only basic to Christian pastoring, but it is also required of us by the State (as in Australia).

We usually start out by assessing their readiness for marriage—how long have they known each other—are they willing to resign their independence and give themselves to one another?

One should also go into the biblical standards for marriage. Passages like Ephesians 5 and I Corinthians 13 are excellent in this regard.

Ask the couple to discuss their own strong and weak points. In other words, guide them in self-evaluation. Try to discern how well they have thought through the "give" and the "take" of marriage.

Encourage them to be open with each other in their communication. They should be willing to discuss feelings, attitudes, expectations and hurts.

Warn them that problems are sure to come. It depends entirely on how they face such problems. Meet them head on together, and with God's help problems can be overcome.

When the above issues have been adequately considered, then it is time to plan the wedding. The minister can guide wisely at this time, encouraging orderliness, discouraging heavy expense and display.

Pre-marital counseling can have lasting effects upon the lives of those who look forward to walking life's road together.

# Chapter 60
# Problems in Marriage

Some researchers discovered that 42% of those who had problems had problems which centered around their marriages. Marital conflict is almost universal. Tensions become apparent when two people with different backgrounds and personalities begin living together in the most intimate of human relationships. Friction and tensions frequently burst into explosions which in turn can create more tensions.

Problems are accentuated by the prevailing views of marriage. Marital separation is common. Divorce is an easy fire escape when marital conflicts get too hot to handle. Defacto living is accepted by many. Marriage is often considered a temporary arrangement, and is not thought of seriously.

Conflict and tensions can be caused by selfishness, lack of love, unwillingness to forgive, anger, bitterness, lack of communication, anxiety, financial problems, sexual abuse, alcohol use, feelings of inferiority, sin, and rejection of God's will.[1]

Counseling in regard to marital problems is best done with both concerned present. Be very careful about taking sides. Seek to be an

---

1.    Collins, op. cit., p. 169

instrument of healing. Recognize that every situation is unique. Set goals for your own approach to them, and then get the couple to set mutually acceptable goals. Even if the practical problems are solved, problems can persist, since many problems are more emotional than rational. As with all helping, empathy, genuineness and warmth are basic to successful marriage counseling.

"Marriage is the most intimate of all human relationships. When this relationship is good and growing, it provides one of life's greatest satisfactions. When it is poor, or even static and routine, it can be a source of great frustration and misery. God surely wants marriages to be good—a model of the beautiful relationship between Christ and His Church. The Christian counselor who understands biblical teaching and who knows counseling techniques is best qualified to help couples attain the biblical ideal for marriage."[1]

### Divorce

Divorce has become a common practice. Although our biblical stance would discourage divorce, we will have to face it in counseling whether we like it or not. We must also reckon with forgiveness. "God hates divorce and forbids adultery, but these are not unpardonable sins. God forgives and expects his followers to do the same—and then to live lives that are pure and free of further sinning."[2]

Divorce is very painful for those who experience it. "It can thoroughly disrupt one's life, routines, feelings of self-worth, and sense of security. It can effect people physically, psychologically and spiritually. Its influence extends to children, parents, other family members, fellow employees, friends, neighbors, and people in the church."[3] Divorce counseling is difficult. It is a crisis time, and counselors must seek to give the support and guidance which people in

---

1.     Ibid., p. 184
2.     Ibid., p. 189
3.     Ibid., p. 191

crisis need. Before remarriage, divorced persons should be encouraged to ponder what they have learned from the previous marriage and divorce.

# Chapter 61
# Child, Youth and Family Problems

Bruce Narramore has an interesting comment about raising children.[1] He states that in our society people are expected to have many years of training before they can teach or practice medicine, and must do years of apprentice work before they can engage in the trades, but for the work of raising a child we give or require no formal training. God entrusts tender young lives to the guidance of adults who have little or no experience in child-rearing. They face a variety of challenges and can often be bewildered by the task of parenthood.

At times the Christian counselor will be involved in counseling children directly, but more often he will be giving parental guidance. The child can be helped indirectly with information, clarification, advice, support, and other counsel.

God placed the solitary in families. He instructed them to be "be fruitful and increase in number, fill the earth."[2] In Old Testament times a large family was considered a special blessing from God, and childlessness was regarded with reproach. In modern times, with problems of over population, many people have limited the size

---

1.     S. Bruce Narramore, *Help! I'm a Parent*, p. 11
2.     Genesis 1:28 NIV

of their families. Children are still of great importance. Jesus had time for the children, and made much of childlike attitudes.

Ephesians 6:1 tells children to obey their parents in the Lord, for this is right. Much of today's problem with children stems from the laxity in discipline, which results in disobedience. Parents are to love their children (6:4) and not to provoke them to anger. Children should not be physically abused or neglected.

When parents don't get along with each other, children develop problems. The stability of the home is threatened. Unstable homes usually produce unstable children. The most basic needs of a growing child have been listed as: the need for significance, security, acceptance, love, praise, discipline, and the need for God. When these needs are not met, maturation is hindered and problems frequently result.

Counseling about children's problems can involve counseling the children themselves, or their parents, or by making referrals. The church is society's greatest institution in its potential influence on childhood and family development.

Adolescence can be a trying period. It is the maturing time when the young person changes physically, sexually, emotionally, intellectually and socially. They move from dependence to independence. During this period three influences can become extremely important: sex, drugs, and motor vehicles.[1] Peer pressures and the need for love and acceptance enter the picture. Choosing higher education, finding a job, and leaving home are decisions of considerable import. Bible teaching can be very helpful to young people struggling through adolescence, as well as helping older folk.

In spite of all that is written and discussed about the problems of youth, it is important to note that most teenagers do grow up into a relatively normal adulthood, sometimes to the amazement of their parents. Others struggle with their problems alone. Some "act out" their problems in socially disapproved ways. Excessive drinking, drug abuse, lying, stealing, violence, crime, and gang behavior are

---

1.    Gary R. Collins, *Christian Counselling*, p. 222

some of them. The increase in teenage pregnancies is one of the serious problems of our day. Every year a large number of youth run away from home. Many of them are frustrated at home and school, lack in self-esteem, and are unable to relate to their parents. Then there are those who attempt to take their own lives. Suicide attempts often indicate a real desire to die, but there is also a cry for help, indicating how much the young person is really hurting.

"The counselor who understands and accepts the problems of teenagers and their parents without taking sides can have a significant impact on both. The impact can be even greater if the counselor is sensitive, calm, and compassionate. Youth and their parents need a caring, wise, self-confident person who provides a haven of calm guidance in times of strong upheaval."[1]

The family can be involved in counseling. They can be a support system in which family members can give help and guidance to one another, and the family as a unit can receive counseling help and treatment.

The family is also the major source of the beliefs, values, and ethical standards that individuals develop. In this respect families and churches work together as a support system. The family and the church together can help people meet crises and cope with the realities of life.

---

1. Ibid., p. 228

## Chapter 62
# Sex Difficulties Before Marriage

Sex apart from marriage is more common and more widely accepted today than before. Cohabitation is increasing in popularity. Both premarital and extra-marital sexual relations appear to be increasing. Homosexuality, although centuries old, has gained prominence as gay liberation groups have surfaced and gained recognition, even in some church circles. Our society seems to be obsessed by sex. That which God created for enjoyment and expression of love has become perverted, a prime example of the moral sickness of our day.

The Bible soundly condemns fornication, which usually refers to premarital sex. It is a deviation from God's plan. We should counsel against it, and encourage waiting until marriage for sex.

Engaging in sex apart from marriage leaves two people abused. The Bible also warns against loose sexual talk.[1] We should counsel that freedom unwisely carried out results in slavery. The exercise of sexual freedom before marriage can result in many sad and serious effects—emotional, physical, and spiritual.

### Sex Adjustment in Marriage

Sexual problems for those married are also very common. It is an underlying cause of much marital strife. Sometimes it is obvious and recognized, and often it is hidden. Unless they are deep-seated, they can usually be solved by knowledge and understanding of the sexual functions, consideration of the partner, and a recognition that love is essential to good sex. Sometimes the orientation to sex before marriage has been so bad that it takes a big adjustment to get the married

---

1.    Ephesians 5:3-4

sex experience in proper focus. There are those who have thought of sex as dirty and shameful who have to learn that it is ordained of God and a thing of beauty.

Counselors need to treat these sexual problems with care and great wisdom. Pastors certainly should not give the impression that they immediately desire to probe into sexual problems, or that they relish such discussion. Collins gives several suggestions. 1) Listen with acceptance and understanding, 2) Be aware of counseling dangers, 3) Gather information about the nature of the problem, 4) Suggest a physical examination, 5) Give accurate information, 6) Deal with related problems, and 7) Be alert to the need for referral.[1]

Adams lays out some good advice in respect to counseling women: 1) Always try to have the husband present, 2) Never counsel a woman alone whom you in any way even suspect to have any improper interest in you, 3) If for some reason such a single woman or a wife must be counseled alone, be sure that your secretary (or wife) is in the next room, 4) Handle the subject matter carefully, 5) Avoid all personal references, and 6) Remember Joseph and Potiphar's wife.[2]

Crabb states that married couples who seek counseling because of sexual difficulties often ask for less than what God wants to provide. He distinguishes between what he calls "Fun Sex" and Body Oneness. To him Body Oneness is different from Fun sex—and better. "Fun sex involves physical pleasure without legitimate personal meaning. Body Oneness involves physical pleasure with personal meaning."[3]

### Homosexuality

The very word today triggers emotional reactions. Until recent years it was rarely mentioned in polite society, and was looked upon

---

1.  Gary Collins, op.cit., pp. 308-311
2.  Jay E. Adams, *Shepherding God's Flock*, 3 vols. in 1, p. 255
3.  Lawrence J. Crabb, Jr., *The Marriage Builder*, pp. 86-7

as sinful, sick and illegal. It was largely ignored. That has changed dramatically.

The Bible discusses homosexuality in seven passages, never with approval. (Genesis 19:1-11, Leviticus 18:22, 20:13, Judges 19:22-25, Romans 1:25-27, I Corinthians 6:9 and I Timothy 1:9-10).

Five other passages refer to it in the context of male prostitution. (Deuteronomy 23:17, I Kings 14:24, 15:12, 22:46 and II Kings 23:7).

Many researchers do not believe that it is inherited, or the result of abnormality, but rather it is learned. Parent dependency, distrust, and fear play a large part in developing homosexual tendencies.

The counselor should remember that Jesus loved sinners. We who follow in His steps should do the same. We need to show compassion toward overt homosexuals and for those with homosexual tendencies. It is not incurable. It is not a disease, but a tendency. It can be helped if the counselee honestly faces his or her problem, has a strong desire to change, is willing to break with homosexual companions, and will avoid drugs and alcohol. Above all, there should be a desire to avoid sin and to commit one's life and problems to Christ as Lord of his/her life.

# Chapter 63

# **Alcoholism**

Drunkenness is clearly condemned in Scripture. See Proverbs 20:1; 23:29-31; Isaiah 5:11; Romans 13:13; I Corinthians 5:11; 6:10; Galatians 5:21; Ephesians 5:18; I Peter 4:3 and I Thessalonians 5:7-8. Ephesians 5:18 presents a life controlled by the Holy Spirit as a superior alternative to a life addicted to alcohol. The Bible also emphasizes that the body is the temple of the Holy Spirit. See I Corinthians 6:19-20. The Bible teaches moderation, and considers abstinence favorably. John the Baptist drank no wine (Luke 7:33) as a special messenger from God. When a Nazarite dedicated himself to God, he abstained from wine and strong drink (Numbers 6:2-4). The matter of example (I Corinthians 8) is one of the strongest arguments against the use of alcoholic beverages by Christians.

Addiction to drink may be rooted in personality and heredity, although there is disagreement on this thought. Parental models can encourage drinking. We have observed Australian parents feeding beer to babies. Unstable and inadequate homes add to the problem. Peer pressure plays a part. Drinking is the "in" thing to do in many circles. It can create a sense of euphoria, and temporarily takes away stress. It can soon become a lifestyle, and addiction takes over.

The problem in alcoholism is to get the patient to recognize his problem. AA will not work with a person who does not recognize that he needs help. He must acknowledge his problem, or help is difficult to obtain.

Alcoholism begins to show up when there is a growing preoccupation with drinking. It is anticipated for regular and special activities. It becomes necessary in times of stress. Soon it is "sneaked" into the home, hid under the bed, etc. It is bought in larger quantities. Then follows loss of control, and harmful consequences result, The family is affected, financial problems develop, fights ensue, and divorce is threatened. Friends drop off, absenteeism appears at work, and jobs are lost.

Physical symptoms also appear. Circulation to extremities may be lost, and brain damage will almost certainly occur. Perhaps the most commonly known symptom is cirrhosis of the liver. Also common is esophagus and stomach damage, generally poor nutrition, and a greatly shortened life span. If left unchecked, alcoholism is a fatal disease.

It is to be hoped that the drinker would seek counseling before it goes too far. Commitment of the life to Christ is basic. Ofttimes this is enough. One can expect relapses in many instances. Prayer is very important.

Collins suggests that the counselor should be: 1) direct, but not D.A. (District Attorney), 2) Persistent, but not threatening, 3) aware of possible distortions due to sincere delusion, and 4) ready to seek out corroborating data from a concerned person if person becomes highly defensive.[1]

Criticism, coaxing, making the person promise to stop, hiding or destroying the alcohol, urging the use of will power, preaching, and instilling guilt usually are not helpful.

Seek to get the addict to a source of help. Get the addict off the alcohol. Detoxification may be necessary. Provide support. Very effective support comes from Alcoholics Anonymous and related groups like Al-Anon. Church support groups can also be cultivated. Offer help in stress management. Encourage changes in lifestyle. Families need to help. Always remember that evangelism and discipleship are basic.

# Chapter 64

# Drug Problems

The problem of addiction is not new. In some cultures opium or marijuana have been the problem drugs. In Western societies hard drugs like heroin or cocaine have been serious problems.

Analysts have found that all addictive chemicals have one thing in common. They change moods. Without a doubt this is what many people are seeking—a change of mood. Some of these changes of mood are very potent and highly addictive, while others are much less powerful. From the highest to the lowest, addictive potential reads as follows: Heroin, morphine, demerol or pethedine, cocaine,

---

1.     Gary R. Collins, op.cit., p. 387

barbiturates, amphetamines, alcohol, tranquilizers, codeine, bromides, nicotine, marijuana, and caffeine. Sufficient exposure to a high dosage of these drugs can make a person psychologically and/or physically dependent on them. For instance, with heroin, addiction can come fast, and with dangerous effects. With caffeine it is much slower, and the effects are minimal. When a drug interferes with our productivity and efficiency and we still persist in its use, we are psychologically addicted. If the drug is withdrawn and we get physically ill, then we are physically addicted as well.[1]

Our era has been described as one of "pill-taking." Children become acquainted early in life with medicines that take away pain, and make them feel better. Teenagers watch their parents consume aspirin, cold tablets, sleeping medications and many other drugs. Millions of people relax with coffee, a cigarette, or a drink before dinner. It is no wonder that young people follow this adult example, and then often get into heavier drugs.

Some religious groups actually use drugs in their worship. Such groups would tend to define religion as a mystical experience. Indiscriminate use of drugs for such purposes can result in serious emotional disturbances.

Some traits which appear frequently in those who abuse drugs are: a high level of anxiety, emotional immaturity, authority problems, and low self-esteem. Impaired personalties are often apparent in drug abusers. Family environment can increase the likelihood of drug addiction. Parental abuse can have its effect on usage by children. Parental permissiveness can stimulate it. A majority of drug problem cases come from unstable and inadequate homes. Peer pressure can play its part. Stress, and a desire to escape from it pushes people into drug use. The lack of spiritual influences can create a vacuum which fosters drug use.

In seeking to help drug users, remember that most addicts have high anxiety and low self-esteem. Be careful not to criticize or condemn in a way that arouses anxiety and threatens. Convey acceptance

---

1.   Quotes from Dr. George A. Mann in Gary C. Collins, *Christian Counselling,* pp. 376-7

of the person but not of the behavior. Listen, but do not give reassurance. Recognize that addicts are specialists in evoking sympathy. Resist the tendency to give advice, preach, or to act like a parent. Show a firm, sensitive attitude which leaves the responsibility for recovery with the addict. The best counselors are gentle, but not soft-hearted.

Experience has shown that only 15 percent of those treated in drug clinics recover, whereas Christian groups like Teen Challenge have had 85 percent success records.

If the counselee is to find new meaning and purpose in life, he or she must come to see that true and lasting fulfillment is found only in Jesus Christ.

# Chapter 65

# Sickness

These bodies of ours are remarkable organisms, but they don't go on forever (at least in this world). Sometimes they are injured beyond repair. If they aren't properly cared for, they can break down. Eventually they wear out.

It is easy to take health for granted. Little bouts with illness cause temporary interruptions in our lives, but when the sickness becomes more serious, one is forced to recognize one's limitations. Sickness can inhibit our activities, slow us down, and make life more difficult. If the illness persists questions can arise such as: "Why did this happen to me?" Other problems follow in the wake of illness. It can become a major challenge to Christian counselors.

The Bible frequently speaks of sickness. Illnesses are mentioned for Miriam, Naaman, Nebuchadnezzar, David's child, Job, Hezekiah, Timothy, Epaphroditus, and Paul, as well as others. Jesus showed a great concern for the sick. From the Bible we can deduce several conclusions:[1] 1) Sickness is a part of life. It crosses nearly every person's path, 2) Care and compassion are important. Jesus demonstrated this concern for the sick ones. 3) Sin and faith are not necessarily related to sickness. Job's friends tried to say they were, but they were wrong. Jesus clearly taught this in John 9:2-3. In some instances of healing in the New Testament the one healed had faith, other times it was the faith of another person, and sometimes there was no faith evident except in Jesus. Paul had great faith, but his "thorn in the flesh" remained. There is no biblical support for those who maintain that sick people are necessarily out of God's will or lacking in faith. It is both incorrect, and it can be cruel, to maintain that health is always available to those who exercise adequate faith. You cannot find a passage in the Bible that says it is always God's will to heal, but charismatics reiterate this again and again as if it is the truth beyond any question, and 4) Sickness raises some difficult questions about suffering. The most common ones are: If God is good, why does He permit suffering?, and if God has all-power, why doesn't He end suffering? The Christian counselor could do well to read *"The Problem of Pain"* by C. S. Lewis on these questions. Suffering is ultimately answered at the cross, as we see God Himself suffering for our sins, in Christ.

Counseling the sick involves the basic principles that apply to all counseling such as warmth and concern, empathy and genuineness, the ability to listen, and encouragement to talk about fears and anxieties. Confidentiality is always important. We certainly must not avoid people who are ill. We must learn to accept the sight of severely ill or injured persons, physical deformities, tubes and machines attached to the body, etc. Understanding is essential. Attempts at light heartedness should be avoided on one hand, and morbid attitudes on the other hand.

The counselor may be asked whether or not a patient should be told the truth about a serious or terminal diagnosis. The answer can

---

1.    See Gary R. Collins, op.cit., p. 397

vary with circumstances. Usually the patient senses the truth before they are told. Honesty can do much to retain the patient's trust.

Christian counselors can instill hope in the face of serious illness. It is basic to our faith. Confidence needs to be placed in the sovereign God who will bring to pass what is best for us. Often it means recovery; sometimes it means years of incapacity; eventually it means passing through death, and, for the believer, into eternal life with Christ.

Illness can teach real lessons, and need not all be bad. It usually slows us down, helps us to recognize our limitations, gives us a different perspective on life, and teaches us more about the love and forgiveness of God. It can be an enriching experience, if seen in the proper light.

# Chapter 66
# Grief and the Sorrowing

Grief is a universal experience. It is felt by every person in the course of a lifetime. Grief and death are difficult issues to face. It has tended to be a subject to avoid. Since 1969, when "Death and Dying" was published by E. K. Ross, there has been an avalanche of publications on these subjects. Thanatology—"The branch of knowledge dealing with the dying and the bereaved"—has developed into quite a field of study.

Grief can involve any kind of loss. Whenever a part of life is removed, there is grief. Most discussions of grief, however, concern losses which come when a loved one or friend has died. Grieving gives counselors a very difficult, but a rewarding challenge—to help people deal with death. It is very much within the province of the minister of the Gospel. It is a time when people need the ministry of the Word of God. Nothing less than a word from God Himself can adequately meet the need of a grief-stricken man or woman.

You can be of help to those in grief over a death only if your attitude toward death is sound, wholesome, and biblical. Otherwise you will only confuse the sorrowing one. Death and grief test a minister's true commitment.

Normal grief is a difficult, long-term process of healing which often needs no special help, since it takes care of itself in time. Discussions about death should occur ahead of the experience, if possible. Anticipatory grief tends to make grieving more normal after the loss has occurred.

Let feelings be expressed. Expect outpouring of crying, anger, or withdrawal. Always let it be known that you are available. Help the grieving person make decisions. Pray for the grieving ones, and comfort them with the words of Scripture. Support the mourner, but do not build an unhealthy dependency. In due time, normal activities will be resumed, and grief will lessen.

Adams sees a time of grief as "an important opportunity for a pastor to reorient lives according to biblical patterns. Death demands changes; why shouldn't those changes be in the direction of greater devotion to Christ?"[1]

Vernon Grounds lists several basic essentials for the pastor in bereavement counseling: 1) The pastor must understand the nature of death, 2) The pastor must understand that his ability to help members of his own congregation in time of bereavement depends largely on the quality of his total relationship with his people, 3) The pastor must understand that bereavement, whether expected or unexpected, often is a sort of emotional earthquake, 4) The minister must understand that his most important function is just to be there with his people, not compulsively talking but helpfully caring and sharing by being there, 5) The pastor must understand that there are occasions when holy reticence is more in order than easy explanations which fail either to convince or to console.[2]

---

1.    Jay Adams, *Competent to Counsel*, p. 171
2.    Vernon Grounds, in *Baker's Dictionary of Practical Theology*, pp. 227-8

Supporting friends can give great support in times of grief. The church can give a fine example of a community of caring, affirming and accepting friends. We need to help the grieving ones to get on with their pilgrimage through life.

# Chapter 67

# Financial Problems

The Bible tells us that "the *love of* money is the root of all evil."[1] The existence of money is not, in itself, a problem. Money is a necessary medium of exchange. The problems develop in respect to our attitude toward money, and our inefficiency in handling it wisely. This problem falls across the pastor-counselor's path frequently.

It is well to begin the issue in premarital counseling. That is a good time to lay groundwork in order to avoid problems later. Proper attitudes toward money, and a good budgeting plan should be discussed with emphasis.

When problems do appear the counselor needs to get the counselees to recognize the reasons for them, and then determine to do something to solve them. The additional problem of worry usually accompanies money difficulties. We can point out that God supplies our needs and that it is possible to get out of debt with proper money management. The solution to financial problems depends less on the state of the economy than on the way individuals and families handle their financial resources.

Certain biblical principles should be considered— a) Everything belongs to God. We are only stewards of our possessions, b) Stealing is wrong, and does not solve financial problems, c) Coveting is

---

1. I Timothy 6:10

forbidden. It implies a dissatisfaction with the possessions and opportunities which God has given. God can help us to be content with what we have, d) Giving is expected of Christians, and e) Management of our money is right.[1] In the parable of the talents it was the poor manager whom Jesus criticized.

A financial plan needs to be laid out which establishes goals and sets priorities. It may be necessary for the pastor-counselor to refer his counselees to others for help, such as bankers or accountants. If financial difficulties can be resolved it often has implications for a variety of other counseling problems.

# Chapter 68
# Retirement and the Aged

The pastor will soon discover that there is much counseling to do for those who are older and in retirement.

Financial circumstances change and often the home environment undergoes a change. These changes come at the time of life when one's body and one's spirit has less capabilities for decisions and adjustments. Advice will often be needed as to housing and medical care. Assistance will often be required because of illness, or the care of a sick one.

The older folk often need to move into smaller quarters, and housing where outside yard work is at a minimum. Varied retirement housing is available today. The pastor should be knowledgeable about what is offered. Some of these homes for the aged offer different stages of care. For instance, one where I ministered weekly for

---

1.    Gary R. Collins, op. cit., pp. 368-9

seven years in Artesia, California offered cottages for couples and singles, the retirement home itself, and a convalescent care unit. This kind of a setup gives a sense of security to older folk, that no matter what may befall, they will be cared for. Counseling may be required to overcome prejudices against such facilities, or to help them through the various steps toward full-time care. It is particularly difficult when the older person is independent in spirit, and tends to reject any help offered in home care or personal care.

All of us need to feel significant. This can pose a problem to one who no longer is the breadwinner, and has laid down his lifelong task. For one to keep well physically and mentally a sense of purpose in life must be felt. The church can offer definite tasks to keep older folk busy, and also fill gaps in the church's program.

Adams makes quite a point of "work" in retirement. "Retirement, as it is currently conceived, is not a biblical option. Indeed, because God made man with the capacity to receive a satisfaction that comes through work, and through work alone, every person needs to work so long as he lives. His work may be remunerative or non-remunerative, but he must work. Work is not the result of the fall; God gave Adam work to do in the garden. The redeemed children of God will work in heaven. So, retirement from a job must not be thought of as a retirement from work. Rather, the Christian must consider retirement from one job as an opportunity to engage in other work which may not have been feasible for him to do before....In this way, many, if not most, of the problems of retirement could be obviated."[1]

One of our good friends, John Boerema, chose to engage in special Christian work every year in many parts of the world, even though his occupation was a farmer and grain salesman. The thrilling story of his sacrificial service is told in a recent book.[2]

---

1.    Jay E. Adams, *Shepherding God's Flock*, p. 269
2.    Lorry Lutz, *An Uncommon Commoner*

Spiritual counseling for the elderly is important. If the counselee has been a Christian for many years, his faith will sustain him. The pastor may even find himself more blessed in receiving than in giving. You'll find others whose faith has wavered over the years who need deeper assurance. There are others, who realize death is always a possibility, who are more ready to face the issues of salvation in Christ. The old stand in need of grace as well as the young.

"Counseling of the aged demands knowledge of their needs and of the resources available to meet them, awareness of the special problems and limitations of the old, and patience in dealing with them. It offers at the same time definite satisfactions in bringing usefulness, enrichment, and joy in the lives of people facing increasing constriction in many aspects of life."[1]

Chapter 69

# Counseling
# Drop-In Strangers

Most ministers have people who drop in to their homes or church offices who come with the usual statement: "I want to talk to the minister about a problem." If it happens at church time, your people will often make a point of bringing them to you, or telling them where to find you. Nine out of ten times it is an effort to beg for money or to take you for a "ride." How to handle this type of case is a perennial problem to ministers. We can find no instructions on this problem in any book on pastoring or counseling. It is more likely in

1.    John D. Frame, in *Baker's Dictionary of Practical Theology*, p. 242

the city than in the country. It comes more often if your church is near a railroad track or a major highway.

They may start out as if they know all about you and throw names at you, or discuss well-known ministers of your denomination. Then the "pitch" for money starts. Do *not* give them money, no matter how big a sob story they give you. I have lost hundreds of dollars in this way, which were never repaid.

Another familiar "pitch" is the one about losing their wallet, or they can't get their car out of hock, or they need money for a bus ticket to their grandmother's funeral, or they have a sick baby, or the family has no place to stay, or they just got out of jail and have no money, or they began a job this week and have to wait for their pay.

It is not unusual to have them quote Bible verses. Some will even go so far as to pray with you for salvation, which is then repeated at the next stop. Some make a regular habit of "taking" as many ministers and churches as they can. We have had them ask for food. When we prepared sandwiches and a hot drink, they turned it down and walked away, stating that they wanted a hot meal.

One approach to them is to ask for an I.D. card of some type. Or you can ask them for a reference. Frequently, when you pick up the phone to check on them, they leave.

In some communities we banded together as churches and set up a system. A card file was kept in a central place, and a phone call could determine whether the individual had received help before. This ferreted out the repeaters. Then "chits" were given for food, lodging, and gas (petrol). The suppliers would bill the fund, which was made up of contributions from the churches. No money would change hands between the minister and the "drop-in."

In other cities referrals can be made to the Salvation Army or the City Mission, which are situated to help drifters and the hungry.

In Orlando, Florida well over 200 churches banded together to sponsor the Christian Service Center. This was an "umbrella" organization to meet varied social needs. Drifters could be sent there to be handled by professional interviewers. Provisions of food and clothing were available, if the need appeared to be real.

Although most of these situations come up with strangers, this can also happen with members or adherents of your church. They can play on your heart strings until you sign a note for them, rent a home for them, or loan them money. I have had a few appreciate it, and return the money, but others have "taken" us for multiplied thousands of dollars. What you do as a gracious Christian act for fellow Christians often ends up as an alienation because they don't repay and don't seem to appreciate it.

Tread with great care in this field, as if you are "walking on eggs."

# Chapter 70

# Depression

Depression as a problem is hardly new. It has been recognized as a common problem for 2,000 years. It certainly is with us today. Some have called our times the age of melancholy. Most everyone experiences depression to some degree in their lifetime. No one is immune from depression or from its sometimes frightening consequences. It affects young and old, rich and poor, loved and unloved. It is also a killer. Suicides among depressed adolescents have increased tremendously in the last forty years. Psychologists link depression to everything from chemical imbalances to sudden trauma. They disagree as much on the treatment of depression as on its cause.

Collins [1] states that the signs of depression include sadness, apathy and inertia, loss of energy, fatigue, pessimism, hopelessness, fear, negative self-concept, loss of spontaneity, and loss of appetite.

---

1.    Gary R. Collins, *Christian Counselling*, pp. 84-5

Depressions can occur at any age and they come in various types. It is not an easy problem to treat.

The Bible does not use the term depression, but it is implied. Consider Psalms 43, 69, 88, and 102. They express despair, but they are set in a context of hope. Jeremiah wrote a whole book of Lamentations. Elijah went through a period of despondency following the Mt. Carmel episode. Jesus' experience in Gethsemane certainly was a time of distress, but He gained the victory.

Jay Adams holds that depression is never an isolated emotion but the result of simply mishandling of an initial problem. "Depression need never result if the initial problem is met God's way. Depression is not inevitable, something that happens and cannot be avoided. Nor is it ever so far gone that the depression cannot be counteracted... The hope for depressed persons, as elsewhere, lies in this: the depression is the result of the counselee's sin."[1]

To us this is too simplistic an approach to the problem. Kirwan points out that the Puritans faced depression (melancholy they called it) head on. They did not try to spiritualize the problem when they didn't understand it.[2]

Crabb states that "it simply is not enough to inform a depressed person that he is sinful and that he must confess his sin to Christ and stop living sinfully. Such an approach presents Christianity as oppressive rather than liberating, an insensitive system of hard to keep rules."[3]

Consider the life of C. H. Spurgeon. He frequently was gripped by a massive depression which laid him aside for days. He fought depressions for many years. Spurgeon would not have labeled his depressions sin. Instead he saw them as a means to reach out to other sufferers. Martin Luther often experienced deep depression.

---

1.     Jay E. Adams, *Christian Counselor's Manual*, p. 378
2.     William T. Kirwan, *Biblical Concepts for Christian Counseling*, p. 64
3.     Larry T. Crabb, *Basic Principles of Biblical Counseling*, p. 18

When you counsel for depression you may ofttimes reach out verbally more frequently than in other situations. Approaches can include optimism, encouragement, asking of questions, giving of compliments, and the sharing of Scripture passages. Confrontation is not wise, and to demand action is not good. If there is any tendency to suicide, try to get the matter out into the open and discuss it. Don't discount the suicide threat. Seek to be available, at least by telephone. Further help may need to be sought.

Faith and trust in God can do a great deal toward overcoming times of depression. I have often used song and music to lift people who are depressed. If we are convinced that God is alive and in control, we can impart hope and encouragement to the depressed.

# Chapter 71

# Anger

Anger is an emotional state commonly experienced. It can vary from mild annoyance to violent rage. It may be destructive, but it can also be constructive, if it motivates us to correct injustice. Paul writes concerning anger: "In your anger do not sin. Do not let the sun go down while you are still angry, and do not give the devil a foothold."[1] A distinction can be made between anger which is justified, such as righteous indignation, and anger which is unjustified and uncontrolled. Adams says: "The idea of allowing anger to break out in an undisciplined manner by saying or doing whatever comes into mind without weighing the consequences, without counting to ten, without holding it back and quieting it, without hearing the whole story, is totally wrong."[2] He also points out that group therapy

---

1.    Ephesians 4:26-27 NIV
2.    Jay E. Adams, *Competent to Counsel*, p. 221

which works on the principle of ventilating anger in order to get something off one's chest, is most unbiblical and unwise. Verses in Proverbs like 14:29, 22:24-25, 29:11, 20, 22 call on us to check our feelings.

Anger can be destructive if it is not expressed in accordance with biblical guidelines. Our human anger often results from distorted perception. Much of this distortion can be placed under a heading of selfishness or self-interest.

Anger often leads to sin. It can result in bitterness, hatred, revenge, and an attitude of judgment. Verbal abuse often follows.

Collins[1] maintains that our human anger can be controlled. It should be acknowledged and admitted. Outbursts need to be restrained. Confession and forgiveness need to be utilized.

Crabb outlines a five step approach to anger when it is experienced in marriage. 1) Be slow to anger, 2) Acknowledge anger. Don't pretend the emotion is not there, 3) Think through goals. Anger generally results when a goal is blocked, 4) Assume responsibility for the proper goal, and 5) Express negative feelings if doing so serves a good purpose.[2]

Counseling in respect to anger won't help much unless there is a desire to change. We need to help them to admit anger, consider its sources, and evaluate the reason for their anger. Counselees need to be helped to gain greater self-control. Venting of anger can often increase instead of decrease hostility. When people learn to communicate honestly and effectively there is a prevention or reduction of destructive anger. When the love of God pervades our souls and we demonstrate it to others, it can melt away angry attitudes.

1.  Gary R. Collins, *Christian Counselling*, p. 103
2.  Lawrence J. Crabb, Jr., *The Marriage Builder*, p. 76

# Chapter 72
# Guilt

Guilt is involved directly and indirectly in many counseling problems. G. Belgum has written a book on guilt which states that guilt is where religion and psychology meet.[1] Bruce Narramore wrote that guilt in one way is involved in all psychological problems. He wrote an article entitled that "Guilt is Where Theology and Psychology Meet."[2]

You can talk with people who are depressed, lonely, struggling with marriage problems, homosexual, alcoholic, grieving, dealing with middle age, or facing almost any other problem, and find that guilt is a part of their difficulty.[3]

There is both objective and subjective guilt. Objective guilt can exist apart from our feelings. It may occur when a law has been broken and the breaker of the law is guilty. Subjective guilt is more of an inward feeling such as remorse and self-condemnation which follows our actions.

In dealing with guilt the Christian counselor has a distinct advantage over the nonbeliever. Guilt is a moral issue, and many guilt feelings arise from moral failures. Secular counselors are not qualified to deal with matters such as forgiveness and atonement for sin.

Early moral teachings (or the lack of them) can have a profound effect on later thinking about right and wrong. Parents need to start early to prevent the development of unhealthy guilt feelings. Children also learn from the climate of the home. If in the home the

1.  G. Belgum, *Guilt: Where Religion and Psychology Meet*
2.  S. Bruce Narramore, *Guilt: Where Theology and Psychology Meet*
3.  Gary R. Collins, *Christian Counselling*, p. 116

attitude is rigid, condemning, demanding, and unforgiving, the children can easily develop a sense of failure. Proper discipline must point out failure, but it should also include abundant love, encouragement, and forgiveness.

Nowhere else is our Christian theology more relevant and meaningful than when we counsel in respect to guilt. The great Bible truths of forgiveness and the atoning power of the cross are the repositories from which we can draw to see the guilty through to peace of mind and heart.

# Part 6

# BOOK REVIEWS

# Chapter 73

## *The Reformed Pastor*
## and
## *Call to the Unconverted*
## by
## Richard Baxter

The *Reformed Pastor* has been considered a classic on the ministry since the late 1600s. It was written in 1656. Without a doubt, it has much good advice to give, but I found it too critical and negative to inspire or to be very helpful. The 1829 edition has an introductory essay by Bishop Wilson of Calcutta which lasts for the unbelievable length of 56 pages!

After a dedication of 16 pages, Baxter takes the passage from Acts 20:28 on taking heed unto ourselves and to all the flock, and develops it at great length. Chapter I goes into the nature of this oversight. 1) is to see that the work of saving grace be thoroughly wrought in your own souls. "God never saved a man for being a preacher, but because he was a justified, sanctified man, and consequently faithful in his Master's work."—"It is a fearful thing to be an unsanctified professor, but much more to be an unsanctified preacher."—"When you pen your sermons, little do you think that you are drawing up indictments against your own soul."—"If you speak of hell, you speak of your own inheritance."—"O what aggravated misery is this, to perish in the midst of plenty—to famish with the bread of life in our hands."—"It is the common danger and calamity of the church, to have unregenerate and inexperienced pastors, and to have so many men become preachers before they are Christians." 2) Be careful that your graces are kept in vigorous and lively exercise. Preach to yourselves the sermons which you study before you preach them to others. 3) Take heed to yourselves, lest your example contradict your doctrine.—"It is a palpable error of some ministers who study hard to preach exactly, and study little or not at all to live exactly."—"Do well, as well as say well; be zealous of good works."—"Abound in works of charity and benevolence." 4) Take heed lest you live in those sins which you preach against in others, and lest you be guilty of that which daily you condemn, and 5) Take heed that you be not destitute of the qualifications necessary for your work.—"Woe to us, if we tolerate and indulge our own weakness."

Chapter II deals with the motives of the oversight of ourselves. 1) You have a heaven to win or lose, 2) You have a depraved nature, and sinful inclinations, as well as others, 3) You are exposed to greater temptations than other men. 4) There are many eyes upon you to observe your falls. 5) Your sins have more heinous aggravations than other men's. 6) Our works require greater grace than other men's. 7) The honor of your Lord, and of His truth, lies more on you than on other men, and 8) The success of all your labors doth very much depend on it. Thus 47 pages are directed to ourselves—to ministers.

Part II emphasizes the oversight of the flock. 1) Flocks must have their own pastors, 2) they should not be too large. He stresses taking heed to *all* the flock. Then we must pay special attention to the unconverted, the inquirers, and build up the already converted. Special help is needed for those who labor under some particular corruption, and those who are fallen or declining Christians. The strong also need our assistance, and we must have a special eye for families. Visit the sick diligently, admonish those who are impenitent, and exercise church discipline.

Ministerial work must be carried on purely for God and the salvation of souls. Carry it on diligently and laboriously, prudently and orderly. Insist upon the greatest and most necessary truths. All our teaching must be as plain and simple as possible. Exercise great humility. Use a prudent mixture of severity and mildness in preaching and in discipline. Be serious, affectionate, and zealous. Express tender love to your people. Manage all your work reverently. Do it spiritually, as by men possessed of the Holy Spirit. Keep up earnest expectations of success. Depend entirely on Christ. Be studious of the unity and peace of the churches.

After heavy criticism of ministers he does come up with a statement like this on page 202: "I do not believe that ever England had so able and faithful a ministry since it was a nation, as it hath at this day; and I fear that few nations on earth, if any, have the like." He then points out deficiencies, such as pride, negligence in studies, lack of vigorous preaching, lack of compassion for the poor, temporizing for secular advantage, minding worldly things too much, barrenness in works of charity, undervaluing the unity and peace of the churches, and neglecting church discipline.

The last 106 pages dwell on personal instruction, with particular emphasis on catechizing. The Sunday School had not yet risen.

The *"Call to the Unconverted"* was written in 1657. He starts out with Ezekiel 33:11, and divides it into seven doctrines.

1. It is the unchangeable law of God, that wicked men must turn or die.
2. It is the promise of God, that the wicked shall live, if they will but turn.
3. God takes pleasure in men's conversion and salvation, not in their death or damnation.
4. (3) is most certain, confirmed by God's oath.
5. The Lord redoubles His persuasions to the wicked to turn.
6. The Lord asks the wicked why they will die.
7. If men perish, it is their own fault, not God's.

Both of Baxter's books are creatures of their time. What they have to say about the ministry and the Gospel are basically correct, but such an approach today would turn people off. It should ever be our aim to be winsome, and to present the Gospel attractively. The negative aspects should be handled with care, ever presenting the truth in love.

# Chapter 74

## *The Mystery of Preaching*
## by
## James Black

Black was the pastor of St. George's United Free Church, Edinburgh. He gave these lectures in 1924 at Union Seminary in Richmond, Virginia as the James Sprunt Lecturer.

Preaching will always remain a mystery. It is tied up with the mystery of personality. It is a big business, and requires hard work. Preaching is the natural overflow of our religion. Having received good news, we long to tell it to others. Preaching is to present Jesus as Lord and Savior. Despite criticism of the church, the Savior stands unblemished. The moral is that the nearer we get to Him, the nearer we shall get to the world. If we preach Jesus, the savior, in the majesty both of His goodness and His pity, we shall have a listening world.

Preaching presupposes an audience. In our preparation there should always be the shadow of a listening people. We will speak to people, not benches. If we would move our audience, we must be immediately understood. We must know the big common heart of those we address. No preacher, however great, can afford to do without the intimate human knowledge which he acquires by visitation. We must be as interested in people as in ideas. Black does not feel that the colleges of Scotland train enough in the technique of preaching. He is astonished at the effectiveness of the average American preacher. The reason is "preachers are really trained in America."

Preaching presupposes a message. It is central. 1) Keep near to the big controlling truths. Preach on issues, not side issues. Men need healing and it is the big truths that heal. Get down deep. You may hurt, but you will heal, 2) Preach nothing other than you believe. Borrowed beliefs have no power. Truth generates its own white heat. If one only is in earnest and speaks as he believes, there will be a ring even in his voice that will command and arrest. Do not be ashamed of the enthusiasm that truth generates. The one sure note of power is sincerity. Without it, preaching is only a noise. 3) Try to preach with interest. Try to help and guide your people in the problems of their tangled life and show them the great way out. Don't presume they know too much. You can easily preach over their heads. Dr. M. Dods is quoted: "Never underestimate the intelligence of your people, but never overestimate the use they may make of their intelligence."

Preaching presupposes a man as its vehicle. The personality should have its share. Be true to your own genius. Cultivate it. There is room for all kinds and types of preachers. Generally avoid mannerisms, but don't be afraid of them unless they offend. After all, the style is the man. Never imitate. The results can be fatal—or funny. Acknowledge your sources. We must live generously on the labors of others, but the difference between theft and honesty must never be obscured. Pass the ideas you borrow from books or men through the magic alembic of your own mind. Be bold with the courage of conviction. We can be gripped and constrained by the love of Jesus. Human life can only be redeemed in terms of Him. We are lost men without His salvation.

A chapter is entitled, "The Smith at His Forge," which discusses the minister at his task of sermon-making. Our work is a vocation, not a job. We are in God's business; we handle His affairs, and we traffic for souls. A minister is continually giving out every week, and there must be some method of continually filling the coffer. A good sermon is never 'worked up,' but worked out. Your richness for future ministry will depend in strict proportion on the richness of your own mind and soul. Cultivate above all things your own devotional and spiritual life, so that your vision becomes clearer and your insight keener each day. Don't wait for 'inspiration.' You can often command inspiration. If honest work will not command it, what will? Claim your morning hours for work. In the ministry, of all places, God has no use for a lazy man. Read widely. Next to work and reading, observe men and things. Books are not a substitution for life. Cultivate the homiletic mind. Know your Bible as a book. Your sermon preparation must be thorough. After getting your subject and your text, know where you are going—get your conclusion. Develop the body of your sermon, and then blue pencil everything that is irrelevant or needless. Get into your subject, and stick to it. Don't spend too long a time on the introduction. Keep alive the element of surprise. Variety is the spice of continuous preaching. There is only one excuse and justification for all this talk about the art and craft of preaching—a love for God and a passion for the souls of men, so that we are willing to submit ourselves and our gifts for the invasion of the Holy Spirit.

Chapter 4 covers "The Marks of Good Preaching." In a true sense, every sermon is only worth the result it produces. Its whole purpose is to effect some influence on the mind, will, conscience, and life. Black discusses the preacher's pitfalls as 1) a young man's perilous gift of sarcasm and innuendo, 2) the young man's undoubted gift of wholehearted scolding. Ian Maclaren made the famous statement that if he had it all to live over again, he would preach more comfort. 3) No fireworks—no personal display. His positive marks are 1) clarify your thought, 2) use clearness of language, 3) employ the art of illustration. Preachers of renown like Chalmers and Guthrie in Scotland, Spurgeon and Maclaren in England, Beecher and Brooks in America used illustration generously and finely. 4) Be direct and pointed, in both matter and manner. 5) Be yourself, be natural. Don't become somebody else when you enter the pulpit. 6) Be men on fire. 7) Be brief. Preach according to the subject, not according to the clock. We never err by conciseness and brevity. Henry Drummond said he could hold an audience for 20 minutes, not 21. Leave your people with an appetite for more.

Chapter 5 deals with the use of our material in preaching. He starts with the Bible as our source and touchstone of truth. Expound books of the Bible, some by the sins and vices they scourge, some by their leading ideas, some by events, or by portraits, or by natural grouping. You will take your people through vistas of Christian truth, and it will be good for you. Don't fail to preach doctrines and also deal with Bible characters.

"The day of action" deals with the presentation. Since preaching is a form of speech, it should be subject to the recognized good laws of effective speaking. Since it is writing and composition, it should observe the rules of good style. Should it not be the best and most effective style within our range? It would be an immense folly to concentrate a solid week's labor and energy on the preparation of a sermon, and give no time at all to its effective delivery. Atmosphere, confidence, earnestness, emotion, and humor are all treated. Gestures and the speaking voice likewise. He spends some time on the question of reading the sermon, memorization, and speaking from a full mind. He recommends using varieties of style.

The last two chapters discuss the theory of Christian worship and common prayer. Black defines worship as the Church on its knees, the ascribing of "worth" to God, and as transcendent wonder. We meet in our Christian service to give and to receive—to give praise and adoring thanks, to receive pardon, direction, and peace from God, and the benefits of communion with our fellow-believers.

In early worship the elements were praise, prayer, testimony, reading of the Word, and preaching and teaching. Such simple forms were largely the outcome of the special circumstances of the day. We are not tied to them. The Holy Spirit did not cease to function at Pentecost! We claim the right to develop. The problem in church worship is to blend the simple, free type with the fixed, formal and ornate service. There is a via media.

The "free" service delights in the ancient simplicities of Christian worship. Grandeur does not depend on external aids, but always consists in spiritual qualities and effects. It is not in the method but in the spirit. The first note in worship is the expression of gratitude. What gave the Calvinistic church its unfailing dignity and power was its sense of awe—wonder at the decrees and sovereignty of God, and wonder at His mercy, so unmerited. This produced a dignity of Christian life and worship that has marked all Calvinistic creed. The secret is amazed gratitude. The next note is that of joy. It should be in every service, even funerals. We tend to confuse reverence with solemnity, and serenity with propriety. Choose triumphant praise, and dwell on thanksgiving in your prayers. The next note should be spirituality. Spiritual worship is the communing of our spirit with His. The next note is reverence or dignity. It should climax so that the worshipper may depart eased of burdens and encouraged in faith. The unity of a service should not carry throughout, so that varied needs can be supplied. Freedom is a privilege we should cherish, which gives us adaptability.

By common prayer Black refers to the congregational prayer, or the offered prayer of gathered people. He contrasts free and prescribed prayer, and spends time on the principles of free prayer. Among them he lists 1) a simple assurance of its need and efficacy, 2) an idea of the nature and purpose of prayer, and 3) a clear idea of our own special function as ministers. Our prayer life must be cultivated in the habit and atmosphere of prayer. Common prayer must be immensely human. A gift of chaste and dignified expression should be acquired. The people must be prepared. He suggests the common divisions of adoration, thanksgiving, confession, pardon, petition or intercession, and supplication.

I find this book to be a classic in Practical Theology, with special emphasis on Preaching and Worship.

# Chapter 75

## *The Fine Art of Preaching*
## *The Fine Art of Public Worship*
## *Pastoral Work*
## by
## Andrew Watterson Blackwood
## 1882-1966

We have selected the three books listed above as typical of some 23 books in the field of Practical Theology by Andrew W. Blackwood. He taught in this field in Louisville, Princeton and Temple University Seminaries. Jay Adams states that "It is a serious question whether any other man in the history of American homiletics has been more influential than he."[1]

Blackwood first approached homiletics as a science, but changed to approaching it as an art. This was reflected in his first book (1937) *"The Fine Art of Preaching."* He describes the background of preaching as a fine art, tracing it through the Old Testament and the New Testament preachers, as well as other great preaching through the years. He defines preaching as "the effective presentation of divine truth so as to move the conscience and the will of the hearer Christwards." (p. 21)

In "The Sermon As a Piece of Art" he defines homiletics as "the science of which preaching is the art and the sermon is the product." (p. 25) "Both in substance and in form the sermon must pass the inspection of God." (p. 26) In the Biblical Texture he states that "every

---

1. Jay E. Adams, *The Homiletical Innovations of Andrew W. Blackwood*, p. 1

sermon is a living being, full of grace and truth." (p. 43) "The preacher uses his imagination for the glory of God." (p. 44) He observes a return to biblical preaching, and encourages it.

Further chapters emphasize the mechanics of sermon preparation, ending with "The Joys of Preparing to Preach." He concludes with this passage: "With many feelings of gratitude, of joy and of holy expectation, the young pastor should finish his tasks in the study knowing that he can sleep well on this Saturday night, and that on the morrow he will enter the pulpit refreshed in body, eager in spirit, ready to pray for the assembled throng, and to preach with joyous abandon." (pp. 167-8)

"*The Fine Art of Public Worship*" followed in 1939. "Among Christians, public worship seems to be the best of all the fine arts." (p. 14) Thus he speaks of the leader of worship as the artist. He suggests a motto for any man who aspires to become a master of the fine art of leading in worship—God first, the people second, self third. (p. 30)

He goes through the worship of the Old and New Testaments and Apostolic days. He sees the era of history which followed as "The Struggle of Religion With Art," with a growing tendency to exalt the externals in public worship. He calls for a semi-liturgical stance. "After a minister has worked at his craft long enough...he ought to find great joy as he learns how to lead in worship in his own way, but ever for the glory of God." (p. 73) Blackwood goes into the bearing of psychology on worship, the fine art of sacred music, the art of selecting the hymns, the public reading of the Scripture, and the fine art of leading in prayer. He also discusses worship in relation to funerals, weddings, baptisms, and especially the Lord's Supper.

He concludes on this high note: "From day to day, let the man ordained of God to lead in public worship dedicate himself anew to his high calling. Here am I, O Lord, an earthen vessel. Take me just as I am, cleanse me by the Holy Spirit, and fill me with Thy blessed Word. Then shall I lead in the worship of Thy House so that the people will lose sight of me, because every eye will be fixed on the Lord Jesus." (p. 238)

"*Pastoral Work*" was printed in 1945. There are 29 chapters on nearly every aspect of a minister's work. Since it was printed at the close of World War II it is dated at times, but much of the material is pertinent and timeless. Very few books are as practical for the ministry. Blackwood states that "anyone called of God to the parish ministry can learn to become a good pastor." (p. 10) Pastoral work can be difficult. "Such service has always taxed a man's time and strength, as well as his brains and perseverance." (p. 28)

Starting with the first day in a new field, he calls for developing a plan for pastoral action. The pastor's wife is given a chapter. Various types of calling are described, as are ways to win children and attract men. He speaks of keeping records as a dreary task, but emphasizes its importance.

The second half of the book is even more unusual, dealing with such matters as having a kit bag, the help of the mail, the blessing on a new house, concern about newcomers, openings for evangelism, dealing with special cases, moral problems, and sex tangles. Community service, paid assistants, and enlisting lay workers are also given chapters. The final emphasis is on "The Rewards of Pastoral Work." "With few exceptions, parish ministers have been radiant." (p. 225) They have the joys of a healthy body, a healthy soul, and of serving Christ.

Certainly Blackwood is stimulating reading. Without a doubt his influence on homiletics and practical theology has been great, and will continue for years to come through his many students and his numerous books.

# Chapter 76

# *The Secret of Pulpit Power*
# by
# Simon Blocker
# 1951

As one reads this book he sees himself back in the classroom again. Dr. Blocker taught sixteen years at Western Seminary in Holland, Michigan. This book lifts you far above the mundane things into the heavenlies with Christ. If you need spiritual exhilaration, here are 209 pages packed with vitamins from above.

This book really explains how to organize a sermon that will be a "thrust" into the hearts of those who listen. His "secret" for pulpit power is "thematic preaching." He defines it thus: "thematic Christian preaching is the proclamation in sermonic form of God's self-revelation as contained in the Bible." (p. 13) By the theme he means one golden sentence which contains the seed thought of the entire sermon, and allows for the development of the points. Each point should be in the theme, either expressed or implied. The theme should be expressed "in universal, timeless terms." (p. 19) "The thing desired is a sentence which members of a congregation will carry home with them to ponder, to remember, to talk over with the family, to live on, to live by, to live with." (p. 36) "A sermon which has a theme, is built on a theme and adheres to it, reiterating the theme in varied language as its unfolding proceeds, is what the very word 'sermon' itself means, a 'thrust.' It is the thrust of the Sword of the Spirit, which is the Word of God." (p. 37)

The book is divided into two general sections—the theoretical and the practical. You first learn the method, and then are clearly shown how to put it to work.

Dr. Blocker had an excellent command of the English language, and had the knack of making his subject live by the use of unusual word pictures. One cannot leave this book without a renewed sense of the greatness of preaching. The need of expounding the Scriptures and of exalting Christ is constantly emphasized.

Sentences like these stick with you: "Many a preacher must admit to himself that his longest sermons have been those when he had the least to say." (p. 51)—"No more important work is done on earth than preaching the Christian Gospel." (p. 58)—"No greater need confronts the world than a revival of apostolic, Pentecostal preaching." (p. 59)—"A sermon is a unity, an integer, an integrated whole, a living organism, a shining highway to and from God." (p. 76)—"Your one object as preacher and Christian is to exalt your Lord and Savior by lip and life, to lift Christ up in sermon and service." (p. 87)

As this man was a great blessing to me, this book can be a real blessing to you.

# Chapter 77

## *Pleading With Men*
## by
## Adam W. Burnet
## 1935

This book is a "classic" in the field, having been presented as lectures to the students of St. Mary's College, St. Andrews, and of New College, Edinburgh by Adam Burnet of Glasgow.

Chapter I is on "The Christian Fellowship." Burnet speaks of the Church as it was in the moving beauty of its childhood, in the New

Testament. The word is Koinonia. New Testament fellowship heavenwards and earthwards, fellowship with Jesus Christ, and fellowship with those who are one in Him. The early Christians had a union of hearts in union with Christ. Pagan writers said: "Look how they love one another." Paul notes the sacredness of the fellowship. It is "in Christ," "in the Lord," and "in Him." The product of fellowship was spiritual growth. Its purpose was to represent Christ, and serve Him in the world. If you are going out to preach, you owe whatever blessedness that has visited your life to the Christian Fellowship. A living Church is developed as Jesus Christ is preached, and men are made to see His magnificence. Koinonia is created when Jesus comes to His Kingdom in His disciples' hearts.

Chapter II details "The Significance of Worship." Christians had come to see in Christ, the Son, the heart of the Father laid bare. Hence they worshipped God. All the well springs of the church's life are involved in worship. People worship out of fear and out of a sense of need. But the highest opportunity that the church affords is not that of getting something for ourselves, but that of giving something to God. A man cannot live without breathing, nor can a church exist without worship. "It is the instinctive and spontaneous outgoing of the soul in salutation to what is all-glorious." Worship brings forth fruits of 1) humility, 2) faith, 3) gratitude, 4) service, and 5) deliverance from self. Majestic worship can catch the soul away into an immeasurably larger world, freeing it not only from *sectarian myopia*, but also from pride and fear, ingratitude and indolence, and all kinds of depression and self-complacency. Noone has a monopoly on the capacity for worship. That belongs by nature to all God's children. Because He is our Father He has made all His children for the vision of His face. Hence our sermons cannot be anything less than an act of worship.

Chapter III concentrates on "Prayers and the Preacher." The conception of Christian Fellowship and Worship leads us at once into Sanctuary Worship and its prayers. It is in the context of prayer that the sermon is delivered. If the prayers have done their work, at sermon time the preacher does not rise to face a casual gathering. There

...y there. They have been to heavenly places ...describes the call to worship, the prayer of invoca-...e various parts of prayer—confession, forgiveness, peti-...anksgiving, adoration, and intercession. Prayer is the great act of Christian fellowship. "There is no part of the whole service that is more Christ-like. It cannot be done too well."

He suggests guiding principles for prayers. 1) They should be an outgoing of the soul to God alone, 2) Prayers are public and communal, 3) Prayers are not an opportunity for bringing in literary effects, and 4) Prayers require all the preparation you can give them.

The preacher "can honor God's trust in Him and fulfill his vocation only as he gives himself to God."—"He will keep his vow not by hoping for the best but by the regular habit of prayer."—"A world of joy in heaven and earth depends on your first-hand acquaintance with Deity."—"Let no man despise what is only to be learned in faithful pastoral visitation. Going with God among His people, he will know where the shoe of life pinches them."—Put yourself at God's disposal.—"What are you there for but to make yourself so pure a mouthpiece of the Spirit that God will never fail to speak when you preach?"

The last two chapters are on the sermon. He deals with general and particular preparation, the use of other people's sermons, illustrations and quotations, choosing the text, construction of the sermon, and preliminary spadework.

Burnet favors writing out the sermon, or at least one per week. In time you can dispense with writing. There is the danger of becoming loose in expression, of multiplying synonyms, of falling back on tiresome phrases, and of being wordy and diffuse. In writing the sermon, say only what is true. Be concrete. The truth must be brought into immediate relation with the lives of our people. Lucidity is important. Be simple. Don't preach above people's heads. Be self-effacing.

He talks about reading sermons well, and also about preaching from notes. "Begin in a conversational voice, and return to it as often as you can. Don't speak too fast. Give people time to take in what you are saying." His suggestions include: 1) Don't worry about any-thing, 2) Use your voice properly, 3) Use gestures only if they are perfectly natural, 4) Be sparing of humor, 5) Keep emotion in its place, 6) Have faith in human nature.

Some notes of true preaching are: 1) Reality, 2) Gravitas (weight), 3) Gladness, and 4) Affirmation. "It is not uncommon for men to succumb to the temptation to be controversial without being confirming, to be destructive without being constructive, to deal with the Scriptures in a spirit of acrid (bitter) modernism, as if the most striking things in the Bible were problems and perplexities, as if they had nothing to preach but permissive hopes and dubious potentialities. Not the diffident subjunctive but the stout indicative in all its tenses is the true mood for the preacher."—"Whatever you do, trumpeter, sound for the Splendour of God."

This book deserves its place as a "classic" in our field.

# Chapter 78

# *Anointed to Preach*
# by
# Clovis G. Chappell
# 1961

This is a small book (124 pages) on preaching by a very well-known Methodist preacher of the last generation in the U.S.A. He wrote many books of sermons (at least 26), and has a popular style.

The first chapter is on "The Preacher's Call." He bases the idea of a call to the ministry on the story of Moses, the call of the disciples, and the vision of Paul. He illustrates the variety of calls by the three blind men who were healed in different ways. Sometimes the call is clear and unmistakable. Other times it comes in terms of human need, through human voices, or parental influence. He calls men into the ministry to be His spokesman. They need such a call to know what they ought to do. It can steady us in our sense of mission. He illustrates vividly from his own experience.

Chapter two is titled "His Major Emphasis." He takes off from the Acts 6 record when the apostles were relieved of mundane duties by the appointment of deacons, and gave themselves to preaching. So we should put our major emphasis on preaching. First, it is our job. Second, if we don't preach to our congregation, nobody else will, and, third, it is so important. God has never run His Church without preachers. He managed 1,700 years without Sunday Schools and 1,850 years without Boy Scouts, but He never managed without the preacher. "Whenever the preacher has failed, the church has failed. Whenever the pulpit has ceased to give forth living water, drought and desert have spread over the earth. But when fountains have flowed from the pulpit, then the desert has become a garden." Without preaching the individual and the world cannot be saved. The result of the apostolic decision was that "the Word of God increased." Every great day of the church has been a day of great preaching. He cites the story of Ezekiel and the valley of dry bones, Martin Luther, and John Wesley. He concludes: "As we ministers face our difficult world today, the greatest service we can render that world is preaching with a mouth and wisdom that men cannot gainsay nor resist."

The third chapter deals with "The Sermon." 1) A sermon ought to be interesting. If we do not win and hold attention, we are wasting time. Our first business is to win and hold attention. To hold interest we must speak with simplicity. We must also preach with a note of authority. 2) A good sermon is constructive. Young ministers often preach a gospel of denunciation. We must preach positively. 3) A good sermon sounds a note of encouragement. Barnabas was named "Encouragement." To hear him preach was to forget your failures in the prospect of future victories. "Every discouraging sermon is a wicked sermon for which the preacher needs to repent in sackcloth and ashes." Jesus was supremely an encouraging preacher. He surpassed all others in putting heart and hope into people. 4) A good sermon will reach a definite destination. It will start, travel, and arrive. Blessed is the minister who knows where he is going before he sets out.

"Preparing The Sermon" is the subject of Chapter four. No man can be a Christian minister unless he is a sound workman. Few men in the community work harder than the faithful minister.

In preparing the sermon, first select a theme. By this he means a topic or subject (which is not what we mean by a theme). He suggests series of sermons, but not long ones. Five to ten is enough, twenty can swamp the interest of the hearers. Always use a text. Bible-centered preaching is the most helpful. Read and reread the text and the context. Then read everything on the subject you can find. You can find real help from the sermons of others. Just don't claim for your own what you have taken from another. Originality is taking an old truth and putting it through your own soul. Now organize your material. An outline is not a luxury, it is an absolute necessity. The number of divisions is not of great significance. Now fill in the outline. Write out the sermon. Lay it aside. Know your outline, and then preach it. Ask God to breathe upon the sermon and upon you that both may live.

"Our Finest Hour" is the chapter on delivery of the message. To make it our finest hour we must realize who we are and what we are there to do. We are God's ambassadors. Don't waste time or be late. Don't make needless announcements. Don't talk about yourself before your sermon, or make apologies. Select good hymns. Read the Scripture to the edification of the saints. Chappell reads it from memory. Don't heap up empty phrases in your prayers. Study to make your prayers helpful in the worship of God. Let the service reach its climax in the sermon. In delivering 1) Keep an eye on the congregation, 2) Be yourself, 3) Use every power that God has given you, and 4) Let us be in earnest.

The last chapter on "Keeping Fit" refers to the preacher maintaining himself. 1) Look well to your physical needs. Your body is the house in which you live. Take care of it. 2) Look well to the cultivation of your mind. Don't stop studying when you leave school. 3) Keep your religious experience vital. This undergirds all else. Live close to the Lord. Maintain the spiritual glow. "If we experience a daily renewal, we can be perfectly sure that we shall never become disqualified."

This book is full of good advice from one who has been through the mill, and is not afraid to speak of his failures. Actually, he was most successful in his chosen profession.

# Chapter 79

# *Nine Lectures on Preaching*
# by
# R. W. Dale
# 1896

G. Campbell Morgan looked upon these lectures as "one of the greatest volumes on preaching." They were nine lectures given at Yale University. He begins by warning against negative preaching which consists of doubts and questioning, and doesn't minister to need. "If a minister forgets that he has to preach to a congregation the chances are that he will soon have no congregation to preach to." (p. 23)

In the second lecture he treats "intellectual sermons." He wants the preacher to use his utmost intellectual strength, but he decries "cold" sermons. A purely intellectual preacher is destitute of some of the brightest and loftiest forms of intellectual power. "The dignity of the pulpit is derived from the grandeur and glory of the truths which the preacher has to illustrate." (p. 35) "If there is any dignity derived from dullness, I care nothing for it." (p. 36) "Every subject on which we intend to speak should be in our complete possession as a whole, and not merely in its various parts." (p. 41) "If you are to preach well you ought to keep your logical faculty bright and clear." (p. 42) Keep your mind awake and active. Imagination must make the facts vivid and real. "There is hardly a page of Holy Scripture which will not become more intelligible to us if we read it with an active imagination." (p. 52) He spoke of imagination as being one of the principal elements of D. L. Moody's power as a preacher. "It is very rarely that a preacher need be afraid of being too brilliant. But if we are loyal to Christ and the Church, we shall use our strength, not to win personal honour, but to prevail upon men to receive the teaching of Christ, and trust in His promises, and to keep His commandments." (pp. 58-59) "Every sermon that we preach should have a relation more or less direct to the rescue of the world from sin and its restoration to God." (p. 61)

In lectures three and four on Reading, Dale is concerned about indolence and the lack of regular reading pursuits in one's ministry. He spends considerable effort to point out proper exegetical procedures, especially being sure to note the context of a passage. Continue to read—we never grow beyond the need to learn more. Read books about preaching. Read sermons of great preachers. Also read great classics. "Vigorous habits of study will contribute to a vigorous habit of thinking and speaking." (p. 113)

Lecture Five discusses the Preparation of Sermons. Read the Bible to supply your minds with the raw material for your sermon. "The substance of our preaching has been given to us in a Divine revelation. For us the Bible is not merely a book of texts, but a text book." (p. 118) Make notes on your reading. Topics for sermons should preferably have a strong moral and religious interest. The text should contain the subject on which you intend to preach. Ask—

What is the sermon to do? Dale does not favor starting with a plan or a skeleton. "The plan of a sermon is the order in which the materials are arranged, and it seems to me that the reasonable method is to arrange the materials when you have got them to arrange—not before." (p. 137) He suggests not announcing the heads (points) until the close of each part, but says that no general rule can be given. "What I am anxious to contend for is variety and freedom." (p. 140) Dale does not think one should plan the introduction too early, nor spend too much time on it. "The style and size of the porch ought to bear some proportion to the style and size of the house." (p. 144) Make sure that the truth taught is properly applied in the conclusion. Don't be afraid of repetition. "We should all preach more effectively if, instead of tasking our intellectual resources to say a great many things in the same sermon, we tried to say a very few things in a great many ways." (p. 150)

Lecture Six—Dale finds the arguments for extemporaneous preaching weighty, but he himself used notes, and occasionally read his sermons. "I do not accept the superstition which implies that the Spirit of God is with us in the pulpit and not in the study." (pp. 157-8) He did not object to preaching a sermon a second or third time in the same church after intervals of seven or eight years. "Reading the sermon lessens the interest and impairs the power of our preaching." (p. 166) "The morality of a minister consists very largely in the way in which he deals with thoughts and words. We must do our best to form a style that shall be an accurate expression of our inner thought and life." (p. 177) Dale rated the merits of the English language very highly, and encouraged the preachers to take care of it. "Your language is not yours—not yours alone; it belongs to your country and to posterity." (p. 180)

Lecture Seven zeroes in on Evangelistic Preaching. Dale's main thrust here is not to give in to the doubts of his age, but to clearly present the Christian faith. He details the various approaches to winning people to the Gospel.

In Lecture Eight Dale calls for pastoral preaching. Don't take your people's knowledge of biblical truth for granted. Teach them.

Cultivate the religious life of your people. Don't just find fault. Give them the Bread of Life. Teach them their moral duties, and also their public duties.

Lecture Nine is about Public Worship. Public Prayer must be well planned as well as sermons. Dale realized the importance of the words and music which we sing. Don't leave all the singing to the choir. Singing develops the conscious fellowship of believers. Use tunes the people are able to sing.

God is still active in human affairs. His activity has never been interrupted. The revelation of Himself in human history is still incomplete. His Gospel continues to triumph. Assert the present authority, preach the present love of the living God. Only in God's light can they see light. Christ will be present with you in your work. "If this presence is revealed to you all your ministerial work will be transfigured." (p. 298)

# Chapter 80

## *Steeples Among the Hills*
## *Highland Shepherds*
## *The Shepherdess*
## by
## Arthur Wentworth Hewitt
## 1890—?

The three books named above, as well as *"God's Back Pasture,"* were authored by A. W. Hewitt, who made the rural ministry in Vermont, U.S.A., his specialty.

"*Steeples Among the Hills*" appeared in 1926. It begins with an explanation of why he stayed in his first rural parish for 18 years. He didn't believe in parish-hopping. He loved the rural pastorate, and stayed there despite tempting offers to city churches. He then illustrates his personal experiences with people in his rural ministry. He decries attempts to downgrade serving rural churches. Hewitt sees needed qualities in a rural pastor as 1) A wide variety of intellectual interests, 2) Imagination, 3) Having power over the primal emotions of man, 4) Evangelistic, and 5) The power of psychological suggestion. He ends the book with answering questions about the country pastorate. Some of them are outdated, but his answers show a deep devotion to the rural ministry.

"*Highland Shepherds*" was printed in 1939. By this time he had moved from Plainfield to Riverton, Vermont. This book developed more as an organized book on the rural ministry, dealing with 1) The Person, 2) The Priest, 3) The Preacher, and 4) The Pastor.

The Person deals with qualities that are essential to the rural pastor as well as elements that are fatal to him. The fatal elements listed are: 1) Stain, 2) Censoriousness, 3) Pessimism, and 4) Selfish ambitions.

The Priest involves such matters as discipline, the ministry of music, worship services, communion, baptism, weddings, funerals, and the prayer meeting. This section includes much homely advice, most of which is just good common sense.

The Preacher section deals with the requisites, the manner, and the themes of rural preaching. "When folks come to church they want to hear about God." (p. 99) "Preaching in a rural pulpit must be done in a natural manner." (p. 100) Hewitt calls for forthright, eye-to-eye, heart-to-heart, conversational method of extemporaneous speech. (p. 101) On sermon content he says that "Death is abroad in any church where the newspaper dethrones the dynasty of prophets and apostles." (p. 110) "Preaching founded on external interests and trivialities of the day is the profane trifling of a fool. Preaching which reaches the great primal needs of the human heart will be up to date today as in the days of Terah...or in the days of those who live a thousand years hence." (p. 122)

He has chapters on Reason and Imagination as Principles of Sermon Preparation. He calls for only reasonable and sensible uses of the text. "What a joy it is when a minister discovers he has a mind and begins to use it!" (p. 143) "It is the imagination which gives beauty to preaching." (p. 146) He points out that illustrations can come from many sources, such as the Bible, literature, history, biography, science, observation, current events, invention, anecdotes, and experience.

"The price of good preaching is utter self-devotion." (p. 164) Carelessness and mistakes in preaching are not justified. Watch out for bad pronunciation and errors of articulation. Our "purpose in preaching is to show forth God and His most holy will." (p. 176)

The Pastor section begins on the Shepherd note. "The work of a pastor is to care for his people." (p. 181) "To be a good pastor is to be like Jesus." (p. 181) "Pastoral work must be the center of all our plans." (p. 182) "If you have any scorn of pastoral work, get out of the pulpit." (p.184) "Pastoral visitation is the only way to reach all your people with the gospel." (p. 185) "The end of any ministry inevitably begins when the shepherd forgets his sheep." (p. 190)

In the rural pastor Hewitt wants to see certain qualities evident. They are: 1) Common sense, 2) He must not be a social moron, 3) He should be a gentleman.

His last chapter is entitled: "How To Be a Good Pastor." Hewitt lists his answers: 1) By having a will to work, 2) By obeying the inner voice, 3) By letting your love be known, 4) By being impartial, 5) By being trustworthy, and 6) By being physician and surgeon to the soul.

In 1943 Hewitt wrote *"The Shepherdess"* for the minister's wife. He thought of it as an excursion into new territory, although *"I Married a Minister,"* edited by Golda Bader, came out at about the same time.

His first chapter describes her as a lover. She became a shepherdess most likely because her lover was a shepherd. Her first duty is that of being a good lover to her chosen mate. "To be his perfect lover is her greatest and most sacred duty." "The romantic love of a husband is kept by the same means through which it is attained." "Woe be unto you if your husband must love you in spite of what you are instead of because of what you are!" "Woe be to you if, while your lover is seeing all others at their very best, he is compelled to see you daily at your worst." He calls for developing these habits: 1) the habit of affection, 2) the habit of respect, 3) the habit of devotion to God. "For a man and a woman to approach the throne of God together every day is a divine safeguard to married love." And 4) the habit of sharing all life.

Chapter II deals with the shepherdess as a helpmeet. Although the word is a misnomer, the chapter is good. Your first field of helpfulness is psychological. You can keep your husband from faults of the ministry such as jealousy, disparagement, discourtesy. Serve his meals on time. Be prompt. Be a good housekeeper. Don't be a "blab" wife.

Chapter III is entitled "The Good Shepherdess." 1) She must be a lover of God, 2) she must have a good mentality, 3) she should be physically fit, 4) she must be a good housekeeper, 5) she must have common sense, 6) she must have good tastes, 7) she must not be jealous, 8) she must be unshockable, 9) she must have a sense of humour, 10) she must be adaptable, and 11) she must have social winsomeness. Be tactful, and go easy on criticism. Be an example of courtesy.

"Economics of the Manse." Being a good economist is not the most inspiring of her requirements, but it is important. "The simple fact is that among those born of women there have not risen financiers more excellent and capable than the average minister and his wife." "One becomes expert in home management, as in all other skills, by practice."

Develop the ability for objective self-inventory. Use honest self-analysis. Keep your activities within the limits of the powers you presently have. If you have qualities for larger duties, and want to do them, the next chapters deal with them. 1) A presiding officer, 2) An executive—at times duty will call you beyond your ability. Do the best you can, it will be good training for you. 3) A hostess—You do not owe a return dinner to everyone who invites you. Have your house in condition. Be ready before the appointed time. Greet your guests with friendliness. Gather a reasonable knowledge of social etiquette. 4) A teacher—You most likely will face this. 5) A public speaker—One preacher in the family is usually enough. But, there are times she will be called upon to speak. She should seek to do it well.

The next chapter calls for her to have love, understanding, trustworthiness, and inspiration. Guide mostly by suggestion. Rebuke rarely, scold never. Never minimize another's trouble. Be positive and instructive in your counsels.

How is a shepherdess prepared? How shall an untrained girl educate herself for the duties of a minister's wife? She needs education, but not necessarily college! All significant people are self-educated. "If your mind is eager for knowledge, nothing under the stars can keep you from it. If not, no school on earth can give you an education." Learn to read, know your Bible. Know the theology of your church. Know church history. Keep up on current periodicals. Be comrades of the cultured. Read classic literature. Slowly, patiently, gradually, whether college-bred or not, you will become educated if you wish it.

"Patience in a Parsonage" contains many illustrated anecdotes, which demonstrate the point. It is a place where rich and lifelong friendships are formed.—What home so privileged in friendships as the parsonage (manse)?

"The Care of a Shepherdess" is the final chapter. Pastors can be selfish. Listen! 1) Be tender with your shepherdess, 2) give her credit for all her good ideas, 3) be appreciative of her, 4) let her know you love her, 5) be thoughtful to spare her anxiety, 6) don't make humour at your wife's expense and 7) guard her health—"Follow the Golden Rule until the Golden Wedding, and then all my be safely left to habit."

Hewitt is an unusual writer. He uses anecdotes and has humor. At times he is quite hard on preachers who don't meet his standards. His long experience in rural parishes gives him insight into this work as a specialty.

# Chapter 81

# *The Romance of Preaching*
# by
# Charles Silvester Horne
# 1914

Horne was a well-known Congregationalist in London. He gave this book as lectures at Yale University, U.S.A. and died three days later. His wife published them.

He begins with a lecture on "The Servant of The Spirit" which deals with the greatness of the preacher's task. "For every voice that carries inspiration to its fellows; for every soul that has some authentic word from the Eternal wherewith to guide and bless mankind, there will always be a welcome." (p. 21) The preacher has superior authenticity to human authority. "The preacher, who is the messenger of God, is the real master of society." (p. 23) "The real romance of history is this romance of the preacher." (p. 27) "Have any of us fathomed the depth of that supreme saying of our Lord's that the real life of man is by 'every word that proceedeth out of the mouth of God?' " (pp. 29-30) "The great empires of yesterday did not go to their ruin because of any lack of wealth. They were on the contrary enervated by luxury...They declined for lack of soul...The appearance of a true preacher is the greatest gift that any nation can have." (pp. 42-43) He called the lectures "The Romance of Preaching" because he feared that we have been losing our sense of the splendid possibilities of our vocation. (p. 44)

The next six chapters are a review of some of the most notable preaching exploits of history. He begins with Moses, whom Horne calls The First of The Prophets. Moses took up his ministry under a sense of compulsion, as has always been true of God's best ministers. "Not natural selection, but supernatural election...God's noblest warriors have felt like pressed men." (p. 62) Moses knew his God and he understood his people. He espoused their suffering. He was a visionary, but he had the wisdom of statesmanship. Next Horne deals with the Apostolic Age. He speaks of the Apostolic Age as the romance of all history. The early Christians were gripped with the truths of Immortality and Equality. Horne liked their "Christian Socialism."

The lecture on Athanasius and Chrysostom is termed "The Royalty of The Pulpit." "The Christian Church has been the nursing home of great orators." (p. 117) Athanasius and Chrysostom were so dissimilar in the externals of their ministry but they vividly exemplified the same supreme power of inspired personality. (p. 120) "The one supreme qualification for the ministry is a soul of flame." (p. 124) When Athanasius rose to defend the faith he was a man of giant stature, although he was physically small. He maintained the royalty of the pulpit as the one place where the truth of God is to be proclaimed without fear or favour. He was endowed with common sense and the gift of humour. He was a controversialist who cared so supremely for the honour of his Saviour that he was prepared to stand alone against the world. Chrysostom has a place of preeminence among Christian preachers and the world's famous orators. His style is a model of what Christian eloquence at its highest can be. "The supreme merit of Chrysostom is that he never for one moment forgets that he is dealing with human beings and human life." (p.142) He knew "that the preacher's lot is a desperate war with organized evil and throned iniquity." (p. 147)

He also lectures on Savonarola, Calvin and Knox. These men veritably became the conscience of the communities where they labored. Each of them dominated the life of a commonwealth. (pp. 161-2) Savonarola of Florence lived and witnessed in a day when the princes of the Church outvied in greed and lust the princes of the State. His ultimate triumph as a preacher, Horne says, is the triumph of naturalism in the pulpit. He relied on plain, searching, and passionate speech. (p. 166) "Judged by the test that a great sermon is to make its hearers ready to fight and die for the faith, Savonarola was a supreme preacher." (p. 168) "To pass from Savonarola to Calvin of Geneva is to pass from a volcano to a well-controlled furnace." (p. 175) His destiny was to inspire a church to become the instrument of freedom and righteousness in the civic life of the city. (p. 176) Calvin can deepen the preacher's sense of destiny today. Knox of Scotland united the fiery eloquence of Savonarola to the statesmanship of Calvin. (p. 182) He was not afraid of Mary, Queen of Scots. He dared to oppose Truth to Error. "What the world owes to the example of Savonarola, to the constructive thinking of Calvin, and to the statesmanship of Knox, can never be told." (p. 189)

John Robinson and the Pilgrim Fathers are described as the Founders of Freedom. When you study Robinson's personality and preaching, you do not wonder at the spirit and exploits of the Pilgrim community. "I imagine John Robinson would have found it difficult to decide whether his people owed most to his preaching, or his preaching owed most to his people." (pp. 209-10) "The part played by Moses in the days of the Jewish exodus towards the Land of Promise is not one wit more notable or significant than the part played by John Robinson in the exodus that landed in this land of promise." (pp. 214-15)

The Passion of Evangelism is exemplified by Wesley and Whitefield. "The ministry that is not an evangelistic ministry is not in the full sense a Christian ministry." (p. 228) Wesley won people by the old fashioned weapons of persuasion, patience, sacrifice, courage, and sympathy. (p. 248) "For dramatic and declamatory power Whitefield had no rival in his age, and no superior in any age." (p. 249) "Let every preacher resolve he will be churchman and evangelist in one." (p. 262)

The final chapter emphasizes the title of the book with "The Romance of Modern Preaching." "Preaching can never lose its place so long as the mystery and wonder of the human spirit remain." (p. 268) "Amid all changes of thought and phrase the wonder of conversion remains." (p. 275) His last two points emphasize new applications of Christ's teaching, which include equal distribution of wealth, and efforts at organized peace.

This book is clearly a classic on preaching, although set in a time when illusions of a Christian Socialism and a universal Peace were being given prominence in the pulpit.

# Chapter 82

# *That The Ministry Be Not Blamed*
# by
# John A. Hutton

This book is a series of five lectures given to divinity students in Aberdeen, Edinburgh, and Glasgow in the Spring of 1921, by Dr. John A. Hutton, who for many years edited *"The British Weekly,"* and also pastored Westminster Chapel in London.

Hutton states that he was not "a born preacher," but had to work to become one. He had varied experiences in the ministry, read a dozen books on preaching, took notes on them, and developed these lectures.

He maintains that congregations make sermons long or short, depending on their interest or want of interest. He says that most volumes of sermons by Scots have a temporariness and a stridency about them, even though there has been a great preaching tradition in Scotland. He deprecates the turning of the sermon into an occasion for discussion. When men have been brought face to face with God, there should be no escape into debate.

Preaching must deal with necessary things. Otherwise we become irrelevant. Only then can our work be worthwhile. We must speak to men about God. There is one solving word for this universe: it is God. There is one solving word for God: it is Christ.

In the twentieth century, the function of good men who speak in the Name of God is to declare that faith in God is not only possible but an absolute necessity. Not only may men have fellowship with God, but they must have. Man must put Christ on the throne, or perish. Hutton discusses the teaching of the forgiveness of sins. He believes that it must be preached, but not in a "cheap" fashion, so that it gives the impression that God does not take sin seriously. Forgiveness is not accomplished unless as a consequence of an agony in man and of an agony in God.

In lecture three, Hutton fears that preaching "nowadays" consists in telling the story of man's achievement, and worship consists in listening to the story respectfully. We must remind our listeners that life is still a good fight. Our belief in God itself is taken far too easily. The whole Bible is the record of man's agony to find God, and having found Him, not to lose Him—No man will have faith who does not acknowledge his need of faith.—Christianity is something which Christ, the Founder of it, thought could be lived in this world.—the Church of Christ is not the mind of the world, but the conscience of the world.—As preachers, we are to declare that to hold on for the highest in this very world is surely of the very essence of Christian faith. There are difficulties, but God sent His Son into the world to tilt the balance to the side of faith.—We vote for God against the insinuation of life and death. Let us vote for Christ against the natural passions of the body and the soul.

Preaching is not only a calling, but it is also a craft. It must be done worthily. Reading is important. Always make notes of your reading. don't read very much with the direct and immediate view to preaching. Read to make an able and wise man of yourself, conversant with life discerned spiritually. Reformed people don't preach in cathedrals, so we have to create our atmosphere. Read deeply rather than widely. Avoid all 'Aids' to Preachers. Read what you like. Then, read what you don't like. And then, read what you ought to like. Never sit down with the newspaper. Read it standing. A man should write out to the last syllable what he plans to speak. This gives proof to himself that he has put his mind to the matter. Having written your sermon, it need not be preached from the paper. If you speak without manuscript, do not memorize. Be anxious only that you have the idea or ideas.

A rule for extemporaneous preaching is to write out what you propose to be your last sentence. Don't expand it, or say any more. Don't roll your eyes while speaking. It pains the people and looks dreadful.

Ours is an art which demands everything of us. Our preaching comes to be our personal confession.

This book is quite different from others we have reviewed. It tends to take a more philosophical approach to the work of the ministry. As such, it has value and is helpful.

# Chapter 83

# *The Preacher, His Life and Work*
## by
## J. H. Jowett
## 1863—1923

J. H. Jowett was a well-known preacher who served churches in both England and the U.S.A.

Chapter I is on the Preacher's call. "It is of momentous importance how a man enters the ministry. There is a 'door' into this sheepfold, and there is 'some other way.' " He may take it up as a result of personal calculation, from secular counsel, as a profession, or as a preference over other tasks. All such reasons miss the appointed door. There is nothing vertical in this vision. "Before a man selects the Christian ministry as his vocation he must have the assurance that the selection has been imperatively constrained by the Eternal God." The call of the Eternal must ring through his soul. "Necessity is laid" upon him. Ultimately he has no alternative. Jowett points out the variety of Scriptural calls, illustrated by Amos, Isaiah, and Jeremiah. "Every genuine call has its own uniqueness. In all genuine callings to the ministry there is a sense of the divine initiative, a solemn communication of the divine will, a mysterious feeling of commission, which leaves a man no alternative, but which sets him in the road of this vocation bearing the ambassage of a servant and instrument of the Eternal God." "The assurance of being sent is the vital part of our commission." Entering the divine vocation you will apprehend the glory of this calling. Paul never lost this sense in the medley of professions. To him it was always a privilege and his work never lost its halo. "Unto me, who am less than the least of all saints, is this grace given, that I should preach among the Gentiles the unsearchable riches of Christ." Sensing the glory of our vocation will keep us humble and will also make us great. The sacredness of this calling leaves us with solemn responsibilities. "It is a great, awful, holy trust." "We are to be the friends of the Bridegroom, winning men, not to ourselves, but to Him, matchmaking for the Lord, abundantly satisfied when we have brought the bride and the Bridegroom together." Jesus said, "As Thou has sent Me into the world, even so have I also sent them into the world." "It means the exaltation of Christian apostleship, the glorification of the Christian ministry. It means that the mystic ordination that rested on the Son rested also on Peter and on Paul and we also share in it."

We are to find our mission in the service of good news. It is the good news about God and the Son of God. It is the good news about the vanquishing of guilt and the forgiveness of sins. Our first mission to the world is to be carriers of good news. We are not only to preach the good news but we are also to incarnate it in vital service. The word of grace is to be confirmed by gracious deeds.

Chapter II is about "The Perils of the Preacher." He begins with Paul's thought about becoming a castaway. Paul sees the insurgent danger of men who are busy among holy things becoming profane. One may lead others into the heavenly way and lose the road himself. None of us are immune from this problem. "Perils are ever the attendants of privilege." "Privilege never confers security; it rather provides the conditions of the fiercest strife." "We may lead people into wealth and we ourselves may be counterfeit."

The first peril discussed is a deadening familiarity with the sublime. "It is possible to be busy about the Holy Place, and yet to lose the wondering sense of the Holy Lord. We may have much to do with religion and yet not be religious." "A man may live in mountain country and lose all sense of the heights."

The second peril is that of deadening familiarity with the commonplace. We can become dead to the bleeding tragedies of common life. The pathetic can cease to melt us, and the tragic may cease to shock us. We may lose our power to weep. We may become "past feeling."

The third peril is the possible perversion of our emotional life. The emotions can become perverted, unhealthily intense and inflammatory. They may become defiled, and one's moral defences are imperilled.

Also, we face the perilous gravitation of the world. "It is round about us like a malaria, and we may become susceptible to its contagion." It involves compromise, taking a medium-line, wearing a grey color, whereas we are called upon to keep our garments white. We are also fascinated with the glittering. We are tempted to a showy eloquence rather than a deep spirit of power. We may become more intent on full pews than on redeemed souls.

All of these perils can snare you away from God. The results are that, 1) We will lose our spirituality, 2) Our speech lacks a mysterious impressiveness, and 3) Our enterprises become pastimes rather than crusades.

To avoid these perils "we must assiduously attend to the culture of our souls, we must sternly and systematically make time for prayer, and for the devotional reading of the Word of God." A restless scattering of energies over many interests leaves no margin of time for communion with God. "We are great only as we are God-possessed." The discipline of the soul must be serious and studious. It is difficult, but its rewards are infinite. Character is disciplined by the culture of the soul. Other virtues such as gratitude, courtesy, patience, consideration, and good temper will follow.

"A calling without difficulty would not be worth our choice. You will have traps and enemies, allurements and besetments all along your way, but 'grace abounds,' and 'the joy of the Lord is your strength.' "

Chapter III—"The Preacher's Theme." "Feed my sheep," said the Lord. The shepherd is to lead his sheep to "green pastures" and "still waters." He guards the church's health by providing against moral and spiritual famine.

There is danger of an emphasis on reform. "Men may become so absorbed in social wrongs as to miss the deeper malady of personal sin. They may lift the rod of oppression and leave the burden of guilt." Some preachers live in the Old Testament with an Amos rather than in the New Testament with John or in Ephesians. The sociologist can impair the evangelist in the preacher. It is for the preacher to keep a true insight into the things that matter most. No "way of the world" seduced Paul from his central themes. Wherever he went he determined to know only Jesus Christ and Him crucified. Despite the changed conditions of our day, we should do the same. "You cannot drop the big themes and create great saints." We must preach upon the great texts of the Scriptures, the fat texts, and the tremendous passages. We are not appointed merely to give good advice, but to proclaim good news.

We must be careful how we proclaim it. "The matter may be bruised and spoiled by the manner. The work of grace may be marred by our own ungraciousness." We must avoid a cold officialism, which recites the evangel of redeeming love with the apathy and coldness of a machine. Also we must avoid the peril of dictatorialism. We must differ between authoritative and dictatorial. The authoritative carries an atmosphere as well as a message. The dictatorial may have the form of truth, but it lacks the grace of the Lord Jesus. To present great themes in a great way we have the abundant resources of a bountiful God.

Chapter IV—The Preacher in His Study. It is imperative that the preacher go into his study to do hard work. No man is so speedily discovered as an idle minister. Enter your study at an appointed hour, one which is as early as your people go to their tasks.

Take advantage of the best scholarship. Cultivate the power of historical imagination, and you can avoid unreality in preaching. Consult other minds, but respect your own individuality.

"No sermon is ready for preaching, or for writing out, until we can express its theme in a short, pregnant sentence as clear as a crystal."

To compel one's self to fashion that sentence is surely one of the most vital and essential factors in the making of a sermon. The preparation of Sunday's sermons cannot begin on Saturday morning and finish on Saturday night. The preparation is a long process.

Relate your sermons to life. The sermon must be a proclamation of truth as vitally related to living men and women. It must touch life where the touch is significant. We must make everybody feel that our key fits the lock of his own private door.

Pay sacred heed to the ministry of style. When you have discovered a jewel, give it the most appropriate setting. A fine thought demands a fine expression.

Illustrations are like street lamps, scarcely noticed, but throwing floods of light upon the road.

Chapter V—"The Preacher in His Pulpit." The pulpit may be the center of overwhelming power, and it may be the scene of tragic disaster. It is our God-appointed office to lead people who are weary or wayward, exultant or depressed, eager or indifferent, into "the secret place of the Most High." "We are to help the sinful to the fountain of cleansing, the bondslaves to the wonderful songs of deliverance. We are to help the halt and the lame to recover their lost nimbleness. We are to help the broken-winged into the healing light of 'the heavenly places in Christ Jesus.' We are to help the sad into the sunshine of grace. We are to help the buoyant to clothe themselves with 'the garment of praise.' We are to help to redeem the strong from the atheism of pride, and the weak from the atheism of despair. We are to help little children to see the glorious attractiveness of God, and we are to help the aged to realize the encompassing care of the Father and the assurance of the eternal home. This is something of what our calling means when we enter the pulpit of the sanctuary. And our possible glory is this, we may do it. And our possible shame is this, we may hinder it. When 'the sick and the diseased' are gathered together we may be ministers or barriers to their healing. We may be added encumbrances or spiritual helps. We may be stumbling-blocks over which our people have to climb in their desire to commune with God."

Jowett deals at length with the Scripture reading, the prayers, and the music. He concludes: "And so with these mighty allies of prayer, and Scripture, and music, all pulsating with the power of the Holy Ghost, we shall give to a prepared people the message of the sermon." In all our preaching, we must preach for verdicts. Our ultimate object is to move the will and to set it in another course. There is no joy on earth comparable to that of the shepherd finding the sheep, and carrying it home.

Chapter VI—"The Preacher in the Home." When the preacher leaves the sanctuary and enters the private home, there is a change of sphere, but no change of mission. The line of purpose continues unbroken.

In seeking communion with the individual, we must bring a ministry of sympathetic listening. We provide an audience for the expression of trouble and difficulty and fear, and also for the transfiguration and enrichment of his joy. We strengthen a man's faith when we give him opportunity of confession; we enrich his joy when we listen to his song in the Lord. We also bring to the individual the strengthening grace of sympathetic speech. Our God will inspire the counsel if we will cherish and seek His glory.

While you give, you will receive. While you comfort, you will be comforted. While you counsel, you will be enlightened. While you lift another's burden your own burden will be made light.

Chapter VII—"The Preacher as a Man of Affairs." Jowett refers here to the Preacher as one who meets and consults with other men in the business management of the church. The children of the world are not to be wiser than the children of light. "We are not to 'scrap' the business gifts, and rely upon some mysterious influence which works without them. We are to be vigilant, punctual, enterprising, decisive, surrendering all our senses to the work, and notably the king of all the senses, the sense which makes all other senses effective, the power of common sense. We are to be as merchantmen, men of sobriety, of wide sanity, of keen but cool judgment, alert but not hasty, zealous but circumspect, doing the King's business in a business-like way."

A primary requisite is to ourselves be *men*. Second, we must have a competent knowledge of men.

General principles he advises to follow are: 1) Never move with small majorities, 2) Avoid the notoriety of always wanting something new, 3) Never mistake the multiplication of organization for the enlargement and enrichment of service, 4) Never become a victim to the standard of numbers, and 5) Never help the business by advertising yourself.

"My brethren, you are going forth into a big world to confront big things. There is 'the pestilence that walketh in darkness,' and there is 'the destruction that wasteth at noonday.' There is success and there is failure, and there is sin, and sorrow, and death. And of all pathetic plights surely the most pathetic is that of a minister moving about this grim field of varied necessity, professing to be a physician, but carrying in his wallet no balms, no cordials, no caustics to meet the clamant needs of men. But of all privileged callings surely the most privileged is that of a Greatheart pacing the highways of life, carrying with him all that is needed by fainting, bruised, and broken pilgrims, perfectly confident in Him 'Whom he has believed.' Brethren, your calling is very holy. Your work is very difficult. Your Saviour is very mighty. And the joy of the Lord will be your strength."

This book is most certainly a classic, and deserves many accolades.

# Chapter 84

# *Preaching and Preachers*
# by
# D. Martyn Lloyd-Jones
# 1971

Lloyd-Jones was the well-known pastor of Westminster Chapel, London for thirty years, 1938-1968. This book was originally given as a series of lectures at Westminster Seminary, Philadelphia. In the preface he admits "to my dogmatic assertions." This would be my criticism of a generally excellent book.

He begins with an emphasis on the primacy of preaching, listing various reasons why he thinks that preaching has been on the decline. He calls for preaching of the Word of God, and believes it is our main business. Reformation and Revival are dependent on great preaching. He sees the need for preaching to be Scriptural and theological. True preaching lays down the essential principles for personal help. Lloyd-Jones maintains that true preaching will draw people to hear it.

The sermon must have good content, showing the relevance of the Word. It should contain the message of salvation and the edifying, teaching aspect. It must not be an essay, or a lecture. It should always be expository, and be in good form. Sermon preparation involves sweat and labor.

The whole personality of the preacher must be involved in the delivery. Freedom is important, and so is seriousness. Never be dull. Urgency needs to be underlined. He stands between God and men, and between time and eternity. Persuasiveness is another characteristic, and so is pathos. Emotion should play a part, and preaching should be in power. True preaching consists of the sermon and the act of preaching combined in right proportions. Preaching is theology coming through a man who is on fire.

Chapter Six deals with the preacher. He is generally opposed to lay preaching. He feels that only "called" men should preach. A sense of constraint is a crucial test.

Lloyd-Jones believes in the basics of seminary (theological college) training. He has a prejudice against homiletics. He suggests listening to great preachers, and reading their sermons.

In the chapters on the Congregation, and the Character of the Message he opposes efforts to cater to and please any types of persons. Rather they should all be addressed as sinners and in need of the Gospel. The pew should not control the pulpit. Preachers must be contemporary, and deal with the living people who listen to us. Don't assume they are all Christians. All who attend church need to be brought under the power of the Gospel. The pulpit needs to speak with authority, not intellectual or cultural authority, but spiritual authority. If Christians recognize this, they should be ready to listen to the preacher.

On the preparation of the preacher, Lloyd-Jones stresses that he should always be preparing, not his sermon, but himself. Get to know yourself, and work out a program for you to do your best work. Pray. Read you Bible. Read devotional material. Read sermons, theology, and Church history. Balance your reading. Think originally. "The preacher is not meant to be a mere channel through which water flows; he is to be more like a well."

The next chapters are on the sermon. Preaching should always arise out of the Scriptures. He is quite favorable to series of sermons.

He never guaranteed finishing his prepared sermon (a never never to us). This he considers "the freedom of the Spirit." He stresses expository preaching (but not in the thematic way which we emphasize). Determine the meaning of the text, and deal with it honestly, always in context. Let the main thrust of the text lead you and teach you, and let that be the burden of your sermon.

The number of heads (points) in the sermon need not be only three. They must arise from the text. Struggle with the form of the sermon until you get it in shape. Clothe your skeletons with flesh. Be practical. Remember the people; you are preaching to them.

Don't overdo the use of illustrations. Imagination is important, but don't let it run away with you. Humor is allowable only if it comes naturally. To try to be humorous is an abomination. He objects to ten minute sermons as well as one hour sermons, and considers time to be relative, depending on the congregation's capacity.

Lloyd-Jones objects to announcing your subject ahead. He calls this practice and choirs and children's addresses "a part of that pseudo-intellectualism of the Victorians." He sees radio and television preaching as inimical to true preaching. In a list of things to avoid he discusses professionalism, pride, too much intellect, too much polemic, the use of irony, and sanctimoniousness.

Lloyd-Jones is not pleased with an emphasis on music in worship. He blames it on the nineteenth century. He also speaks of an "organist tyranny," and choir problems. He would prefer to abolish choirs, since all the people should lift up their voices in praise and worship. Music must be kept in its place.

He discuses the decision call at the close of a sermon. He lists ten reasons why there should not be a public call for decisions. The appeal should be a part of the message. He also warns against the pitfalls of using other men's sermons, and has a very interesting story to tell about Spurgeon.

He speaks of the romance of preaching. It is the greatest and most thrilling work in the world. He closes with an emphasis on the importance of the Holy Spirit's power on our preaching.

As I close this book of 325 pages I feel I have read a book which clearly deals with homiletics in nearly every aspect of the subject. Strange, isn't it, that the author states on page 118 that homiletics to him is almost an abomination, and that books such as "*The Craft of a Sermon*" are to him a prostitution.

# Chapter 85

# *Preaching*
# Edited by Samuel T. Logan, Jr.
# 1986

This is a sort of anthology on preaching which emanates from Westminster Theological Seminary in Philadelphia. Of the twenty different contributors, eleven of them either trained or taught at Westminster. Of the other nine there are some well-known names such as: James M. Boice, Donald Macleod, Joel Nederhood, James I. Packer, and R. C. Sproul. Two listed as contributors do not have a chapter in the book, R. M. Craven and W. R. Godfrey. They apparently participated in the compilation. Logan himself died in 1985.

This book is a big one—469 pages—and is a "heavy," from the intellectual viewpoint. The cover states that it is a "a major new guide-book for ministers and lay preachers." Some ministers will wade through it, but very few lay preachers are likely to tackle it.

Haddon W. Robinson, president of Denver Seminary, and himself the author of "*Biblical Preaching*" writes in a review[1] that "after working through this collection of essays, the reader may struggle

---

1.    In *Eternity* magazine, June 1987 issue

with the question, 'Have I ever seen a preacher?' Even worse, he may ask, 'Could I ever pass as a preacher?' According to these writers, a preacher must measure up to a breathtaking array of skills and virtues. (Then he lists nineteen of them found in the book.) A minister, attempting to apply all this counsel, suffers burn-out merely reading it."

The total viewpoint of the book is evangelical and Reformed. Many of its suggestions and advice are well-taken. We shall attempt to cull only a few of them from amongst the many.

Packer defines preaching as "the very essence of the corporate phenomenon called Christianity." He says "that preaching is more caught than taught." (p. 2) Preachers must have a vision that 1) Scripture is revelation, 2) God is glorious, 3) People are lost, 4) Christ is unchanging, 5) Persuasion is needed, 6) Satan is active, and 7) God's Spirit is sovereign.

"Preaching is sacred eloquence through an ambassador whose life must be consistent in every way with the message he proclaims." (Hulse, p. 62) Piety and holiness are all-embracing. Ministers should emulate Christ in love, self-sacrifice, prayer and fasting, a humble and joyful service of others, and a faith to persevere. (p. 80) If we abide in Christ we can derive from Him the spiritual power to live holy lives and to preach powerful sermons. (p. 87)

"A sermon is not a lecture. It is exposition of a text of Scripture in terms of contemporary culture with the specific goal of helping people to understand and obey the truth of God...To do that well the preacher must be well-studied." (Boice p. 91) Suggestions in re scholarship are 1) Get all the formal training you can, 2) Never stop learning, 3) Set aside specific times for study, and 4) Tackle some big problems.

"God has chosen preaching as a means to save the world. The same God takes a dim view of false preaching." (Sproul, p. 120) Because understanding is crucial to the preacher and the hearer, good biblical preaching must be from the whole man to the whole man. "Preaching is far more than an art or a science—it is a spiritual exercise, a holy vocation." (pp. 124-5)

Clowney wants Christ preached from all of the Scriptures. "When the Old Testament is interpreted in the light of its own structure of promise and when that promise is seen as fulfilled in Jesus Christ, then the significance of the Old Testament can be preached in theological depth and practical power." (p. 183) "Christological preaching calls for patient comparing of Scripture with Scripture, extensive use of concordances, and a lifetime commitment to Bible study, meditation and prayer." (p. 190)

Under exegesis Ferguson states that exegetical preaching should not be confused with a homiletical running commentary, and that it is not merely the preaching of a course of sermons on a Bible book. He finds six primary elements in preparing and preaching exegetical sermons: selecting, understanding, crystallizing, structuralizing, concretizing, and delivery.

Two theses are laid out in the hermeneutics chapter: 1) The biblical text has a single meaning determined by the will of the author and 2) The text has a manifold significance that is squarely based upon the meaning of the text. (p. 213)

D. Macleod writes a good chapter on the relation of systematic theology to preaching. He concludes that we must preach all the theology we know. We must preach with authority, born of the confidence that what we are proclaiming is the Word of God. When dealing with the profoundest themes of revelation, we should strive for lucidity. We are to preach lovingly, especially when we handle controversial and polemical subjects.

"Preaching is driving home the Word of the living God to the lives of His people. It is declaring 'Thus says the Lord' to people who constantly hear other claims for allegiance and direction." (Bettler, p. 332) "Storytelling is the life blood of a message...The preacher will do well to use them freely." (Adams, p. 352) Adams also calls for sense appeal in preaching. "Through sense appeal, the preacher is able to help his audience see, feel, or otherwise experience what he is talking about in a way that closely approximates the reality about which he is preaching." (p. 354) "For a revival of powerful preaching in the church we must be diligent in the Word, and in the exercise and proclamation of faith, and in prayer. These are the only means of power that the church has, or ever will have." (Thomas, p. 396)

Vosteen argues against the use of children's sermons, since worship is a convenantal, family event. The regular sermon is for the whole family. He takes times in his regular sermon to address the children. (p. 409) "When Scripture makes a direct application of truth to our lives, we make a direct application to the congregation." (p. 412) "The preacher...stands in a unique place. He stands before God with the responsibility to be absolutely faithful to His truth...At the same time he stands before his congregation with the responsibility to address their lives and needs with concern." (p. 417)

A rather technical chapter follows on "Reading the Word of God Aloud." Rather strangely for such a learned anthology on preaching, the final chapter deals with "The Body in the Pulpit." This book contains much that is helpful for our ministry. Some chapters are more practical than others.

# Chapter 86

# *Preaching Without Notes* by Clarence E. Macartney 1946

Clarence Macartney was an outstanding preacher, who served Presbyterian churches in Paterson, New Jersey, Philadelphia and Pittsburgh, Pennsylvania. He wrote his life story, "*The Making of a Minister*," which was published in 1961, four years after his death. Many of his sermons are in book form.

The title of the book is a bit misleading, since it refers to only one chapter. The book is an approach to the total ministry of the pulpit.

The "Recall to Gospel Preaching" is a trumpet call to vital preaching of the gospel, over against liberal failures. "Christ did not say that He was *a* way, but that He was *the* Way, *the* Truth, and *the* Life." (p. 14) "Too many of our sermons lack that which is distinctly Christian." (p. 15) "One of the conditions for successful gospel preaching is a concern for and desire for the salvation of souls." (p. 18) "Successful evangelical preaching is the presentation of the cardinal doctrines and truths of the Christian faith." (p. 19) True preaching must recognize, honor, and invoke the Holy Spirit, and must be a result of prayer. "When we step into our pulpit, we go as men who have been trusted of God to declare the glorious gospel of the blessed God." (p. 28)

The chapter on illustrations is indicative of Macartney's genius for finding illustrations everywhere. He found them first in Bible stories. "People like to hear the stories of the Bible told and interpreted." (p. 37) "A vigorous, imaginative presentation of any great Bible scene leaves a wholesome impression." (p. 38) He also seeks illustrations from biography and autobiography, mythology, fiction, poetry, philosophy, nature and common life, metaphors, and personal experience. "The average preacher does not make enough use of his imagination. He can use it either in describing a Bible scene or in a flight of pure fancy." (p. 68) "The preacher of imagination is the prince of the pulpit." (p. 75)

In "Getting Ready for the Pulpit" Macartney states that wide reading should begin with regular devotional reading of the Bible. Then read a good newspaper, history, biography, and poetry. He demonstrates his ability to form interesting series on Bible events and characters, and on life situations. Although he emphasizes proclamation of the Gospel, he also believes he should defend it against doubt, misrepresentation, and unbelief. He quotes Patton "that if our faith cannot be vindicated at the bar of reason it will be ruled out in the experience of life." (p. 101)

A chapter follows on Bible Biographical Preaching. "God is the great, original, and continual biographical preacher." (p. 121) God revealed Himself in a life, that of Jesus Christ. "The Bible is the supreme book on human personality." (p. 121) "An advantage of preaching on Bible characters is that the sermon will have a freshness about it. It is no longer wise to take for granted any wide degree of knowledge concerning the Bible." (p. 128) "Many a preacher, after wandering into the far country and feeding his people and himself on the husks which the swine did eat, has returned again to the Bible and been surprised to discover how new, fresh, and powerful it is." (p. 130) This chapter is fertile with preaching ideas and suggestions.

"Preaching Without Notes" emphasizes Macartney's approach to preaching. "There can be no question that the sermon that does the most good is the sermon which is preached without notes." (p. 145) The reading of a sermon is never preaching in the highest sense. "The highest preaching and the highest oratory is the impact of one soul upon another in free and open address." (p. 147) It can give "great and stirring pulpit appeal." (p. 169)

Macartney was without a doubt a prince of the pulpit, and this book gives us an insight into his message and method.

# Chapter 87

# *Expository Preaching Plans and Methods*
# by
# F. B. Meyer
# 1954 edition

This well-known English preacher and writer of another generation lays out his idea of preaching and how to do it. Each one of the six chapters discusses the philosophy, and then contains a sermon as an example. "The aim of this book is not only to demonstrate the value of expository preaching, but to show how." (p. 5)

"The one supreme object of the Christian ministry is to preach Christ and Him crucified...All sermons must culminate and find their loftiest purpose in the Divine Redeemer." (p. 11) In our ministry we are in partnership with the Holy Spirit. "Our mission to the world is only possible of fulfillment in so far as it represents the union of the human and Divine." (p. 15) To receive the Holy Spirit's power we must be spiritual men, we must seek only the glory of Jesus, and we must honour the Scripture.

Meyer defines "expository preaching as the consecutive treatment of some book or extended portion of Scripture." (p. 32) "Each sermon should not be required to be propped up against another to make it stand." (p. 35) We must apply God's Word to each individual in the audience. "We must preach to the people as well as before them." (p. 37)

Meyer lists the advantages in the expository method as 1) It saves the preacher from getting into ruts, 2) Continuous exposition compels the preacher to handle big themes, 3) The expositor will be led to handle subjects which would not otherwise occur to him, and, 4) It gives immense force to the ministry that is based upon it. (pp. 49-56)

Jesus set the example in His use of Scripture. "No disciples were ever so saturated with their master's thoughts or so steeped in their spirit as Jesus was with Scripture." (p. 72) "Our Lord's profound reverence and love for the Scripture should make every minister desire that during his pastorate he should succeed in leading his people to a well-balanced and intimate acquaintance with the entire range of the Word of God." (p. 78)

Meyer lists "five considerations that must be met in every successful sermon. There should be an appeal to the Reason, to the Conscience, to the Imagination, to the Emotion, and to the Will; and for each of these there is no method so serviceable as systematic exposition." (p. 93) The Bible has inexhaustible riches, which gives the expository method a perennial interest. "It is difficult to conceive of any process which will more magnify the Scriptures, more unfold their truth, more explain their method, more saturate our congregations with their essence and spirit, than the habit of continuous exposition." (p. 118)

What Meyer has to say in his plea for expository preaching is true and is well said. However, the six sermons he includes, one after each chapter, are hardly homiletic examples of exposition of Scripture, even though they express evangelical truth.

# Chapter 88

## *Preaching*
## by
## G. Campbell Morgan
## 1937

This is a short book by the famous preacher and Bible expositor, G. Campbell Morgan, which sets forth some of the principles vital to expository preaching.

In "The Essentials of a Sermon" Morgan begins with Ephesians 4:9-10 and Romans 10:12-15 to set "an atmosphere." "The supreme work of the Christian minister is the work of preaching." He sees preaching as the declaration of the grace of God to human need on the authority of the Throne of God. Preaching should be addressed to the will of man. His message is from a King. Men are waiting for preaching of the New Testament kind. Morgan sees Truth, Clarity, and Passion as the essentials of a sermon. We are stewards of the mysteries of God. We have to deal with the supernatural. We move in the realm of truth revealed. Originality in preaching consists in the interpretation of revelation. The Word is authoritative. The sermon must be clear enough so that people may apprehend. Preach words that are understood. And then preach it with passion. We cannot handle great themes of the Gospel without passion. No preacher can lift his hearers above the level of his own experience. In Christ we have the power of truth in life illustrated. That has to be reproduced in all who are really preaching.

Chapter Two deals with the Text. He defines text as something that is woven. The text, taken from Holy Writ, is then woven into the web of the sermon. You need a text to have the authority of the Word in your message. It helps the sermon to be definite, and maintains variety. Make sure that your text is a complete statement.

Chapter Three is about The Central Message. Every sermon must have a scheme or plan. The purpose should be defined. It should always meet a need. First, work on the text itself. Master its real meaning. Use scholarly commentaries, not devotional ones. Bring order out of chaos. Keep imagination in its proper place. You need an introduction, the message itself, and a conclusion. For clarity, nothing is more important than divisions. He cites numerous illustrations of the misuse of texts. The divisions will take on color from our intention and purpose. Let them be clearly stated, and at the beginning of the sermon.

The final chapter deals with the introduction and conclusion. The introduction calls attention, and prepares the mind of the hearers. It is like a preface to a book. It can overcome the preoccupation of the audience, as well as their indifference. Simplicity, pertinence, and courage should be the properties of an introduction.

The conclusion must bring everything to an end. It must stir the human will. Preach for a verdict. The best note is, "Thou art the man." Make the last sixty seconds intense with all the power of the message.

This is a good book from a master preacher.

# Chapter 89

## *Heralds of God*
## by
## James S. Stewart
## 1946

Stewart was a preacher in Edinburgh of considerable renown. This book divides into five parts about the Preacher.

The Preacher's World: "Our basic message remains constant and invariable, but our presentation of it must take account of, and be largely conditioned by, the actual world on which our eyes look out today." (p. 11) "The Church needs men who, knowing the world around them, and knowing the Christ above them and within, will set the trumpet of the Gospel to their lips, and proclaim His sovereignty and all-sufficiency." (pp. 12-13) "It is quite impossible to preach Christ faithfully without saying many things which will sting the natural heart of man into opposition and rebellion." (p. 30) "Resist all temptations to dilute your Gospel." (p. 31) He suggests the following maxims: 1) Be real in worship, 2) Be real in language, and 3) Be real in your total attitude to the message. "The longest ministry is too short by far to exhaust the treasures of the Word of God." (p. 46) " 'I came into the town,' wrote John Wesley in his *Journal*, 'and offered them Christ.' To spend your days doing that—not just describing Christianity or arguing for a creed, not apologizing for the faith or debating fine shades of religious meaning, but actually offering and giving men Christ—could any life work be more thrilling or momentous?" (p. 57)

The Preacher's Theme: "We have no right in our preaching to waste time on side-issues and irrelevance." (p. 61) The Apostles presented the death and resurrection of Jesus as nothing less than

God in omnipotent action. Their stupendous tidings dwarfed all other facts "that the sovereign Power of the universe had cleft history asunder, travelling in the greatness of His strength, mighty to save." (p. 64) It is wrong to segregate preaching from worship. "The sermon is divinely intended to be one of those high places of the spirit where men and women grow piercingly aware of the eternal and where a worshipping congregation sees no man, save Jesus only." (p. 72) "To the supreme facts of the Cross and the Resurrection, our preaching must ever return." (pp. 74-75) The herald of the Cross must preach the Cross in the context of the world's suffering and also in the context of the world's sin. Preach the cross as revelation, victory, and challenge.

The Preacher's Study: "It is one thing to learn the technique and mechanics of preaching; it is quite another to preach a sermon which will draw back the veil and make the barriers fall that hide the face of God." (p. 101) People are wanting to be told what God has said in His Word. Let the Bible speak its own message. Observe the Christian Year. The great festival days suggest basic themes that keep us close to the fundamental doctrines of the faith.

"Make sure every sermon you preach has a definite aim." (p. 120) "It ought to be our one consuming ambition to help men and women, through the services of the sanctuary, to meet the living God." (p. 121) Stewart has doubts about announcing the main divisions of a sermon at the very outset. Construct your sermon so that it will lead men through the outer and inner courts to the Holy Place, and the very presence of the Lord.

The Preacher's Technique: "Profuse and indiscriminate quotation is a mark of bad preaching." (p. 147) "It is only as we live in the Bible-devotionally, and as students of the sacred Word—that we can hope to find the manna falling regularly for our people's need." (p. 154) Some sermons proceed quite flagrantly to violate the intention of the original writer of Scripture. "Resolve that every sermon you preach shall be in the truest sense your own." (p. 174) In delivery use every faculty God has given you, but in the end the messenger shall be nothing and the message everything.

The Preacher's Inner Life: "It is no trouble to preach, but a vast trouble to construct a preacher." (p. 190) "First, the true preacher will be a man utterly dedicated to his work. This one thing I do." (p. 194) "Second, the herald of Christ will be a man of prayer." (p. 201) "The third characteristic note of the preacher's inner life—He will be a man marked by a great humility of heart." (p. 205) Fourth, "He will be a man of authority...Humble and self-forgetting we must be always, but diffident and apologetic about the Gospel never." (p. 210) Last, "he will be a man on fire for Christ." (p. 219) "Yours is the greatest of all vocations. You will stint no pains or labour to prepare for it." (pp. 221-2)

Stewart writes very well. His emphasis is wholesome. This book is worthy of being a classic.

# BIBLIOGRAPHY

Adams, Jay E.

    *Communicating With 20th Century Man*, Phillipsburg, N.J.: Presbyterian and Reformed, 1979.

    *Competent to Counsel*, Grand Rapids, Mich.: Baker Book House, 1970.

    *Meaning and Mode of Baptism*, Phillipsburg, N.J.: Presbyterian and Reformed, 1976.

    *Preaching With Purpose*, Phillipsburg, N.J.: Presbyterian and Reformed, 1982.

    *Pulpit Speech*, Philadelphia, Pa.: Presbyterian and Reformed, 1974.

    *Shepherding God's Flock*, 3 vols. in 1, Grand Rapids, Mich.: Baker Book House, 1979.

    Vol. 3, Philadelphia, Pa.: Presbyterian and Reformed, 1975.

    *The Big Umbrella*, Philadelphia, Pa.: Presbyterian and Reformed, 1972.

    *The Homiletical Innovations of Andrew W. Blackwood*, Nutley, N.J.: Presbyterian and Reformed, 1977.

Bader, Golda Elam (ed)

    *I Married a Minister*, Nashville, Tenn.: Abingdon Press, 1942.

Baumann, J. Daniel

    *An Introduction to Contemporary Preaching*, Grand Rapids, Mich.: Baker Book House, 1972.

Baxter, Richard

    *Call to the Unconverted*, New York, N.Y.: American Tract Society, 1830.

    *The Reformed Pastor*, New York N.Y.: American Tract Society, 1829.

Belgum G.

    *Guilt: Where Religion and Psychology Meet*, Minneapolis, Minn.: Augsburg Press, 1970.

Berkhof, Louis

    *Systematic Theology*, Grand Rapids, Mich.: Wm. B. Eerdmans Publ. Co., 1941.

Black, James
> *The Mystery of Preaching*, New York, N.Y.: Fleming H. Revell Co., 1924.

Blackwood, Andrew W.
> *Evangelism in the Home Church*, Nashville, Tenn.: Abingdon-Cokesbury Press, 1942.
> *Expository Preaching for Today*, New York, N.Y.: Abingdon-Cokesbury, 1953.
> *Pastoral Work*, Philadelphia, Pa.: The Westminster Press, 1945.
> *The Fine Art of Preaching*, New York, N.Y.: The Macmillan Co., 1937.
> *The Fine Art of Public Worship*, Nashville, Tenn.: Cokesbury Press, 1939.
> *The Preparation of Sermons*, New York, N.Y.: Abingdon Press, 1958.
> *The Funeral*, Philadelphia, Pa.: The Westminster Press, 1942.

Blocker, Simon
> *The Secret of Pulpit Power* Grand Rapids, Mich.: Wm. B. Eerdmans Publ. Co., 1951.

Bodey, Richard Allen (ed)
> *Inside the Sermon*, Grand Rapids, Mich.: Baker Book House, 1990.

Boice, James Montgomery
> "The Preacher and Scholarship" in *Preaching*, edited by S. T. Logan, Jr.

Breed, David R.
> *Preparing to Preach*, New York, N.Y.: George H. Doran Co., 1911.

Bridges, Charles
> *The Christian Ministry*, Edinburgh, Scotland: The Banner of Truth Trust, 1980. Reprint from 1830.

Broadus, John A.
> *A Treatise on the Preparation and Delivery of Sermons*, Philadelphia, Pa.: Smith, English, and Co., 1876.

Burnet, Adam
    *Pleading With Men*, New York, N.Y.: Fleming H. Revell Co.,
    1935.

Burrell, David James
    *The Sermon—Its Construction and Delivery*, New York, N.Y.:
    Fleming H. Revell Co., 1913.

Chappell, Clovis G.
    *Anointed to Preach*, Nashville, Tenn.: Abingdon-Cokesbury
    Press, 1951.

*Church of England Newspaper*: 9 January 1977 issue.

Clowney, Edmund P.
    *Called to the Ministry*, Phillipsburg, N.J.: Presbyterian and
    Reformed, 1964.

Collins, Gary R.
    *Christian Counselling*, Waco, Tex.: Word Publishing, 1980.
    *Helping People Grow*, Vision House, 1979.

Crabb, Lawrence J., Jr.
    *Basic Principles of Biblical Counseling*, Melbourne, Vic.: S.
    John Bacon, 1975.
    *Effective Biblical Counseling*, Grand Rapids, Mich.: Zondervan,
    1977.
    *The Marriage Builder*, Grand Rapids, Mich.: Zondervan, 1982.
    *Understanding People*, Melbourne, Vic.: S. John Bacon, 1987.

Cuyler, Theodore L.
    *How to be a Pastor*, New York, N.Y.: The Baker and Taylor Co.,
    1890.

Daane, James
    *Preaching With Confidence*, Grand Rapids, Mich.: Wm B.
    Eerdmans Publ. Co., 1980.

Dabney, Robert L.
    *Sacred Rhetoric*, Edinburgh, Scotland: The Banner of Truth
    Trust, 1979. Reprint from 1870.

Dale, R. W.
*Nine Lectures on Preaching*, London, Eng.: Hodder and Stoughton, 1896.

Davis, Henry Grady
*Design for Preaching*, Philadelphia, Pa.: Fortress Press, 1958.

Devan, S. Arthur
*Ascent to Zion*, New York, N.Y.: The Macmillan Co., 1942.

*Eternity Magazine*, Philadelphia, Pa.: June 1987.

Ferris, Theodore P.
*Go Tell the People*, New York, N.Y.: Scribner, 1951.

Ford, Leighton
*The Christian Persuader*, New York, N.Y.: Harper and Row, 1966.

Frame, John D.
"Counseling the Aged" in *Baker's Dictionary of Practical Theology*.

Grounds, Vernon
"Counseling the Bereaved" in *Baker's Dictionary of Practical Theology*.

Gunn, Arthur
*Biblical Baptism*, Auckland, N.Z.: G. W. Moore Ltd., 1983.

Hewitt, Arthur Wentworth
*Highland Shepherds*, Chicago, Ill.: Willett, Clark, and Co., 1939.
*Steeples in the Hills*, New York, N.Y.: The Abingdon Press, 1926.
*The Shepherdess*, Chicago, Ill.: Willett, Clark, and Co., 1943.

Hodge, Charles
*Epistle to the Romans*, New York, N.Y.: A. C. Armstrong and Son, 1906.
*Systematic Theology*, 3 Vols., New York, N.Y.: Charles Scribner's Sons, 1906.

Hoeksema, Herman
> *The Biblical Ground for the Baptism of Infants*, Grand Rapids, Mich.: First Protestant Reformed Church, ab. 1932.

Horne, Charles Silvester
> *The Romance of Preaching*, New York, N.Y.: Fleming H. Revell Co., 1914.

Hutton, John A.
> *That the Ministry Be Not Blamed*, New York, N.Y.: George H. Doran Co., 1921.

Jefferson, Charles E.
> *The Minister as Prophet*, New York, N.Y.: Thomas Y. Crowell Co., ab. 1910.
> *The Minister as Shepherd*, New York, N.Y.: Thomas Y. Crowell Co., 1912.

Johnson, John Scott
> *Baptism*, Weaverville, No. Car.: The Southern Presbyterian Journal.

Jowett, J. H.
> *The Preacher, His Life and Work*, New York, N.Y.: Harper and Brothers, 1912.

Kirwan, William T.
> *Biblical Concepts for Christian Counseling*, Grand Rapids, Mich.: Baker Book House, 1984.

Kubler-Ross, Elizabeth
> *On Death and Dying*, New York, N.Y.: Macmillan, 1969.
> *Questions and Answers on Death and Dying*, New York, N.Y.: Macmillan, 1974.

Leach, William H.
> *Church Administration*, New York, N.Y.: George H. Doran Co., 1928.

Leavell, Roland Q.
> *The Romance of Evangelism*, New York, N.Y.: Fleming H. Revell Co., 1942.

Lloyd-Jones, D. Martyn
*Preaching and Preachers*, Grand Rapids, Mich.: Zondervan Publ. House, 1971.

Logan, Samuel T. Jr. (ed.)
*Preaching*, Hertfordshire, England: Evangelical Press, 1986.

Luccock, Halford E.
*In the Minister's Workshop*, Nashville, Tenn.: Abingdon-Cokesbury Press, 1944.

Lutz, Lorry
*An Uncommon Commoner*, Langley, B.C.: Credo Publ., 1987.

Macartney, Clarence E.
*Preaching Without Notes*, Nashville, Tenn.: Abingdon-Cokesbury Press, 1946.

Martin, Al N.
*Prepared to Preach*, Strathpine, Australia: Covenanter Press, 1981.

McGinnis, Alan Loy
*Bringing Out the Best in People*, Adelaide, Australia: Lutheran Publishing House, 1985.

Meyer, F. B.
*Expository Preaching*, Grand Rapids, Mich.: Zondervan, 1954.

Morgan, G. Campbell
*Preaching*, New York, N.Y.: Fleming H. Revell Co., 1937.

Muller, John H.
*A Plan for the Building Up of the Body of Christ*, 1977 (doctoral dissertation).
*Exciting Christianity*, New York, N.Y.: Vantage Press, 1973.

Murray, John
*Christian Baptism*, Philadelphia, Pa.: Presbyterian and Reformed, 1974.

Narramore, S. Bruce
*Help! I'm a Parent*, Grand Rapids, Mich.: Zondervan, 1972.

Newman, Bill
*Called to Proclaim*, Toowong, Qld., Australia: BNC Publications, 1986.

Osterhaven, M. Eugene
*What is Christian Baptism?*, Grand Rapids, Mich.: Society for Reformed Publications, 1956.

Packer, J. I.
"Why Preach?" in *Preaching*, edited by S. T. Logan, Jr.

Parrott, Lora Lee
*How to Be a Preacher's Wife and Like It*, Grand Rapids, Mich.: Zondervan Publ. House, 1956.

Pieters, Albertus
*Why We Baptize Infants*, New York, N.Y.: Board of Publications, Reformed Church in America, ab. 1935.

Richards, Lawrence O.
*A Theology of Christian Education*, Grand Rapids, Mich.: Zondervan, 1975.

Robertson, James D.
"Sermon Illustration" in *Baker's Dictionary of Practical Theology*.

Robinson, Haddon W.
*Biblical Preaching*, Grand Rapids, Mich.: Baker Book House, 1980.

Roddy, Clarence S.
*We Prepare and Preach*, Chicago, Ill.: Moody Press, 1959.

Sangster, Paul E.
"Pulpit Speech and Rhetoric" in *Baker's Dictionary of Practical Theology*.

Shelley, Marshall
*Well-Intentioned Dragons*, Waco, Tex.: Word Publishers, 1985.

Skinner, Craig
*The Teaching Ministry of the Pulpit*, Grand Rapids, Mich.: Baker Book House, 1973.

Spurgeon, Charles H.
   *Lectures to His Students*, Grand Rapids, Mich.: Zondervan reprint, 1955.

Stewart, James S.
   *Heralds of God*, New York, N.Y.: Charles Scribner's Sons, 1946.

Stott, John
   *Between Two Worlds*, Grand Rapids, Mich.: Wm. B. Eerdmans Publ. Co., 1982.

Swaim, J. Carter
   "Preaching Doctrine" In *Baker's Dictionary of Practical Theology*.

Taylor, William M.
   *The Ministry of the Word*, London: T. Nelson and Sons, 1876.

Tucker, Louis
   *Clerical Errors*, New York, N.Y.: Harper and Brothers, 1943.

Turnbull, Ralph G.
   *A Minister's Obstacles*, Westwood, N.J.: Fleming H. Revell Co., 1964.

Turnbull, Ralph G. (ed.)
   *Baker's Dictionary of Practical Theology*, Grand Rapids, Mich.: Baker Book House, 1967.

Unger, Merrill F.
   *Principles of Expository Preaching*, Grand Rapids, Mich.: Zondervan Publ. House, 1955.

Webber, Robert E.
   *Worship Old and New*, Grand Rapids, Mich.: Zondervan, 1982.

Whitesell, Faris D.
   *Power in Expository Preaching*, New York, N.Y.: Fleming H. Revell, 1963.

# You may order this book from:

Dr. John H. Muller
17500 Hickory Road
Spring Lake, MI 49456

or

Companion Press
P.O. Box 310
Shippensburg, PA 17257-0310

Retail price: $11.95 Australia, $10.50 Canada, $8.95 U.S.A., plus shipping and handling of $2.00 for single books, or $1.00 each for orders of four or more books.

Special consideration given to distributors and bookstores.